CONELY BRANCH LIBRARY
4600 MARTIN
DETROIT, MI 48210
(313) 224-6461

The Complete Guide to
Personal and Home Safety

DEC   07

MAR - 2006

Also by Captain Robert L. Snow

Family Abuse: Tough Solutions to Stop the Violence

Looking for Carroll Beckwith:
The True Story of a Detective's Search for His Past Life

Stopping a Stalker:
A Cop's Guide to Making the System Work for You

SWAT Teams:
Explosive Face-Offs with America's Deadliest Criminals

Terrorists Among Us: The Militia Threat

The Complete Guide to Personal and Home Safety

What You Need to Know

———— ⌇ ————

Revised Edition

CAPTAIN ROBERT L. SNOW

PERSEUS
PUBLISHING

A Member of the Perseus Books Group

Many of the designations used by manufacturers and sellers to distinguish their products are claimed as trademarks. Where those designations appear in this book, and where Perseus Publishing was aware of a trademark claim, the designations have been printed in initial capital letters.

Copyright © 1995, 2002 by Robert L. Snow

The previous edition of this book was published as *Protecting Your Life, Home, and Property.*

All rights reserved. No part of this publication may be reproduced, stored in a retrieval system, or transmitted, in any form or by any means, electronic, mechanical, photocopying, recording, or otherwise, without the prior written permission of the publisher. Printed in the United States of America.

Cataloging-in-Publication Data available from the Library of Congress

ISBN 0-7382-0786-1

Perseus Publishing is a member of the Perseus Books Group.
Find us on the World Wide Web at http://www.perseuspublishing.com

Perseus Publishing books are available at special discounts for bulk purchases in the U.S. by corporations, institutions, and other organizations. For more information, please contact the Special Markets Department at the Perseus Books Group, 11 Cambridge Center, Cambridge, MA 02142, or call (800) 255-1514 or (617) 252-5298, or e-mail j.mccrary@perseusbooks.com.

Text design by Janice Tapia
Set in 10.25-point Meridien Roman by the Perseus Books Group

First printing, September 2002

1 2 3 4 5 6 7 8 9 10—04 03 02

MAR   2006

CONELY BRANCH

*Dedicated to the memory of Sergeant Richard Combs,
detective, gentleman, role model*

CONTENTS

ACKNOWLEDGMENTS

A BOOK OF THIS TYPE, of course, can never be written in isolation. Many people and agencies very kindly assisted me in its completion. My heartfelt thanks go particularly to my editor, Linda Greenspan Regan, who not only shared my vision for the book but also forced me to perform at only my absolute best, which is the greatest help anyone can give a writer. In addition, many thanks go to Mr. John Rodzvilla of Perseus Books Group for seeing the need and pushing for a second edition of this book. I also want to thank my agent, Fran Collin, for all her hard work in placing this book. And I especially want to thank my wife, Melanie, and my children, Alan and Melissa, for putting up with a husband and a father who had to closet himself away for months in order to write this book.

I naturally also received a large amount of technical assistance with this book. No police officer, no matter how competent or how many areas of law enforcement he has served in, can know enough to a write a book of this breadth. And so, I want not only to thank my brother and sister officers of the Indianapolis Police Department, but also those of the police departments of Los Angeles, California; Santa Ana, California; Chicago, Illinois; Takoma Park, Maryland; Colorado Springs, Colorado; Maricopa County, Arizona; Virginia Beach, Virginia; and Columbus, Ohio. I want all of the officers who helped me to know that I truly appreciate their patience with and understanding of my incessant questioning about their particular law enforcement specialty.

I also want to extend my appreciation to Mr. George Sunderland, Manager of Criminal Justice Services of the American Association of Retired People, for his input, and I particularly want to acknowledge the Department of Justice's *Research in Brief* documents, from which I extracted many of the statistics for this book. Lastly, I want to extend my deepest appreciation to Alice K. Turner for her inspiration.

PROLOGUE

FEW PEOPLE KNOW THE TRUTH.

As a police officer for over thirty years, I have found that few people know the truth about cops, crooks, and crime. Few people know, for example, that the way the media portray police and police procedure is seldom accurate. Few people know that even though there were more than 11.5 million crimes reported to the police in 2000, this number represents only a small percentage of the actual total. The actual total, according to the U.S. Government's National Crime Victimization Survey, is closer to 26 or 27 million. And even fewer people know that police protection in most parts of the United States is spread so thin that there is actually very little protection at all. Few people, I have found, have much correct information about the police and crime.

This lack of accurate information is never more evident than when citizens see flashing lights in the rearview mirror; find themselves or someone close to them about to be arrested (yes, even good citizens get arrested); or discover that they have been, or are about to become, the victim of a crime. In such circumstances, citizens will very often do the wrong thing. If, however, these same citizens had accurate information about cops, crooks, and crime, they would know the right thing to do and could greatly increase their chances of avoiding the ticket, the arrest, or even the crime. The purpose of this book is to tell readers how to do just that.

I wrote *The Complete Guide to Personal and Home Safety* to correct the huge amount of misinformation I see perpetuated every year by the hundreds of articles, books, and movies written about police, police procedure, and crime, produced for the most part by people who have obviously had little contact with the police and even less contact with crime and real crime victims. By contact with real crime victims I don't mean speaking to them days or weeks after the crime has occurred, but talking to them as only a police officer can: while they are still bleeding, while they are still grieving and in shock, or while they are still in the middle of a crime scene. I wrote *The Complete Guide to Personal and Home Safety* because, given the vast preponderance of misinformation and the omnipresent portrayals of the media version of police, police procedure, and crime, the average citizen makes costly mistakes when confronted by criminals or the police. I hope that this book will correct some of these misconceptions.

There are a number of compelling reasons why all of us must be more knowledgeable about protecting our families and property. U.S. Department of Justice statistics show that 99 percent of all the people alive today will be the victim of a crime at some point, that more than three-fourths of us will be a victim several times, and that a person has a better chance of becoming the victim of a violent crime than being injured in an automobile accident. The same statistics show that although overall reported crime in the United States has increased more than 600 percent during the past 40 years (which accounts for a whopping additional 9.67 million reported crimes a year), violent crime during the same 40 years also jumped a staggering 575 percent. Startling as these statistics are, the fact is that much of the future crime in our country will occur because people simply don't do enough, or anything at all, to deter crime or protect themselves. People believe the job of protection belongs to the police. But the truth is that there are simply not enough police around to handle the amount of crime that exists.

In most areas of the United States the average police-to-citizen ratio is about 1 to 500. However, this reported number really isn't an accurate figure because this ratio includes *all* of the police officers in a particular local police department, including officers working in support positions, administration, and technical spots. The actual number of uniformed police officers who patrol the streets is roughly half to two-thirds of a police department's officers, which puts the ratio closer to 1 police officer for every 750 to 1,000 citizens. But these uniformed police officers are split into at least three shifts, and every day a percentage of them have the day off, are sick, or work in areas such as traffic enforcement, motorcycle escort, and parking enforcement, which have little to do with crime prevention (stopping and questioning suspicious people, patrolling neighborhoods, and so on). So the truth is that the ratio is probably closer to 1 police officer actually designated for crime prevention for every 3,000 to 4,000 citizens. This is not really much protection, and even less when we take into account the actual time an officer has available out of an eight-hour shift for crime prevention. The time available during the most crime-prone shifts is zero. The officers are simply too busy racing from one call for the police to the next, so that most lives, homes, and property are left unprotected.

Citizens must learn to protect themselves. The police can't do the job unaided by the public. This does not mean I advocate citizens carrying guns. Far too many tragedies have shown that a gun is several times more likely to injure or kill an innocent person than to protect its owner. Rather, I believe citizens need to be prepared in other productive and effective ways to forestall the dangers of crime.

Before any readers think that because of their position or where they live, they are immune to America's crime, let me say that *no one, absolutely no one,* is immune to crime. Nuns get robbed and raped; congressmen get mugged; women have their purses snatched in the finest, most exclusive stores. There is simply no act too despicable for criminals to commit. I had a case once in which a Vietnam veteran who had lost his legs to a Viet Cong mortar shell was wheeling down the sidewalk in his wheelchair. A car stopped alongside him and two men got out, knocked the disabled veteran (who was wearing camouflage fatigues with his medals attached) out of the chair and onto the ground, folded up the wheelchair and put it in the trunk of their car, then drove away. *No one* is immune to becoming a crime victim.

In addition to the possibility of becoming a crime victim, many readers may have a future encounter with the police for other reasons, such as a traffic ticket, an automobile accident, or being arrested or having someone close to them arrested, all of which are usually painful experiences. Knowing how to deal effectively with cops, crooks, and crime can make these experiences a little less painful.

America's insecurity about crime and the police wasn't always the way it is today. At the beginning of the twentieth century the officer on the beat was a fixture in every neighborhood. Citizens knew him and how to deal with him. They knew what they could and could not get away with. Crime was a personal matter to the neighborhood beat officer. He knew all of the people, both good and bad, and he took pride in keeping the neighborhood safe, giving families who had often lived there for generations a feeling of security.

Increased social mobility, however, has erased that feeling. The population of most neighborhoods today is no longer stable, criminals may come from across or out of town, and police officers may often be seen only as fleeting faces behind a passing windshield. Consequently, citizens today often feel isolated and powerless when dealing with police officers, the criminal justice system, and crime.

That feeling, though, is illusory. In this book I will tell readers, as only a police officer can, how they may protect themselves against crime and criminals and how they may, if the need arises, sail smoothly and effectively through the criminal justice system. I will also offer practical advice on dealing with modern-day police officers, advice on such things as how citizens can control the outcome of a traffic violation stop by the police, how they can minimize the damage of being arrested, and how they can even talk an officer out of an arrest (or a traffic ticket). In addition, I will offer advice on how citizens who do become crime victims can get the best service possible from the police and hence greatly increase their chances of having the perpetrator caught and their property returned.

The outcome of almost all police-citizen encounters, readers will find, is controllable by anyone who is knowledgeable about police officers and police procedure. This book will give readers that knowledge. And since it is a sad truth that the police are able to offer very little actual protection against crime, readers will also find out how they can, with the proper information, successfully protect their own lives, homes, and property. This book will provide readers with the critical information they need to help them survive unscathed in a time of increasing criminal activity. It will arm readers with vital information on how to deal successfully with cops, crooks, and crime.

1

THE TRUTH
ABOUT THE POLICE

THE SCENARIO

Jake, an overweight police detective quickly approaching retirement, and Danny, a brash young investigator, stand at the rear of a pawnshop rumored to be involved in selling illegal drugs. Nodding to each other, the detectives pull out their 16-shot Glocks, drop out the magazines to check them, and then slam the ammunition back up into the pistol handles as Jake steps forward and kicks the door in. A moment later, Jake and Danny both suck in a sudden gasp of air, adrenaline chills racing out their fingertips, when they find the proprietor of the pawnshop, obviously dead for some time, lying on the floor just inside, a bloody knife nearby.

Slipping his pistol back into the holster, Jake steps cautiously inside and kneels down next to the body. "Looks like whoever killed him hadn't planned on it."

"What makes you think so?" Danny asks.

To avoid smearing any fingerprints, Jake pulls out his handkerchief and uses it to pick up the knife. "This is part of an expensive carving set. Aren't too many people that carry these things around with them. I'll bet whoever killed him probably grabbed it out of the pawnshop." He glances around for a second. "Hey," Jake says, nodding toward several bags of white powder sitting on a nearby counter, "looks like the rumors about this place were true."

Danny starts toward the counter. "What do you suppose it is?"

Stepping over and opening one of the bags, Jake sticks his finger into the powder and then touches it to his tongue. "Pure heroin," he says, compressing his lips and giving a knowing nod to Danny.

Several days later, on Jake and Danny's day off, Danny receives a telephone call from Jake, who asks him to pick up their unmarked Crown Vic and meet him at a tavern several blocks from the pawnshop. A half-hour later, Danny finds Jake sitting at the bar; it appears he has been drinking for several hours, but he seems to be holding his liquor well.

"Come here often?" Danny asks, looking around at the surly-faced customers, his nostrils burning from the smell of stale perspiration.

"I like places like this," Jake answers, downing the last of his Seagram's. "The people that come here don't pretend to be anything but the scum they are. See that drunk over there in the corner?" Jake hooks his thumb at an elderly man holding a glass of whiskey with trembling hands. "Claims he used to take stuff all the time to the pawnshop. Says our murdered guy was having some pretty nasty arguments with his son-in-law, a real scumball named Nick. What do you say we go have a talk with this Nick?"

Ten minutes later, Jake and Danny pull to the curb in front of a small brick home just as a man is getting into a red Camaro.

"Nick?" Jake calls as he and Danny climb out of the police car.

The man stops half in and half out of the Camaro. "Who wants to know?"

"Police!" Jake and Danny both flash their badges at him.

Looking around for a second, Nick yanks out the Beretta he has been carrying since murdering his father-in-law and fires a wild shot at the two detectives, then jumps into the Camaro and races away.

"Come on!" Jake shouts as he and Danny both leap back into the Crown Vic.

After a mile-long, high-speed chase during which both cars sideswipe several other vehicles and force a half-dozen pedestrians to leap for their lives, Nick's Camaro crashes into a parked car. With blood now streaming down his forehead, Nick jumps out and fires another shot at Jake and Danny before fleeing between two buildings.

"Head him off!" Jake shouts to Danny as he jumps out of the police car.

Running after Nick, Jake has to leap to one side several times when Nick turns and fires at him. As they come out onto another street, it appears that Nick, now 75 yards ahead, is going to escape if Jake doesn't do something. Jake, dripping with sweat and breathing hard, stops, takes aim, and fires his Glock, hitting Nick in the leg and sending him crashing to the sidewalk. With an expression of obvious pain, Nick struggles back up to his feet and aims his pistol at Jake, who has now almost caught up with him. Jake, however, fires first and shoots the pistol out of Nick's hand, but Nick scrambles across the sidewalk for it and picks the pistol back up. Jake fires a third shot and this time hits Nick squarely in the chest, sending him crashing backward through a plate-glass window.

A moment later, as a crowd begins gathering, Danny pulls up in the Crown Vic. Jake looks at Nick for a second, then sticks his pistol back into the holster and walks over and climbs into the police car. "Come on," he says. "I don't know about you, but I need a drink."

The Truth

Anyone who has read a detective novel or been to a crime movie in the past 20 years undoubtedly recognizes this sequence of events. It has been used in various forms at least hundreds, and probably thousands, of times and continues to be used every year—even though most of the things described above never actually happen in real life. And yet, even though completely wrong, plots such as this, used for years in books and movies, are often the source from which many people get their preconceptions about police and police work.

Because this source of information is filled with mistakes and distortions, it can contribute to problems between the police and the public. Many people believe, through the misinformation they receive from the media, that they know exactly how police officers think and act, but unfortunately they often find out too late that they've been misinformed.

When citizens interact with the police, either they want the police to correct a wrong or they want to be able to remove themselves from the interaction with the least amount of harm possible: without a ticket, without being arrested, and so on. What many citizens may not realize is that the police have a large amount of discretion in these areas and that most officers work with only minimal supervision and review of their work. So, in correcting wrongs the police can either take a report and simply file it away or, if they want, they can conduct an in-depth investigation, canvass a neighborhood for witnesses, make arrests, and recover property. And in situations where the police are the ones who initiate the contact, they have the discretion to write the ticket, make the arrest, or simply let the citizen go with a warning. But the decision as to which course of action the police will take is not so much up to the police as it is up to the citizens they've stopped. Citizens who know how to interact effectively with the police can control the outcome. But still, every year millions of people talk themselves into a ticket or an arrest, even though the officer had originally intended only to give a warning.

To be able to deal effectively with the police, citizens must first understand the true nature of police officers and their job, and not depend on the information they get from movies and novels, information more often wrong than right.

Mistakes and Distortions

The first paragraph of the scenario at the beginning of this chapter contains a major mistake often seen in novels and movies. The police, working simply on rumors, cannot legally kick in a door as Jake and Danny did at the pawnshop. If they do, nothing they find inside, no matter how incriminating, can be used as evidence. Without the permission of the owner, only in exigent circumstances (for example, life in danger, important evidence being destroyed, etc.) can the police forcibly enter a private residence or closed place of business without a search warrant. And in order to obtain a search warrant they must have more evidence than just rumors.

Another frequently occurring scene that will usually bring a groan from police officers is the one in which, like Jake with the carving knife, an officer, in order to avoid smearing fingerprints, handles a piece of important evidence with a handkerchief. If picking up an object with one's bare hands will smear fingerprints, then what is to stop a handkerchief from doing the same thing? The public, however, firmly believes that the police actually do this, and will often use their belief to the detriment of a criminal investigation.

"It's happened to me more times than you'd believe," says a veteran homicide detective. "You get to the scene of a murder and some witness'll hand you the murder weapon wrapped up in a handkerchief."

Not only don't police officers handle evidence using handkerchiefs, they actually seldom pick up or immediately handle evidence at all. Instead, they usually just leave it where it was found and guard it until an evidence technician can arrive to fingerprint and process it (remove any hair or blood, photograph its position, etc.). Then, after the technician has finished, the detectives can handle and examine the evidence. But if for some reason a piece of evidence must be picked up or moved before an evidence technician arrives, police officers don't use handkerchiefs; instead they use their bare hands or, because of the AIDS scare, rubber gloves. In this situation, they pick the evidence up by a part unlikely to contain fingerprints, or which wouldn't be able to contain them anyway, such as the rough portion of a gun handle. Police officers don't pick up handguns by inserting a pencil or metal rod in the barrel, as I have seen done in many movies. Doing this could damage the rifling in the barrel and make it difficult to prove a bullet was fired from the gun.

A third frequent mistake is the one where an officer, like Jake, tastes drugs in order to identify them. While I understand that this scene is used by writers to demonstrate the hero's competence through the ability, for example, to identify heroin by its bitter taste, officers simply do not identify drugs by tasting them. The reason for this is simple: street drugs, because they are often manufactured under very crude conditions, usually vary considerably in color and texture. And so, if police officers routinely tested for heroin or other drugs by taste, how could they be certain they weren't actually sampling powdered LSD, PCP, or some other hallucinogen? This is important because, though ingesting heroin orally, for example, will usually have no ill effect on a person, many hallucinogens when taken orally, even in minute quantities, are extremely potent. As a police officer, whenever I read a novel or see a movie in which an officer tastes drugs, I always imagine us having to call for the fire department's hook-and-ladder truck to pull the officer down from the top of a lamppost, where he or she was perched howling at passing cars. An unknown substance, incidentally, could just as easily be strychnine, arsenic, or cyanide as a street or prescription drug. Police officers have field drug-testing kits, and every police department usually has access to a forensic laboratory, which can confirm the field kit's findings and do the more elaborate testing needed for presentation of evidence in court.

While these are only a few examples of the dozens of mistakes and distortions found in the media, perhaps an even bigger disservice to law enforcement comes from the novels and movies that stereotype the "typical" police personality. Many books and movies portray police officers, as Jake was portrayed, as caustic, cynical, hard-drinking workaholics, and as with any stereotype this is not based on a true picture of the whole group. While it is true there are many caustic and cynical police officers, there are also many sensitive and feeling police officers; and while there are some hard drinkers, there are also many teetotalers; and while it is true some police officers are workaholics, there

The Police Lifestyle

In addition to the stereotyping effect of police novels and movies, there is another reason many people believe all police officers act and think the same. Many people believe this because most veteran officers, they find, have no close friends other than police officers, and because police officers seem to socialize mostly with each other.

Police officers, however, don't do this because they are all identical, but because officers find that after entering law enforcement their old friends treat them differently, as though they were no longer the same person, but now someone around whom they have to watch what they say and do. This makes most police officers feel very uncomfortable. New police officers also find that their former friends can seldom understand their new job or their motivation for doing it.

It is difficult to say where more information on the police lifestyle can be found, because even writers who are former police officers seldom tell the truth about what it's like to be a police officer. One of the very few exceptions I have found to this, however, is Joseph Wambaugh, a former Los Angeles police officer. When his books first appeared they caused a stir in the law enforcement community because they portrayed police officers as they actually are, warts and all. And so, for anyone interested in not only some fascinating reading but also more information on police officers, police work, and particularly the police lifestyle, I heartily recommend two of Joseph Wambaugh's earliest books, *The Blue Knight* and *The New Centurions*.

are just as many lazy officers. Interestingly, a number of police movies and novels each year are written by former police officers, and unfortunately many of them also use these stereotypes, not because they're true but because they're what the public expects.

As with any group, the members of the law enforcement profession simply cannot be stereotyped. Police officers come from many different backgrounds and each officer has a different psychological makeup. Without knowing an individual officer personally, it is impossible to predict how he or she will react to a particular situation. And so, if during interactions with the police, citizens use the Hollywood stereotype rather than treating the officers as individuals, the outcome will often be negative.

Almost as bad a disservice as the stereotyping of the police personality are the many car-chase scenes in police novels and movies because they portray police officers as callous and unconcerned about public safety. I saw a movie recently in which, like the chase of Nick, the officers, driving with complete abandon, wrecked not only their own car but a half-dozen private vehicles, including a large boat and a passenger bus full of riders. This was not supposed to be a comedy but a serious movie. Yet it was so unrealistic that it bordered on comedy. I don't think the moviegoers realized that while replacing or repairing these vehicles would certainly be expensive to a police department, their cost would seem minimal compared to the lawsuits that would undoubtedly be brought on because of the reckless disregard for life and property the police officers displayed. No officer, no matter how competent, no matter how many arrests he has made, or how many cases he has solved, would be allowed to drive with the reckless abandon and complete disregard for public safety often portrayed in novels and movies. That officer would soon find himself either in another occupation or walking a lonely beat somewhere.

Another major stereotype, similar to the car-chase scenario, involves police officers and firearms, a distortion that again leaves a false image in the public's mind. Practically no police novel or movie would be complete without at least one scene involving a police shoot-out. Yet in truth, most police officers go through their entire careers without ever shooting anyone, even though the police in novels and movies are often portrayed as trigger-happy. And regardless of what the media would have the public believe, shooting someone, even a hardened criminal, is not done lightly. Being forced to take a life in the line of duty can often haunt police officers for many years, and can cause these officers serious psychological problems, even though the person they shot may have been trying to kill them or someone else.

One police officer I interviewed for this book, for example, had the misfortune of being involved in a fatal police-action shooting a little over five years ago. The man he shot had just robbed a filling station and pistol-whipped the attendant, then tried to shoot the officer. Regardless of the viciousness of the man's crime, the officer told me that he still wakes up at night dripping with sweat and his heart palpitating from recurring nightmares of seeing the holdup man's face as he grabbed his side and then fell dead to the pavement. Other officers report daytime flashbacks of their shooting someone, while many suffer through alcohol and drug abuse, failed marriages, and even suicide attempts as a result of being involved in police-action shootings.

But in addition to distortions about the frequency and casualness of police shootings, many of the things fictional police officers are made to do with firearms are not only completely wrong but often ridiculous.

"I always love the scene where a cop chases some guy on foot for a mile or so, then stops and fires at him, hitting the guy right in the leg, all from about 75 or 80 yards," said a 20-year uniformed district sergeant.

Most police officers are not in fact expert shots, and few could do what Jake did, that is, purposely hit a subject in the leg at 75 yards with a pistol, especially after having just run some distance, and particularly if, like Jake, they are overweight and getting along in years. Most police-action shootings don't even happen like the one in the scenario. The majority take place within 10 feet and are usually over in just a few seconds, and I've never known of a single police officer who has ever intentionally shot a weapon out of a suspect's hand.

Yet despite all of this, the Annie Oakley marksmanship fostered by hundreds of police novels and movies is so entrenched in the public's mind that each year many police officers appear before grand juries or civilian review boards who very sincerely ask them why they didn't just shoot the gun out of the suspect's hand. The officers, after a few moments of stunned silence, usually answer with an unbelieving "Huh?"

Other examples of ridiculous misinformation about police officers and firearms include, of course, the revolver or pistol that can fire several dozen times without reloading, or bullets that can send people crashing backward through windows or over tables, as happened to Nick. There are no handgun bullets that have this kind of power. Isaac Newton's third law of mechanics states: "To every action there is always opposed an equal reaction." This means that if there was a handgun bullet powerful enough to send someone flying backward, the recoil from the firearm would also have to send the person firing it flying backward. Quite often, people who are shot not only don't fly backward, they don't even fall down.

During our twice-yearly trips to the police department's firing range to demonstrate proficiency with the department's weapons, the range staff always tries to also present videos that add to the actual hands-on training. One year they presented two videos that were especially enlightening concerning the effects of being shot by handguns. The first was an actual video shot by store security cameras of the robbery of a convenience store. The holdup man, armed with a .357 Magnum revolver (a very powerful handgun), for no apparent reason leaned over the counter and shot a young woman standing at the cash register. The shot was delivered from less than a foot away, yet the woman didn't fly backward or even fall down. Except for a slight movement of her hair when the bullet passed through her chest, there were no apparent signs that she had been shot (even though a few minutes later she sat down and died).

In the second video a police officer told the story of a case in which he and his partner encountered a mentally disturbed man who suddenly flew into a rage and killed the officer's partner. The officer subsequently shot the deranged man 10 times at close range, once even in the top of the head, but the man did not fall or stop trying to kill the other officer. The only thing that finally stopped the man was a lucky shot by the officer that shattered the man's hip socket and consequently kept him from being able to get off the floor.

Interestingly, not only don't people always fall down when they're shot, they often don't even know they have been shot. I had a good friend who, as a police officer, was shot through a door on two different occasions. He told me that both times he didn't feel anything or even know he was shot. He just heard the bang and when he looked down he found he was bleeding.

But even more ridiculous than the bullets that send people flying backward is the scene in which police officers, just before getting ready to break through a door to arrest someone, pull out their weapons as Jake and Danny did and either flip open the revolver cylinder or drop out the pistol magazine, apparently checking to be certain the weapons are loaded. Readers can be sure that police officers are not so simple-minded that they would carry firearms around in their holsters, often for hours, without knowing whether they were loaded or not.

There is one final distortion involving police officers and firearms that, though perhaps not the most ridiculous, is still certainly one of the worst because, more than most, it stereotypes police officers as hardened and cynical. This distortion is the scene in which an officer, after finally winning a gun battle, calmly walks away from the dead and wounded, or worse, after shooting the bad guys sticks his revolver or pistol back into the holster, and then goes home, goes back to work, or, as Jake did, goes somewhere for a drink. The officer is never shown calling for medical help or giving the bad guys first aid, which a real police officer is both legally and morally required to do. More importantly, a real police officer never leaves the scene of a police-action shooting until the ensuing investigation is completed, and there is probably no more complex, complicated, or time-consuming investigation than that of a police-action shooting.

Many large police departments now use "shoot teams" to handle the investigation of all police-action shootings. These teams are made up of homicide detectives, crime lab technicians, prosecutors, and other specialists. The police officer who did the shooting, of course, must be present for this investigation. The shortest time an officer can expect before being released by the homicide detective in charge, even on a shooting that appears to be legal and uncomplicated, is four or five hours. During this time the officer will be questioned, and then will assist the shoot team with the on-scene investigation, written statements, reports, and the dozens of other legal and department requirements. And this is just what takes place on the day of the shooting. The process can, and usually does, go on for weeks afterward, with more statements, more interviews, and more paperwork.

A number of years ago, when I was working as a uniformed district sergeant, one evening around 7:00 P.M. I was standing in a parking lot talking with one of my officers. Suddenly, over the police radio came the report that a passing motorist had seen what appeared to be a holdup in progress at the fast food restaurant only a block and a half away from where we were. The officer and I naturally jumped into our police cars and sped toward the restaurant, pulling into the parking lot just as the holdup man, gun in hand, came running out the door.

Seeing the two marked police cars, the holdup man fled around to the rear of the restaurant, and the officer and I both jumped out of our cars and chased after him, yelling for him to halt. The man jumped over a small, chain-link fence and was heading for a passageway behind the restaurant. As I climbed over the waist-high metal fence to go after the man, the other officer fired his .357 Magnum revolver and struck the holdup man just below his buttocks. The man, apparently out of fear that he was seriously injured, though it later turned out his injuries were very minor, stopped and gave up.

Even though this was a clean case of catching a robbery suspect in the act, I didn't get to leave the scene of the shooting until almost 2:00 A.M. The next day, the officer and I were called

Why Become a Police Officer?

A question often asked of police officers is why would anyone, considering the job conditions, want to become one? From the hundreds of police applicants I have interviewed while serving on applicant review boards and from the hundreds of officers I have worked with, I have found that there are basically four types of individuals who seek law enforcement as a career.

The first type is those who have apparently wanted from their earliest years to become police officers and see it as the only career conceivable for them. These individuals have usually taken law courses in high school, majored in criminal justice during college, worked summer law enforcement internships, and immediately upon graduation from college applied for and joined a police department.

A second type enters law enforcement for reasons that have nothing at all to do with a burning desire to be a police officer, but rather with seeing law enforcement as a secure, fairly well-paying job with good benefits and, most important, work that won't be boring or monotonous. These people have usually worked at a number of other jobs and have either been laid off or become so bored they had to get out.

The third type enters law enforcement for the same reason I did, which is for no reason at all, but simply by falling into it by accident. Like many other young men during the late 1960s, I had returned home after a tour in the military and needed a job. My brother mentioned that the police department was hiring, and not knowing anything about the pay, benefits, or actual working conditions, but thinking that law enforcement sounded exciting, I applied and found I loved the work.

Unfortunately, there is a fourth type that no amount of psychological screening seems to be able to completely *(continued)*

Why Become a Police Officer? (continued)

weed out. These are people who have either personality inadequacies or large amounts of suppressed anger, and who want very much the power that comes from being a police officer. These individuals usually cause police departments a large amount of embarrassment before they can be fired.

Interestingly, very few of the people who apply to be police officers consider the possible dangers of the job as a barrier. Actually, the possible danger is one of the things that attracts them. But even more interesting is that very few of the people who do become police officers, regardless of what they might tell the applicant review board, do so because of a burning desire for public service. Most join because of the perceived excitement and prestige of law enforcement, even though public service is a large part of actually being a police officer.

---

in for more statements and more reports, and several weeks later we had to appear before the Firearms Review Board. Interestingly, at the Firearms Review Board they played a tape of my radio transmissions after the shooting. Although I didn't remember being that way, on the tape I was screaming and sounded almost hysterical. Hardly the picture of a calm, cynical, hardened officer, even though I had been involved in many other stressful and dangerous situations before this, including other police-action shootings. Few books or movies portray police officers in this way.

There is a final distortion that appears in practically every police story, namely, the belief that the police solve nearly every crime they come in contact with, no matter how scant the evidence. This distortion is particularly damaging because, while fictional police almost always catch the bad guys and solve the case by the end, the actual average solution rate for all crimes by the police is only about 20 percent. But because of this distortion, if a solution is not forthcoming, many citizens feel as though the police are just not doing enough and are not working hard enough on their case. The truth is that some cases, actually many cases, simply cannot be solved. This includes both minor crimes and the most heinous ones. Many criminals simply get away with it. This is a sad, but simple, truth that makes it even more imperative that citizens learn all they can about how to avoid becoming the victim of a crime.

Successful Interaction

The examples I have given of the many distortions that appear regularly in novels and movies are not intended to keep people from reading or from going to the movies, but only to emphasize the need not to use the stereotypes they present as the basis for actions when dealing with the police. To be successful in their interactions with the police, members of the public must, besides using the information given in the following chapters, also realize that police officers are not all recruited from some small pool of identical candidates, but from the public at large, from all levels and all backgrounds. And because police officers come from all segments of society, a police department is not a homogenous group, but only a collection of individuals, each with a distinct personality, who all simply share the same job. There is just no typical police officer. Some are outgoing, others are introverts; some are extremely bright, others are only average; some are nice people, others are not so nice.

Best Advice

As a general rule, stereotyping any group is dangerous because very few members of the group will actually fit the stereotype. The best advice I can offer for dealing with police officers is never to depend on the stereotypes depicted in the media. Any dealings with police officers will be much more positive and productive if readers, besides using the advice given in the following chapters, treat police officers as individuals with distinct personalities, and not simply as members of a group who all act and think the same.

2

ASSAULT AND MURDER

WHO COMMITS ASSAULT AND MURDER?

There is an old saying that "familiarity breeds contempt." Every year in our country the crimes of assault (an unlawful attack for the purpose of inflicting injury) and murder (the unlawful killing of another) continue to prove the truth of this old saying.

According to the FBI's national crime statistics, the United States has for the past decade averaged over 20,000 murders and over 1,000,000 serious assaults annually, with the majority of these being committed by family members, lovers, friends, and acquaintances of the victim. In 2000, for example, family members committed over 13 percent of the reported 15,517 murders. They also committed almost 20 percent of the nearly 1,000,000 serious assaults, and probably at least twice as many serious assaults by family members went unreported. Lovers, close friends, and acquaintances added to these figures by committing an additional 31 percent of these 15,517 murders. According to the FBI, only 13 percent of the murders in 2000 could be documented by the police as actually being committed by strangers (usually during the commission of another crime, such as robbery, rape, etc.).

A study published in the *Journal of Trauma* that examined over 215,000 murders found that women were more likely than men to be killed by acquaintances, and that when a woman was the killer she was more likely than a man to kill a spouse, lover, or family member. Another study, this one by the Bureau of Justice Statistics, of 10,000 murder defendants in America's 75 most populous counties, also revealed some alarming statistics about murder in our country. The study found that females were four times more likely than males to die from strangulation or from being struck by a blunt object, and that a third of the murder victims in our country are murdered in their own home.

"Most murderers have some sort of acquaintance with their victims," said ex–homicide captain James Wyatt. "If they're not family, they at least know each other. The same's true for most of the serious assaults."

As might be expected, males are more often the murderer (more than nine times as likely as females) or the murder victim (more than three times as likely). Also, over three times as many males kill females as the reverse (91 percent of female victims were murdered by males).

Tragically, a growing number of the victims of assault and murder in the last few decades have been children. For example, Children's Memorial Hospital in Chicago reported that during a 12-year reporting period they saw an almost 700 percent increase in the number of children under 16 being treated in their emergency room for gunshot wounds. A more recent study by the U.S. Department of Justice shows that children aged 12 to 17 are almost three times as likely as adults to be the victim of an assault. And as with adult victims, a large percentage of these assaults were committed by family, friends, and acquaintances of the children.

According to *Kids Count*, a report compiled by the Annie E. Casey Foundation and the Center for the Study of Social Policy, in 1990, black teenagers were twice as likely to be murdered as to die in an accident. Statistics show that from 1980 to 1997 nearly 38,000 murder victims in the United States were age 17 or younger. Consequently, homicide is the third leading cause of death for those ages 10 to 14, and second for those aged 15 to 24.

Motivation for Assault and Murder

Once arrested, people give numerous reasons for assaulting or killing others, but most, it has been found, assault or kill because of money, romantic triangles, or arguments, with arguments leading by a large margin as the main cause for many of the assaults and murders every year (28.4 percent of the murders in 2000). Whether it is an argument between a husband and wife over domestic matters, between friends over something as minor as borrowed money, or between two strangers over something as trivial as an automobile accident, disagreements are the leading cause for assaults and murders in the United States.

Murder, however, despite what years of Hollywood movie plots would have the public believe, is generally not a planned and plotted crime. The truth is that it is, instead, like many of the serious assaults, often an impulsive act committed in the heat of an argument or fight, with the perpetrators seldom in full control of their faculties, which is why murderers often receive less than the full penalty. (Thirty-two percent of the murders and 38 percent of the assaults committed each year are committed while the perpetrator is either under the influence of drugs or very drunk. These figures, incidentally, come from self-reports, which nationwide drug testing of new arrestees shows are grossly low, probably half or less of the true total.) And yet, even considering the harsh penalties for murder (death in 37 states), and the very small likelihood of getting away with most of them (murder has the highest solution rate of all crimes), the fact that over 15,500 people still did it in 2000 indicates its impulsive nature.

Testifying to this impulsiveness, murders have been committed for things as trivial as a parking space. In Indianapolis several years ago, we had a case in which a teenager bought a pizza and then offered a piece to a homeless man. When the man instead took two pieces, the teenager allegedly went home and got a gun, then came back and killed the man. In San Pablo, California, a mother of four who was asked to stop smoking in the nonsmoking section of a Denny's reportedly returned with a 12-gauge shotgun and murdered one of the patrons.

Warning Signs

Because of the impulsive nature of most assaults and murders, it might seem to readers that there is very little protection against them. Bolstering this belief, most police departments don't even consider murder and assault as preventable crimes since they are usually done on a sudden impulse without any thought. But there are two clear signs that can predict the likelihood, and consequently prevent the occurrence, of an assault or murder.

Since many of the assaults and murders occurring every year are committed by family members or lovers, it follows that one of these signs would be related to probably the most common type of dispatched run that uniformed police officers are sent on: domestic disturbances or family fights. On any weekend night a third to half of all the runs police officers receive can be domestic disturbances, and often they are at the same addresses, over and over. Many times, these are just shouting matches that have finally reached the level where someone has called the police, and occasionally they involve some type of minor violence that results in no serious physical injury, such as pushing or shoving. With this type of domestic disturbance, seldom do the police make any arrests. Instead, they usually try to act as mediators and attempt to bring about some type of peaceful settlement. But occasionally, police officers find, the characteristics of certain relationships cause domestic disturbances that start out as only shouting matches to build over time into minor physical abuse, then into more serious violence, and finally into the use of some type of weapon, such as a gun, knife, or blunt instrument. This final stage often leads to serious injury or death.

This tendency toward progressive violence is one of the clearest signs that a serious assault or murder is an imminent possibility, particularly for those living close to the person exhibiting this behavior. Police officers, particularly when they are rookies, will usually try to warn victims when they see this type of behavior building in a relationship, but find that seldom do the victims of progressive violence heed their warnings or do much at all to protect themselves. Like every other police officer in the United States, I have seen literally hundreds of spouses and live-in lovers who have been clubbed, slugged, and seriously beaten, yet refuse to leave the relationship. Most instead stay in the same violent environment, always insisting that the person doing the assaulting really loves them and will eventually change. Many of these victims, particularly those with little children, also stay because they feel they have very few options. Only when the violence at last reaches very serious levels do they finally consider ending the relationship. By then, however, the violence often results in a death or serious injury before they actually do leave.

"Recent research into domestic murders has produced some interesting findings," said Professor David Ford, a nationally recognized sociologist at Indiana University who has done long-term research into domestic violence. "Most domestic killings occur during or after a spouse or lover has indicated the intention to break up the relationship and move out."

There is a catch22, however, in this finding. What often causes a spouse or live-in lover to decide to end a relationship is that the violence has suddenly evolved beyond simple shouting or minor assaults and has reached serious and often very dangerous levels. Often the decision to break up and move out precipitates even more violent, and sometimes deadly, behavior. In many of these cases, however, serious injury and even death could have been prevented if only something had been done early in the relationship, before the violence had progressed to these very dangerous levels. A slap, shove, or punch should always be considered serious.

When I was a rookie officer on my first permanent beat, I had two public housing projects in my district that usually took up 75 to 80 percent of my time. In one of these projects a woman lived with a man who, almost every weekend it seemed, would get drunk and then assault her. At first this involved slapping or an occasional punch, and when I would get there the man was usually very calm and rational and she would always change her mind about wanting him arrested or even put out for the evening. But soon the violence started increasing, and the victim began receiving black eyes, broken teeth, and once even had a pot of boiling water thrown on her. The man also became smarter and began disappearing as soon as she called the police.

Every weekend, it seemed, I would make a report and she would swear she wanted him arrested and that she would be down at the prosecutor's office the first thing Monday morning to sign a warrant, but she never showed up.

Finally, one Friday night I received the run of a woman who had been knifed. I figured it would be her, but while the address was in the project close to where she lived, it wasn't her apartment. However, when I got to the address I found the woman's boyfriend there with a bloody butcher knife threatening the residents, who he claimed were hiding his girlfriend, which they were. The woman was cowering inside the apartment with a number of slash wounds, though luckily none of them deep enough to be life-threatening. I arrested the woman's boyfriend, and then sent her to the hospital to get sewed up. The next day (being still a rookie then), I was stunned when the woman told the prosecutor that she had changed her mind and didn't want to prosecute. After I went into a raging fit and threatened to refuse to come to her aid in the future no matter what he did (which of course was a bluff), she changed her mind again and signed the complaint. Her boyfriend was eventually convicted of the assault and sentenced to a year on the state penal farm.

Six or seven months later, I was in the project on another run close to the woman's apartment and saw her and her boyfriend, who had recently been released from the state farm, standing in the crowd watching me. A little over a year later, he beat her to death with a frying pan.

In addition to episodes of increasing violence, as in the example above, there is another type of behavior that can indicate an assault or homicide is likely. Individuals who react to what most people would consider only minor or medium stress with sudden, violent, and irrational outbursts are, from a police officer's perspective, persons who should be viewed with serious concern. Assault and murder are impulsive crimes often committed in a sudden, violent, and irrational outburst. I recall, for example, a case in which I was involved where a man who had a long history of screaming at his neighbors and destroying their property had a difficult day at work, and when he came home and found his wife hadn't cleaned the house, he beat her so severely she died. Although later, when he found that she had a good reason for the delay—not that this should have mattered—he was very repentant, it was too late for his wife. Statistics show that over 30 percent of the women murdered in the United States each year are killed by either their husbands or boyfriends, often as a result of a violent outburst. The percentage committing serious assaults is even larger, though no one knows the real magnitude of this problem.

And since research shows that homes experiencing domestic violence against spouses are much more likely than others to also experience domestic violence against children, there are also thousands of cases every year in which adults, in a sudden, violent outburst of anger and frustration at some action, seriously assault or kill their own children. This behavior pattern is one of the reasons why statistics show that homicide is a leading cause of death for children under the age of one.

This second warning sign, though, while often applying to domestic relationships, can also apply to friends, acquaintances, and even strangers. Becoming embroiled in an argument with anyone who appears prone to sudden, violent, and irrational outbursts is not advisable since this type of person is dangerous to frustrate and seldom swayed by logic. When encountering a person who exhibits this type of behavior, readers would do well to avoid getting into any type of confrontation, since these can often lead to violence.

These two behavioral patterns—episodes of increasing violence and sudden, violent, irrational outbursts—are two of the clearest indicators of future assaults or murders. There are, of course, some assaults and murders that take place each year with no indications they were ever going to happen, and there are some individuals who demonstrate one, or even both, of these behavioral patterns, yet never assault or murder anyone and may, for example, take out their violence on the furniture.

But since many assault victims every year are scarred or crippled, and since murder victims don't get a second chance, any clues to the likelihood of another's potential for violence should be taken seriously and acted upon immediately.

Many victims of domestic abuse, however, stay in the relationship because they believe they don't have any other options. In most large communities, though, there are now shelters for the victims of domestic abuse. Many of these shelters do not advertise their address since they don't want abusive spouses coming there. However, most of these can be found through the local victim's assistance group. Also, victims of abuse should never hesitate to request that the police take them and their children to one of these shelters. The police know where they are. Most of these shelters are affiliated with social service agencies and, along with giving victims a safe place to stay, will also provide counseling for abuse victims. Women who detect either of the two signs I have given above would be well advised to find out about the shelters and services in their community—just in case—even though they may not feel in danger yet and are not ready to give up on the relationship.

In addition to these two signs, there is another sign that parents in particular should be concerned about. While not as clear as the two above, and not a sign that always means violence is in the future, it should still be given a serious look. Children who suddenly begin missing school and begin having serious disputes with other students can be exhibiting signs that they are in fear of physical violence at school. Some children skip school because they are afraid of other students—and with good reason. A Harris poll found that 15 percent of the schoolchildren questioned nationwide said they had carried a handgun in the previous month, while 4 percent said they had actually carried a handgun into the school. The FBI reports that from 1985 to 1991 the arrests of 15-, 16-, and 17-year-olds for murder more than doubled, while a third of high-achieving high school students said in a recent survey that they knew someone who had brought a weapon to school. A more recent study by the U.S. Department of Justice found that one in five of all juveniles arrested in the United States said they carried a gun all or most of the time. These are frightening developments because 10 percent of all murder victims in 2000 were under the age of 18, and it has been found that young people are three times more likely to be slain today than were those in 1950. All of this means parents should take any sign their children are afraid of other students very seriously, and immediately take action by meeting with school administrators or the police. By making the police and school administrators aware of students who are threatening others with physical violence, parents can allow the authorities to take action before a tragedy occurs. Administrators who have probable cause to believe a student is carrying a weapon have the right to search for that weapon. Also, many times it is helpful for the authorities to let a person know, without naming their source, that they are aware he is threatening others. He then knows he will be a suspect if anything happens. This is particularly effective if the person doing the threatening is on some type of probation that a misdeed will revoke.

Weapons of Assault and Murder

Many citizens, especially those concerned about gun control, make the claim that the most important factor causing the high number of murders and serious assaults that occur every year in the United States is the ready availability of firearms. They point to the fact that well over 200 million guns are now owned by Americans and that every year Americans purchase millions of new guns.

There is evidence both for and against this argument. Of the over 15,500 murders committed in 2000, for example, over 65 percent were committed by firearms, while a little over 13 percent were committed by cutting or stabbing, almost 5 percent by blunt instruments, and the remainder by some other device (poison, strangulation, etc.).

These statistics, though, can be viewed two ways. Some would say that without firearms 65 percent of the murders committed in 2000 would not have occurred. But most police officers are not really convinced of that. The fact that almost 35 percent of the murders were committed by some method other than a firearm could also mean that these people simply didn't have a firearm readily available and so used something else. Would the 65 percent of the murderers who did use firearms have also simply used whatever else was available if no firearm had been? I don't think anyone really knows for sure how many of them would have, certainly not all, but most police officers suspect it would still be a large number. Murders and serious assaults are often committed in a fit of rage, and with whatever happens to be close at hand.

There is, however, a very revealing statistic that argues for the other viewpoint, for the fact that the availability of firearms is responsible for a large number of murders. A study of police officers murdered in the United States and in Great Britain (where gun ownership is much less common) shows that American police officers are over 100 times more likely to be murdered (mostly by firearms) than are their British counterparts.

But the most frightening statistic shows that firearms in the United States are available not just to adults. A recent Harris poll found that almost 60 percent of youngsters from the sixth to the twelfth grades said they had ready access to a handgun. This is certainly an alarming statistic when one considers the growing number of young murder victims there are every year. From 1986 to 1991, for example, the murder rate for youths aged 14 to 17 grew by 124 percent. In 1999, nearly 1,800 children 17 and younger were murdered in the United States; over 50 percent of these were killed with firearms.

Likelihood of Assault and Murder

But just what exactly is the risk of assault or murder to the average citizen? How likely is it that a person in our country will be seriously assaulted or murdered?

According to the FBI's national crime statistics, over a person's lifetime, males in the United States have about a 1 in 100 chance of being a homicide victim (over three-fourths of the murder victims in the United States during 2000 were male), while females have about a 1 in 323 chance. The chances of being the victim of a serious assault, since serious assaults are almost 60 times more common than murder, are, of course, much larger, with the average person having a 40 percent probability of being seriously assaulted sometime during his or her life. Statistics from the Centers for Disease Control show that in 1999, murder ranked as the second leading cause of death in the United States for those aged 15 to 24, third for those from 10 to 14 and from 25 to 34, and fourth for those from 1 to 9. In 1996, according to the National Crime Victimization Survey, there were over 2,000,000 incidents of violence in the workplace, ranging from assaults by other employees to murders by spouses and lovers who came to the workplace. These incidents of violence caused over 1,000 deaths, which made attacks on women the second leading cause of women dying on the job (after traffic accidents). Though in 1999, 80 percent of the workplace homicide victims were men, a woman, researchers found, was 40 times more likely to be killed at work by her husband than was a husband by his wife.

There are several factors, however, that can affect the likelihood of being assaulted or murdered. For instance, a person has the greatest likelihood of being murdered in the southern states, less in the western and midwestern states, and still less in the northeastern states. And as certain areas of the country are more dangerous than others, so certain times of the year are also more dangerous. In 2000, for example, more murders occurred during the summer months than during any other season. Yet still, a high number of murders occurred during the month of December (highest after the summer months). While there are no statistics available that tell what part of the month murders occur in, readers can draw many inferences from this. Most police departments receive a large number of domestic disturbance runs whenever people are off work for the holidays and spending more time with their families. December is also the time of year that many distant relatives who don't see much of each other suddenly spend time together, and quite often suddenly remember why they don't like to spend much time together. For serious assault, as with murder, summer was again the time of highest probability.

Homicide Investigation

Since murder is a crime usually committed between people who at least know each other, it would seem that murder should be the easiest crime to solve. The national crime statistics each year demonstrate that, in fact, this is the case. In 2000, for example, approximately 9,800 of the 15,517 reported murders in the United States were solved by arrest.

While many readers may be shocked that the police solved only 63 percent of the reported murders in 2000, meaning that over 5,700 went unsolved, this is actually a very good solution rate when compared with the 25 percent solution rate for robbery, the 14 percent solution rate for vehicle theft, or the 13 percent solution rate for burglary. Also, an important variable affecting the percentage of unsolved murders is the fact that an increasing number of the murders committed each year (estimated to be at least one-fourth of the total) are drug-related, and being drug-related they simply do not receive the same emphasis and commitment from the police that other murder investigations (with innocent or at least semi-innocent victims) do. In addition, drug-related murders often involve only a vague "relationship" between the perpetrator and the victim, which adds to the difficulty of solving them.

But to obtain a better picture of the national crime solution rate, readers must look at the total figures. There were an estimated 26 million crimes perpetrated in the United States in 2000, with fewer than half, or about 11.6 million, reported to the police. However, only around 20.5 percent, or around 2.38 million of the reported cases, were solved. This means that

Serial Killers

Every year a small number of homicides in the United States are committed by serial killers (for example, John Gacy, Wayne Williams, Ted Bundy), murderers who seldom know their victims and often simply pick them at random, killing most using the same pattern of approaching their victims, murder methods, and locations for leaving the body. Some of these murderers, such as Wayne Williams, pick all of their victims from one community, while others, like Ted Bundy, may travel cross-country looking for victims. The Department of Justice recently estimated that there are presently 35 to 40 such serial killers in the United States, killers who many times terrorize communities, causing residents to barricade themselves in their homes until the murderer is finally caught.

But even though they are given extensive press coverage, serial murders are actually very rare when compared with the total number of murders committed every year. When the probabilities are compared, serial killers shouldn't overly concern readers. What should concern readers is living with people like R. Gene Simmons of Arkansas, who was found guilty of killing 14 members of his family; King Edward Bell of Indiana, who, in a fit of rage, killed his four small children; or Richard Crafts of Connecticut, who was convicted of murdering his wife and then running her body through a wood chipper. The reality of homicide is that people don't have to be nearly as concerned about being murdered on the street by serial killers as they do about being murdered in their own homes by their own family members.

But regardless of possibilities, likelihoods, or percentages, no one is immune to the possibility of murder. Even cardinals of the Catholic Church are not immune, as was proven when Cardinal Juan Jesus Posadas Ocampo was *(continued)*

Serial Killers (continued)

gunned down by hired killers from San Diego, who mistook him for a drug lord at an airport in Guadalajara, Mexico. Murder recognizes no territorial, social, or economic boundaries.

Another case proving this point was that of Francis and Helen Benefiel. This elderly couple was part of a typical middle-class American family. The two had known each other since grade school and had been married for 47 years. To everyone who knew them this midwestern couple seemed the perfect example of two happily married people who had no enemies and had never hurt anyone. However, they were brutally murdered in their home, allegedly gunned down by an ex-boyfriend of their granddaughter. The police believe he murdered them because he thought they would try to talk their granddaughter out of taking him back as her boyfriend.

actually only a little over 9 percent of the total 26 million crimes were solved. And so, in comparison with the overall crime solution rate, the 63 percent solution rate for murder (which, unlike other crimes, has a near 100 percent reporting rate) is actually quite good.

But how were these 9,800 murders solved? Are the methods used to solve murders in both crime movies and mystery novels a true reflection of how real murders are actually solved? (The investigation of assaults follows much of the same procedure as that of homicides, except that they are both easier and more difficult. They are easier because there is a live victim to give a description of the perpetrator, but more difficult because of the reluctance of many victims to cooperate with the police after enough time has passed for the pain to be forgotten and for the perpetrator to swear that he or she will never do it again. And of course many are afraid that prosecution will only lead to more violence.)

Most homicide detectives smile and shake their heads when asked about the realism of crime movies and mystery novels. While they will admit there are some surface similarities, fictional detective stories seldom show the routineness of actual murder investigation. In most real homicide investigations there are no gun battles or high-speed car chases. Most gun battles and high-speed car chases take place between criminals and uniformed beat officers. There are also no battles of wit with master criminals. Occasionally, the crime is already solved by the time the homicide investigator arrives at the murder scene, the uniformed officers having the suspect (usually a spouse, lover, or friend) in handcuffs. And even in those cases with no suspect yet under arrest, often there are witnesses being detained by the uniformed officers, witnesses who saw what happened and know who the murderer is. In these cases, the only real task a homicide investigator has is the preparation of the case for court.

"The movies never show the tons of paperwork we go through," said one veteran homicide investigator. "They never show the hours of questioning. But the part in movies I always love best is where the homicide detective drops by the murder scene for a few seconds to glance at the body, and then takes off to go hunt for the murderer. On most investigations we're at the scene for hours, going over everything. Homicide investigation just isn't always as exciting as it looks in the movies. It can be occasionally, but mostly it's just Ma and Pa killings."

Another misconception that movies and novels have fostered about homicide investigation is that, contrary to what the writers of these would have people believe, the crime lab or coroner is seldom able to pinpoint precisely the time of death. He or she can estimate the time of death from body temperature, but only estimate, because there are many variables that can affect a murder victim's body temperature, such as air-conditioning, wind, and the surrounding air temperature. Also affecting the body temperature of a murder victim are both how the victim was dressed when murdered and the amount of body fat the victim has. Although seldom mentioned in the movies, the coroner or crime lab many times also uses the body's state of rigor mortis (which usually begins in the jaw area after several hours) to estimate the time of death, but again can only estimate. One last trick, also seldom in movies, is checking to see if the lights in the house were on or off when the body was found, suggesting whether the crime was committed during the day or at night, and checking such things as when the mail and newspaper were last picked up by the victim. There are also a number of exotic ways to determine the time or day of death, such as counting the number and measuring the size of the maggots in the corpse (insects quickly make use of any available corpse) and measuring the loss of chemicals from the bones.

A further misconception about homicide detectives is that seldom are they the first ones on the scene of a murder or the ones to find the body. Usually, they are summoned to the murder scene by uniformed officers, who answered a call from someone else who found the body.

So how do real homicide detectives solve murders in which there are no suspects already named or being detained by uniformed officers?

Most homicide detectives first seek a motive for the murder. This will usually lead to a suspect. Although each homicide detective has his or her own minor variations, most generally follow a certain set of steps in the investigation. First, if not already done by the uniformed officers, most homicide detectives secure the crime scene so that no evidence will be trampled or destroyed. Next, again if not already done by the uniformed officers, the investigators gather up all of the possible witnesses, and then immediately separate them so that they can't compare stories and, either intentionally or unconsciously, change their version. Following this, homicide detectives, in order to get an overview of what has happened, usually talk to the first officer to arrive at the scene and the person who found the body.

After this initial questioning, most investigators survey the crime scene, but do not touch or move anything until after the crime lab has videotaped and photographed the entire area. A number of homicide detectives, even though the murder scene has been photographed and videotaped, also draw a diagram of the murder scene in their notebook. Yet, even after the murder scene has been recorded on film and videotape, the investigator still doesn't touch or move anything until after the crime lab has processed any possible evidence (fingerprints lifted, hair or body fluids removed, the evidence marked and bagged, etc.). While physical evidence alone is not as valuable as having an eyewitness to the murder, it still serves several very crucial purposes. It can establish the elements of a crime (which must be done in court in order to get a conviction), it can connect the suspect with the crime, and it can be used to reconstruct the crime itself. But probably most important, it can be used to show a judge or jury the severity of the crime, and can convince them that the defendant was the perpetrator. A recent study has even shown a strong link between the amount of forensic evidence recovered in a crime and the length of a sentence a defendant receives. This connection probably exists because physical evidence tends to corroborate the prosecution's case.

Once the scene has been recorded on film and the obvious evidence processed by the crime lab, the investigator examines the body. While examining the body the homicide detective looks for any obvious wounds that would indicate the cause of death, looks for defensive wounds (wounds sustained trying to ward off the attack), and always checks for lividity (settlement of blood). After death, a person's blood will settle into the part of the body closest to the ground, discoloring the skin. If the detective finds this discoloration, or lividity, on an upper surface of the murder victim's body, it can be assumed that the body was moved after death. Next, the crime scene is searched and examined in more detail, and the detective will have the crime lab process and bag any further evidence he or she finds and wants to save. To find this evidence, there are various search methods detectives use, such as the spiral, which starts from one central point and spirals outward; the point to point, which moves from one piece of evidence to another, hoping to follow the suspect's path; the wheel, which starts at one central point and radiates outward like the spokes of a wheel; and several others, depending on the size and nature of the crime scene being searched.

A significant part of any homicide investigation is the canvassing of the neighborhood for anyone who might know something about the murder or might have seen something that could prove important to the investigation. This canvassing includes not only the houses on the street where the murder occurred but also those on the street behind the murder scene. Often, people will have seen things they didn't realize were important at the time, or, just as often, people will only talk to the police when canvassed because they don't want others to tag them as "snitches," which they fear would happen if they initiated the contact with the police. In addition, a good source of information for detectives who are canvassing the neighborhood is the "neighborhood gossip," the person who knows the dirt on everyone. This person can often be a real asset when trying to find a motive for the murder.

"We had a case once," a homicide detective told me, "where our victim was a real salt-of-the-earth type. Almost a saint, it seemed. Worked for the church, was a Boy Scout leader, patted stray dogs, you name it. Didn't seem to have a single enemy. We were really stumped because they found our guy face down out behind his house, shot four times in the back. It didn't look like robbery though because he still had his wallet in his pocket. But no one we talked to seemed to have a clue why anyone would want to kill him. That is, until we found the neighborhood snoop. This guy knew everything that went on in the neighborhood and told us that he had seen our victim sneaking in and out of the house of a divorced woman who lived on the street behind him. Turned out our murder victim was having an affair with the lady but wanted to break it off. We brought in the woman for questioning, and she finally broke down and admitted the affair and the murder. She said she told him that she would see him dead if he tried to leave her. And she did."

In addition to the neighborhood gossip, detectives often find that they can get more information on the murder victim by talking to the neighbors than they can by talking to the family. Family members usually want to protect the family's reputation and will often leave out anything that might tarnish their name.

Following this on-scene investigation, which generally takes several hours, a homicide detective usually has all of the witnesses, even though sometimes already initially questioned on the scene, taken to police headquarters or to the precinct house for more extensive questioning. It is easier to break a suspect if the detective takes him or her off home turf and into a strange environment. The suspect is easier to fluster if he or she no longer enjoys the feeling of security that the home provides.

Depending on the size of the police department and the number of homicide detectives it has, occasionally one detective may immediately take the witnesses to headquarters for questioning, while another detective stays at the murder scene. It is during this questioning that homicide investigators are often able to establish a motive and, if none has already been named, a suspect.

Whenever a suspect in a murder is identified, quite often skillful questioning by homicide investigators will bring either incriminating evidence or an admission. Any suspect has the right to remain silent and refuse to be questioned, but since most are pretending to be innocent, and believe that an innocent person wouldn't refuse to talk to the police, suspects usually talk until they make a slip. Often, all a homicide detective has to do is catch a suspect in a lie or an inconsistency and the suspect will then break down and confess. It is during questioning that many murders are solved.

A veteran homicide detective tells, for example, of the case of a 70-year-old woman who had been found strangled. After the initial investigation, it was determined that her 35-year-old boyfriend was the last person to see her alive. From the police questioning him, the suspect apparently guessed that the police believed she had been murdered sometime after 8:00 P.M. He admitted to the police that he had seen her on the day she died, but claimed he had left her apartment at around 6:00 P.M. He stated he knew it had to be around that time because it was just beginning to get dark, and so he turned on the outside light as he left. The detective did a little investigation and found that all of the outside lights in the apartment area were on a timer and not controlled by the tenants.

"When I confronted him with this," the detective said, "he at first tried to explain his way out of it, but then finally broke down and confessed to the murder."

While all homicide investigators usually follow certain standard procedures, each also has a repertoire of little tricks or devices that have solved murders in the past. One detective, for example, always immediately tries to find the last person who saw the murder victim alive. That person is often, he has found, the murderer, or has information that will lead to the murderer. Another detective does a complete neighborhood search, even if the murder occurred inside a building. Many times, he has discovered, a murderer will discard incriminating evidence once outside of a building. One veteran homicide investigator always has the crime lab technician videotape the crowd of spectators that inevitably gather at any murder scene. Often, the murderer will be there, standing far back in the crowd, wanting to find out how much the police know. This has proven to be especially helpful if later the suspect attempts to establish an alibi of being out of town or far away at the time of the murder. Another homicide detective has found it useful to check the criminal records of all witnesses. This has often proven helpful in identifying suspects when it is believed that the murder was drug-related.

In addition to these tricks and devices, though, clues to the identity of the murderer can also come from many other sources, such as a DNA analysis of body fluids left at the murder scene, buttons torn from the murderer's clothing, footprints or tire tracks left by the murderer, and any evidence gathered at the autopsy, which homicide detectives attend.

Most homicide detectives agree that seldom are murder investigations as exciting and glamorous as they appear to be in the movies. Instead, most murders are solved by a lot of footwork, questioning, and paperwork coupled with ceaseless cigarettes, coffee, and late hours.

Best Advice

While murder is the smallest of all major crimes in the actual numbers reported each year (totaling less than 1 percent of all the major crimes reported in the United States), it is obviously the most serious of the major crimes. And so the best advice available is that any evidence of any of the warning signs I have given should be taken very seriously and acted on immediately. Even individuals who might believe the warning signs indicate that only an assault, and not a murder, is a future possibility, and for the sake of their relationship who are willing to risk that for themselves, would still be wise to extricate themselves from the relationship as early as possible. Violence-prone people tend to strike out not just at spouses and lovers, but also at others, including children and the elderly.

3

RAPE, CHILD MOLESTATION, AND OTHER SEX CRIMES

MOTIVATION FOR RAPE

Rape may be defined as sexual intercourse by force or threats and against a person's will, and is probably the most misunderstood crime committed in our country. Although popularly believed to be an act of lust or passion, in truth it actually seldom is. Many rapes, investigators find, are not even acts of sexual gratification, but simply acts of violence in which sexual intercourse is the weapon. Most rapes are simply attempts by men with serious emotional adjustment problems to compensate for their inadequacies by exerting power and dominance over women. In an FBI study of 41 serial rapists, which will be detailed below, it was found that over a third of the men had some type of sexual dysfunction during the rape, and that most reported low levels of pleasure from the sexual act itself.

This finding simply reinforces the truth that rape isn't for the sex, it's for the power. If rape really was predominantly an act of lust and passion, mainly young, attractive women would need to fear it. But this simply isn't the case. The truth is that rape victims can range from the newborn infant to the bedridden elderly, from the healthy to the handicapped, and from the beautiful to the plain. The reality of rape is that its motivation seldom has as much to do with sexual gratification as it does with violence, power, and dominance. This is the reason why the often-heard recommendation for legalizing prostitution would not prevent rape.

FBI Study of Serial Rapists

Several years ago the FBI's National Center for the Analysis of Violence conducted a study of 41 serial rapists, who had committed a total of at least 837 sexual assaults and more than 400 attempts. Through this study, researchers found that the location of a victim and her accessibility to being raped were overwhelmingly more important in her selection as a victim than was any physical quality she had. A fourth of the rapists studied said they had no special physical reasons at all (age, race, physical characteristics, etc.) for selecting their victims. They simply took a victim who happened to be there.

"Any woman is a potential rape victim, and most rapists, we find, have committed or tried to commit the crime at least two or three times before we catch them," said former sex crimes Detective Linda Roeschlein. "Unfortunately, we often don't know about many of the rapes because the victims haven't reported them."

Most sex offense investigators agree with Officer Roeschlein that, like the rapists in the FBI study noted above, the majority of rapists commit or attempt to commit the crime more than once, often dozens of times. Rapists, however, even though convicted of one rape, often don't tell about the others, and, just as often, the victims have not reported them either. It should be pointed out, however, that most sex crime detectives believe there are also the occasional one time rapists, usually men involuntarily being divorced or who perhaps have been fired or reprimanded by a woman, and who commit a single act of rape in a twisted attempt to compensate for the psychological problems caused by their inability to deal with the stress. These men hope that by violently forcing themselves into a position of dominance over a woman they can feel in control again. Still, one cannot predict with accuracy that such a perpetrator will not deal with stress the same way in the future, and so single cases of rape are believed by many sex crime investigators to be much less common than serial rapes.

Fear of Rape

Probably more than any other crime, women fear rape. A recent national poll, for example, found that 62 percent of the respondents said they worry regularly about the possibility of someone raping them or a member of their family. Authors Margaret T. Gordon and Stephanie Riger state in their book *The Female Fear* that two-thirds of the women they interviewed were afraid to walk or jog after dark in their own neighborhoods because of the fear of rape. This constant fear, the authors go on to say, can rob its victims of their freedom, forcing them to often restrict activities, and occasionally even to isolate themselves. Women fear rape, it has been found, not only because of the very real threat of physical harm or disease but also, and sometimes more, because it is not just an assault on their bodies but also an assault on their dignity and feelings of self-worth.

This fear of rape by many women is not just a baseless anxiety, but rather a fear well founded in fact. A researcher at the University of California in Los Angeles found that 40 percent of the men surveyed said they might force a woman to have sex if they were sure they could get away with it. And many men try. In 2000, there were over 90,000 rapes reported to the police (one every 5.8 minutes of the year, though rapes actually tend to occur more often in summer than in winter), and, depending on whose research we believe, this is anywhere from 20 to 75 percent of the actual number of rapes in our country, with half probably being a good guess.

Statistics compiled by the U.S. Justice Department also substantiate this fear of rape. The department's figures show that over a lifetime a woman has an alarming 1 in 12 chance of being raped, while, even more alarming, other figures show that from 1960 to 2000, reported rapes in the United States increased almost 600 percent.

But if single, isolated rapes, such as those described above, are less common than serial rapes, what kind of man commits serial rapes?

The results of the FBI's study of serial rapists were surprising in this aspect. Researchers found that the majority of the serial rapists were neat, well-groomed men who tended to meet people easily. A majority also held steady jobs, had been married at least once, were above average in intelligence, and had been raised in average to above-average socioeconomic environments. Other studies have found that most rapists are either married or involved in a consensual sexual relationship with a woman when committing the rapes.

However, not as surprising, the FBI study also found that most of these men were seen as being macho, and they often tried to further this image of themselves through their dress and attitude. Additionally, a majority of the men had been sexually abused as children, had poor relationships with their parents, had been in trouble with the law, had been institutionalized at some point during their youth, and had committed a number of less serious sex crimes, such as flashing, window peeping, and obscene telephone calls. What the results of the study show are that, while outwardly appearing normal, in truth serial rapists are maladapted, immature, and certainly violent men who commit rape and other sexual crimes in an attempt to deal with serious emotional adjustment problems.

Reporting Rape

Another obvious conclusion of the study above that can be drawn from the large number of rapes committed by these men, is that they would have undoubtedly continued with their crimes if not arrested by the police. Yet for every crime these serial rapists committed that was reported to the police, at least two or three went unreported.

"We find that victims will more likely report rapes committed by strangers than those by acquaintances," said Lieutenant Teresa

Deal. "But unfortunately, we find that an awful lot of both types go unreported."

For those women who don't report rapes committed by strangers, the reasons given are usually embarrassment or shame, worry of exposure in the press, and fear that the attacker will return. While this fear of a rapist's return is usually baseless, it isn't always. When I was a rookie officer I worked for a while guarding prisoners at the county hospital. One evening the ambulance brought in a man with severe head injuries who was barely clinging to life (actually, the entire left side of his skull was missing). I received the paperwork since the man was under arrest for burglary and rape, and from the officer who accompanied the ambulance I heard the man's story.

Reportedly, the injured man had raped a woman a week or so before in her home, and when he left he threatened to come back and rape her again if she called the police. The woman, however, did call the police. She also called her brother and asked him to stay with her for a while. A week or so later, unable to sleep because of the trauma of the rape, the woman was looking out of her upstairs bedroom window at around one o'clock in the morning when she saw the rapist slipping up the walk toward her house. The woman quickly ran downstairs and aroused her brother, who got his shotgun. The rapist, looking around, crept up onto the porch and jimmied a front window. As he eased the window up and then stealthily stuck his head in through the opening, the woman's brother placed the shotgun up next to the rapist's head and fired both barrels.

The rapist died several days later, but before he died I had a rather enlightening experience. The rapist's family came to see him, and, amazingly, they were infuriated that he had been shot. Although they made no attempt to deny that he was a serial rapist, they didn't think it was fair that he had been shot because he hadn't injured the woman when he had raped her, but only threatened to. Despite such rare cases, the threat of a rapist returning is not as great as many victims believe. To a rapist the victim isn't a person, just an object. But still, far too many women sexually assaulted by strangers don't call the police because of this fear.

Women sexually assaulted by acquaintances often don't call the police because they either feel it is a personal matter that they don't want dealt with publicly or, because the rape was committed by someone they know, they blame themselves and don't want to see the rapist arrested. But for rapes committed by both strangers and acquaintances, victims often don't call the police because they fear the criminal justice system will be unsympathetic to them. This last reason, unfortunately, was very true for many years. Rape victims were often in the past treated rudely by the police and, once in court, many times made to feel as though they were the ones on trial when defense attorneys began aggressively questioning them about their past sexual activities.

But much of this attitude has changed in the last few decades. Police departments are now much more sensitive to rape victims, with most large departments having female detectives to do the questioning since they realize that many women simply cannot talk to a man about what happened during a rape. Any rape victim, therefore, who doesn't have a female officer assigned to her case, and wishes one, should not hesitate to request it or insist on speaking to a supervisor if the request is not honored. A key point not just rape victims but all crime victims should be aware of is that during the 1960s and 1970s the police received some very bad press, some justified, some not. But because of this bad publicity, most police departments have worked diligently during the last few decades of the twentieth century to improve their public image. As a part of this effort most police departments want to be as compassionate and accommodating as possible to crime victims.

In addition, and again in an effort to improve their public image, most police departments now also recognize and make allowances for the effects of rape trauma syndrome. This condition, resulting from feelings of guilt and self-blame, can often cause rape victims to distort details of the crime since they fear society will blame them if they admit, for example, that they accepted a ride from a stranger or that they met the rapist in a singles bar. In years past, victims suffering from rape trauma syndrome were considered unreliable and their cases often not prosecuted, but now this too has changed.

Along with police departments becoming more compassionate, most states have now instituted rape shield laws, which prevent defense attorneys from questioning rape victims about their past sex lives. Judges and juries too have changed, and have in recent years become much more stern in dealing with rapists. Recent figures from the U.S. Justice Department, for example, show that 88 percent of those convicted of rape are now sent to prison, with only homicide convictions having a larger percentage. In the National Survey of Crime Severity, forcible rape was ranked as tenth most serious among 204 illegal acts, which ranged from murder to truancy, while in the even more recent National Survey on Punishment for Criminal Offenses it ranked fifth out of 24 criminal acts, ranging from murder to burglary. And yet, while all of these changes should encourage more victims to report rape, they often don't, for many women still apparently fear the stigma of having been raped.

Resisting Rape

Because of the stigma attached to being a rape victim, many of the rapes that are reported to the police every year, we find, are only done so because the victim has been injured. During the reported 90,000+ rapes in 2000, one-fourth of the victims were injured seriously enough to require medical attention. Sex crime detectives theorize that the reason so many rapes result in serious injuries is that rape is not an attack on property, but on a woman's body, on her dignity and self-esteem. Because of this, over 75 percent of rape victims each year, even those confronted by an armed rapist, resist in some way, ranging from attempting to talk the rapist out of the crime to actual physical resistance.

Rapists generally use one of three methods to get hold of their victims, and each one requires a different type of resistance or prevention (which are detailed in the section below). The first method involves the rapist convincing a woman through some subterfuge to accompany him to a secluded spot, where he assaults her. Rapist and murderer Ted Bundy reportedly wore a fake arm cast and worked on a woman's sympathy to persuade her to feel safe accompanying him. A second method used by rapists is the sudden attack or blitz, in which the rapist suddenly and unexpectedly attacks a woman, usually sexually assaulting her right at the spot of the attack or somewhere nearby, often close to where there are witnesses. The third method involves hiding and surprising the woman in her home or in some out-of-the-way spot where there are no witnesses.

Rape Safety Tips

Most investigators feel that if women follow the tips below, they can lessen their chances of being a rape victim:

- Be aware of your surroundings. Particularly at night, when the majority of rapes occur, check out a parking lot or street before entering it. Don't walk blind. Know who is around you. Awareness is the key to safety. Never be so preoccupied with other matters that you don't notice your surroundings. Wearing a Walkman or talking on a cellular telephone will make you inattentive and a good target for a rapist.
- Since a lone woman is the most common rape victim, use a "buddy system" for walking to cars, or ask for an escort. Have your car keys ready. Carry the keys positioned between your fingers so that they can be used as a defensive weapon if necessary. Check the cars around you as you approach yours. Are there people loitering around them? Carry a small flashlight and check *under* the car as well as the interior before getting in, and then lock the car doors once you're inside. Could anyone be hiding behind the car next to yours?
- When traveling to visit family or friends at night, advise them of an arrival time so they will be watching for you. Don't

drive through areas that you wouldn't walk through. You are just as exposed in your car as you would be walking. We had a case recently of a woman assaulted while driving through a bad neighborhood. She had followed most of the safety rules and had her doors locked and windows rolled up, but an attacker jumped in through her open sunroof. Many women feel safe driving through a bad area so long as they're on a major highway, or simply have no choice but must use a major highway that cuts through a bad district. However, don't forget, if your car stops running on this major highway, then you're now stranded *in a bad neighborhood.* Therefore, if traveling through a bad district is a must, you should have a cellular telephone. With it you can call for assistance if your car breaks down or call for help if you feel threatened. Also, when a highway is stalled or congested, *never* take a shortcut through unfamiliar streets.

If, however, you do find yourself in a bad area, and an attacker somehow gets into your car, probably the best action to take is to ram your car immediately into a nearby parked car (at a speed that won't kill or seriously injure you). This will attract the attention of anyone close by and also allow you a few seconds to get out of the car and away. This may sound drastic, but we're talking about raw survival. Many women are abducted, raped, and killed every year in their own cars. Also, if you're in a bad neighborhood, stay in the center lane and leave space between your car and the car in front of you at stop signs and lights in order to give yourself room to maneuver if necessary. Otherwise you can be trapped when a car pulls up to your rear bumper. Give yourself room to pull your car over into the next lane and away from danger. In bad districts don't stop in the event you are involved in a minor accident, but signal the other driver to follow you to an open filling station or store. Bumping cars is a tactic used by criminals to force the driver to stop and get out of the car. In addition, while driving, be cautious of lonely interstate rest stops at night. If a man is accompanying you, have him check the rest room or wait outside the rest room door for you.

- If your car breaks down, put up the hood and remain inside with the doors locked. If you do not have a cellular telephone and someone stops and offers help, ask him or her to call for a service truck. Do not get out. In addition, don't stop to offer help to disabled motorists, but instead stop at the next telephone and call the police. Most important, if a car pulls up alongside you while you are driving and the driver indicates that something is wrong with your vehicle, do not stop but instead drive to the nearest service station. Serial rapist and murderer Steven Judy used this ruse to persuade Terry Lee Chasteen and her three small children to pull over and allow him to look under the hood of her car, which he then covertly disabled. Finding herself stranded, Mrs. Chasteen accepted the offer of a ride from Judy to a telephone, but instead was driven to a deserted creek bank, where she was brutally raped and murdered, and her three small children were tossed into the swollen creek and drowned.

- Even short trips on elevators can be dangerous. I had a case come across my desk when I was a district detective captain in which a young woman got onto an elevator with a lone man in an exclusive women's clothing store. The man suddenly pushed the stop button, pulled out a revolver, and raped the woman. He then threatened to kill her if she said anything, and started the elevator again, getting off at the next floor. By the time the victim was able to find and notify the store security of what had happened the man had escaped. Women by themselves should always avoid getting onto an elevator with a lone man, but if you do so, you should stand close to the alarm button.

- Public transportation, particularly late at night, can always be hazardous to women. Isolated bus stops or subway stations in the evening or early morning hours are often used by rapists as locations for attack. If possible, use a well-lit one, and don't get off at a darkened stop if you feel threatened, but ride on to a well-lit, busy one. Sit close to the driver or conductor or next to the door if the occupants of a bus or subway car appear threatening. At subway stations, stay within sight of the toll booth operator.

- Since many rapes occur in a victim's home, be certain your home is secure against break-ins. Not all rapes are spontaneous, and some rapists, it has been found, in order to familiarize themselves with the interior, have previously gained entry to the home when no one was there. If you're alone at night, draw the curtains. Two-thirds of all rapes occur at night, and some rapists like to scout their victims before attacking them. As a side note, the Boston Strangler reportedly located his victims from women's names on mailboxes, so it is advisable to use only a first initial on the mailbox and in the phone book.

- Never admit strangers into your home, particularly when you are there alone. I investigated a case once in which a woman, home recuperating from an operation, admitted a man who told her his car had broken down and that he needed to use the telephone. Once inside and certain she was alone, he pulled out a revolver and ordered her to disrobe. She pleaded with him that she had just gotten out of the hospital and wasn't well, finally having to show him the bandages. As occasionally, but rarely, happens, the rapist was persuaded not to go through with the crime. When he walked out the front door, though, he turned and said, "Lady, from now on don't be letting strangers come in your house like this." Sound advice from someone who knows.

  Women should always be certain to lock the door to their house or apartment when leaving, even if they are only going to be gone for a few moments. In a number of cases, the police have found that women were attacked by men who have sneaked into homes after they left the doors unlocked while going to the laundry room, taking out the trash, or working in the yard.

- Don't answer the door if you are alone and not expecting anyone. Tell friends always to call first. And don't depend on door chains. They are unbelievably fragile. If you feel you must answer the door, a rubber doorstop or wooden wedge adjusted with your foot will prevent someone from forcing the door open. Also, if you do answer the door, never indicate that you are home alone. Call over your shoulder as though you were talking to someone.

- Be alert to the surroundings when entering your home or apartment. Often attackers will lurk nearby and shove you inside after you unlock the door. Have a key chain with a small light attached. This allows you to enter your home or car quickly. Be aware of people loitering in an apartment lobby. If you must return late at night to an apartment building, have someone come down to meet you. Also, have a table inside your home close to the entry door so that you can put packages down and immediately shut and lock the door. And *never, never* go into a house or apartment that appears to have been burglarized. Go to the nearest telephone and call the police. A little side note about human nature: if you are attacked in a building where you think the people might be reluctant to come out and help you, yell "Fire!" rather than "Rape!" or "Help!" The shout of "Fire!" will arouse even the most lethargic person. This may not be completely legal, but again we're talking about raw survival, about the strong likelihood of being raped or murdered, and legal niceties at a time like this should not be a consideration.
- Know a man before accepting a date or ride with him. While date rape has been a popular subject in the news media, the occurrence of a rape by someone a woman has been dating for a long time is actually rare compared with rape by a new acquaintance. Most of these new acquaintances are men whom women have met and accepted dates or rides from at parties, singles bars, etc. For the first few dates with a new male acquaintance it would be wise to go only to places where there are other people you know. Do not accompany a new male acquaintance to his apartment, even if he seems

to have a good excuse for stopping there, because he can say later that it wasn't rape. He can claim that you agreed to sex. Why else would you have gone to his apartment? Also, never accept a drink from a stranger. The use of "rape drugs" slipped into an unsuspecting woman's drink has increased in popularity. These drugs render a woman unconscious and helpless. If you do suspect someone has slipped something into your drink, immediately tell your friends or even the bartender so they can get you help.

- Interestingly, though, while studies show that rapes are not often committed by long-term boyfriends, they are many times committed by someone known and often related to the victim. In any case, whether he's a long-term friend or a new acquaintance, when a man begins making unwanted sexual advances, the woman should tell the man firmly that she doesn't want to have sex. Men can, and often do, later claim that they thought a woman was just being coy when she said, "We shouldn't be doing this." Any woman experiencing unwanted sexual advances should say, "Stop this right now! I mean it! This is rape!" Later on, the man cannot say he didn't know the woman didn't want to have sex. While this won't stop anyone determined on rape, it will stop most aggressive men who think a woman is just playing hard to get.

- Don't be afraid to take action on your fears or thoughts. Many times, rape victims will tell the police that the rapist had made them feel uncomfortable beforehand, or that they thought he might be following them, but that they didn't do anything about it. Don't get onto an elevator or enter a building if it feels wrong. Trust your feelings.

- Also, be alert to the fact that occasionally rapists work in pairs. One will threaten a woman, while the other pretends to be a passing Good Samaritan who offers to let the woman into his car or building. Rapists have also been known to answer Lost and Found ads, saying they have found a lost dog or kitten and suggesting that the woman come to an address to retrieve it.

Purchase a small, inexpensive air-horn, such as the ones used on boats and bicycles, or any device that makes a loud noise and can be carried in your purse or coat pocket. If approached by a suspicious person, attempt to either get away to a populated area or use the noisemaker to draw attention to yourself. At this point the person, if a potential rapist, has not done anything unlawful and will usually just want to get away so as not to come to the attention of the police. A convicted serial rapist I spoke with one time while visiting the state prison told me that his main concern was always not getting caught, and if anything went wrong before the actual attack, he would usually just run. If you happen to be mistaken and the person is completely innocent, it is much easier to apologize than to undergo the trauma of a rape.

The observant reader will notice that I haven't included in this or the preceding section any advice about physically resisting a rapist once an attack is imminent, even though 75 percent of rape victims report taking some type of self-protective measures. Most sex offense detectives I have spoken with agree that the type of self-protective measures taken should be the decision of the woman, based on the circumstances of the attack. Some rapists can be successfully resisted, and occasionally even talked out of an attack. Other rapists, however, have shut out any remorse, or simply have none, and are extremely prone to violence. These rapists consider any resistance, even the slightest, as an affront to the power and dominance they are attempting to exert through the rape. Resisting one of these rapists can be very dangerous, and perhaps even fatal, since resistance will often send them into a maniacal fury. This is even more frightening when it is revealed that by self-report 40 percent of rapists are either very drunk or under the influence of drugs when they commit the crime. And since these are self-reports, the figure of 40 percent is probably much lower than the actual percentage.

A number of women, because of the fear of rape, arm themselves with self-protection devices such as Mace, pepper gas, knives, and so on. Some women also take self-defense courses, such as judo or karate. Still other women, when confronted by a rapist, have claimed to have AIDS, have pretended to faint, or have purposely vomited. While all of these measures have occasionally proven effective, I must give a note of caution. *Never, never* become complacent and believe that these will get you out of any situation. Police officers carry chemical weapons much more potent than those sold to the public, yet even these are not effective all the time. Some people sprayed with these chemicals become even more enraged. And though I was trained thoroughly in self-defense tactics in the police academy, I found that only a few of these actually work in real life, because the person doesn't stand still or attack you at normal speed, but instead rushes at you from different angles with arms flailing.

Very few weapons are of much value against a man with a gun who knows how to use it.

Therefore, the decision of whether or not to resist a rapist should be based on the chances of success. How close is help if you can break free and get away? Do you know the rapist and therefore can you possibly persuade him not to go through with it? Are you risking imminent death or serious injury by resisting? If you have a weapon, do you know how to use it? Will it likely be turned on you? How confident are you of your chances?

While all of the above factors should be considered, the decision of whether to resist a rape or not must be the woman's, and any decision she makes should be supported by her family and friends.

I realize that based on the length of the list above, it seems that in order for a woman to be safe from rape she has to be almost paranoid. But following this advice is not paranoia. It is simply a matter of being cautious. The next time you see a police officer stop a car late at night, watch what he or she does. The officer, even though carrying a weapon, approaches the car with caution, usually keeping his or her gun hand free while talking to the motorist from a position behind the driver's door, always maintaining a tactical advantage over the driver. While drivers who have no aggressive intent at all may think that the officer is being overly cautious and perhaps even a bit paranoid, these are only commonsense precautions, like those in the list above.

After a Rape

If, through a lapse of caution or through unavoidable circumstances a rape does occur, it is imperative that it be reported to the police. Most rapists will continue committing rapes until they are finally caught, and only through reporting rape can the rapist be stopped and other women spared. Rapists, the police find, often follow a stringent modus operandi, and information provided by their victims can lead to their apprehension.

When I was working as a uniformed district sergeant, late one evening I heard on the police radio that a naked woman, severely injured, was at an address close by. When I arrived at the home I found a nude woman who had been stabbed several times in the chest and had her throat slashed (though luckily not deep enough to be fatal). While I was administering first aid, the woman told me she was in the parking lot in back of her workplace when a man came up behind her with a knife and forced her into her car. Ordering her to drive to the alley behind the house she was now in, he took her into a nearby garage and, after brutally raping her, tried to kill her. Playing dead, she waited until he left in her car and then ran to the first house she saw with lights on.

After the ambulance took her to the hospital, I obtained a description of her car and its license number from our computer, and then began a block-by-block search, finally locating the vehicle parked in a business loading dock about a mile away. Once the sex crime detective came to the scene and heard what had happened to the victim, he knew who the most likely suspect was, a man who had been paroled just a month before for a very similar rape at the same location, and who lived less than a block from where I found the car.

The victim recovered from her wounds, identified the suspect from a lineup, and was an excellent witness in court. The man was convicted of attempted murder and rape and received a prison sentence that in Indiana means he will become eligible for Social Security long before he has his first parole hearing, the hefty sentence undoubtedly due to the viciousness of the crime.

The solving of a rape case by the police involves many of the same investigative procedures and techniques that are used in solving a murder, with the critical exception that there is usually a victim's description of the suspect. An interesting sidelight to the study of serial rapists by the FBI was that very few of the rapists had done anything at all to alter their appearance. Therefore, rape victims can greatly assist the police in apprehending the perpetrators if they try to memorize the rapist's appearance and anything distinctive about them—their clothing, their car, etc. As in the case above, many sex offenders are known to the police, and any description given can often lead to an apprehension. Also, rape victims, if they are to assist the police in apprehending the suspects, must resist the natural inclination to bathe, wash their clothing, or clean up evidence of the rape. With the new DNA analysis techniques now available, any body fluids recovered can solve the case by identifying a suspect as the likely perpetrator. Also, with a laser print finder and other devices, locating a rapist's fingerprints is much easier now, provided the scene hasn't been cleaned up.

I had a case recently that vividly illustrates the value of DNA evidence in rapes. On April 13, 1985, Indianapolis police officers found the body of 15-year-old Tracey Poindexter in a creekbed on the north side of the city. Autopsy results showed that she had been raped and murdered. Although Detective Sergeant Mike Crooke thoroughly investigated this case, no arrest came from it. And while the semen recovered during the autopsy was saved, it held little evidentiary value without a suspect in 1985. However, in early 2001, Sergeant Crooke attended a conference where a speaker discussed the FBI's new Combined DNA Index

System (CODIS), which allows federal, state, and local crime laboratories to exchange and compare DNA profiles electronically and thereby link DNA recovered at a crime scene to a specific person.

Sergeant Crooke also learned that Indiana now required all persons convicted of a violent crime to give a DNA sample for the State Police DNA Bank. Remembering the Tracey Poindexter case and retrieving the semen sample, he sent it in for DNA analysis. A few weeks later, the state police reported that they had matched the DNA in the semen sample to a convicted rapist named Sterling Riggs, who had just been paroled from prison after serving 15 years for a very similar kidnapping and rape. In November 2001, a jury convicted Riggs of the Tracey Poindexter murder and a judge sentenced him to 130 years in prison. In Indiana, this means Riggs will have his first parole hearing in 2066, when he is 110 years old.

It is interesting to note here that some rapists have begun wearing condoms, both to escape DNA detection and because of the fear of AIDS and other diseases. However, DNA can also be obtained from sources other than semen, such as hair and saliva.

In the hope of obtaining DNA and other evidence, the police send most rape victims immediately to a hospital for examination and treatment. Any bathing beforehand will make this exam useless, and perhaps destroy the chances of catching the suspect. Like police departments, most hospitals have also instituted procedures in the last decade or so that ensure that the treatment of rape victims is humane and courteous.

If a rape occurs in a location unknown to the victim, she should attempt to leave her fingerprints everywhere possible, and perhaps leave behind a personal item that can be identified, such as an earring. As was mentioned in the preceding chapter, it has been found that in serious criminal cases the larger the amount of physical evidence recovered, the more serious the court considered the crime to be and the more severe the sentence the perpetrator received.

A rape victim's assistance in these matters is vital to the police's ability to solve rape cases; an interesting finding of the FBI's study of serial rapists was that half of the rapists fully admitted the crime when questioned by the police. Therefore, any assistance a rape victim can provide that will help the police locate a suspect may solve the case.

But in addition to a rape victim helping the police, family and friends of the victim should help her. They should be available if the rape victim wants to talk in the days or weeks afterward. After a rape a woman needs considerable support and understanding, but often finds that family and friends will try to do anything to keep from having to talk about it (with the exception of the ghouls who want to know every intimate detail). Family and friends often don't understand what happened or why the victim didn't do something more to protect herself, even though doing anything more may not have been possible at the time. It is easy, of course, to imagine what you would have done, but it is always different when the situation actually arises. For example, as a rookie police officer I always imagined how heroic I would be if I was involved in a gun battle. The first time it happened, though, my bladder let go and I shook for the rest of the day. No one really knows what he or she will do in a situation until actually faced with it.

Family and friends of rape victims should also be aware that for some time afterward the victim will likely feel insecure and will be easily frightened. This is the time to give the victim as much support and understanding as possible. This is the time when the victim's self-esteem may be shattered, when love and understanding by family and friends are the best medicine. Counseling can often prove helpful, and if not sought by the victim, it should be encouraged by those who love her.

Child Molestation: A Hidden National Problem

While there were over 90,000 rapes reported to the police in 2000, there is a related sex crime probably several times more common than rape and also very destructive to its victims: child sexual abuse. Child sexual abuse can be something as minimal as sexual innuendoes, in which the perpetrator is aroused by talking dirty to children, or can be more serious behavior, such as exposing children to pornography, touching over the clothing, sexual intercourse, or even sexual sadism. Like those who commit rape, most of the people who commit child sexual abuse also suffer from serious emotional adjustment problems. Studies show that most child molesters are very immature sexually and usually very uncomfortable with their adult sexual role.

As with the crime of rape, far too many child sexual abuse cases go unreported. Actually, no one is really sure just how much child sexual abuse takes place every year, but most sex crime investigators believe the amount would shock the American public. These detectives find that child molesters come from all age groups, from as young as 6 or 7 to as old as 90. When I was in charge of the police department's identification and records branch, one of my lieutenants kept a special rogue's gallery of sex offenders aged six to nine years old. Child molesters also come from all social and economic classes. No segment of our society, police officers find, either high or low, is immune from it, though most people would like to believe it really doesn't happen.

"The biggest problem in trying to prevent child molesting is the 'ostrich syndrome,'" said Sergeant Terry Hall, a police officer formerly in charge of presenting a molestation prevention program in Indianapolis called Good Touch–Bad Touch. "Most people just don't want to believe that this sort of thing happens as much as it does."

People, the police find, also don't like to talk about child molestation. People will talk (and talk and talk) about having their car stolen or having their garage broken into, but will not talk about their child being molested. For many people it is simply too painful to talk about, and many people are silent because they feel guilty about not preventing the molestation of their child. Even adult victims of child sexual abuse often don't tell or talk about it. As a part of the research for the first edition of this book I attended several sessions of Sergeant Hall's Good Touch–Bad Touch program. The first session I attended was the one he presents to adults to show them what he will be telling the children. At the end of the program two adults from the audience came forward, a man and a woman, both child molestation victims who until that day had never told anyone because they felt it was a shame they couldn't share, that is, until they heard Sergeant Hall tell of his own molestation as a child. Unfortunately, along with the adult presentation, at almost every program given to children Sergeant Hall also finds at least one case of unreported child sexual abuse. He finds children who until that time didn't know that they had the right or the power to say no, who didn't know that what had happened to them also happens to others, children who until that time didn't realize how important it is to tell someone what happened.

How prevalent is child sexual abuse? Several years ago, an HBO *America Under Cover* episode on child sexual abuse stated that at least 1,000 children are sexually molested in our country every day. Most people working in the field of child abuse, however, believe that this is probably a very conservative estimate. Sex crime investigators say that when a "neighborhood child molester" is arrested, and one, two, or even a dozen victims are identified, this is usually only a fraction of the actual number of victims. It is predicted that one out of every four girls and one out of every five boys in this country will be sexually molested before they become adults.

Molester-Victim Relationships

Much more disturbing than even the statistics above is the fact that sex offense detectives find during their investigations that at least 90 percent of the people committing child sexual abuse are not strangers, are not degenerates who hang around school yards in long trench coats. The truth many people don't want to face is that child molesters are usually either family members or friends of the family, and are quite often people with considerable stature in the community, and usually with a reputation as being very good with children. Because of this close relationship between child molesters and their victims, and because of many molesters' reputations, child sexual abuse is probably one of the most under-reported crimes in our country.

Methods Used by Child Molesters

In addition to the often close relationship between most child molesters and their victims and the fact that many child molesters have good community reputations, there are a number of other reasons why child sexual abuse cases are not reported. Child molesters, for example, will use several methods to keep children from reporting them, including physical threats against the victims and their family, instilling fear of what the exposure will do to the victim and his or her family's reputation, bribery with money or presents, and other methods. The molested children themselves many times don't report sexual abuse because they have been made to feel that they are at fault, have been convinced that their family will blame them for it, or think they won't be believed if they do tell. Parents, on the other hand, often don't report child sexual abuse because they consider it degrading to the family and know that the details of the molestation will be exposed to public scrutiny if the molester is arrested and the case heard in court. Also, many parents worry that the trauma of a trial will only aggravate the injuries already suffered by the molested child.

Additionally, if the molester is closely related to the victim (a very common occurrence), the family realizes it will be torn apart by the repercussions of having a family member arrested, tried, and imprisoned. Because of all these reasons, many parents try to handle the problem within the family. But this secrecy is what allows child molesters to thrive. While child molesters may stop sexually abusing the child they have been accused of molesting, they will usually just move on to a new victim, knowing they will never be exposed. But even worse than all of the above, and certainly more disastrous for children, occasionally parents will suspect that child sexual abuse is occurring, yet be so horrified by it that they will simply refuse to admit that it is happening, or will convince themselves that the children are lying when they try to tell about it.

One of the things that parents of molested children find hardest to accept is that their children haven't been molested by some degenerate in a dirty trench coat, but instead by a "pillar of the community" who has a reputation as being exceptionally good with children. Parents are usually stunned when such a person is exposed, and often ask themselves, "How could he have turned into a child molester?" But this isn't what has happened. What has actually happened is that rather than a pillar of the community becoming a child molester, a child molester has become a pillar of the community. Child molesters will often purposely work themselves into positions of trust with children, and then will use this trust to their own advantage. This was demonstrated recently in a report from the Boy Scouts of America that admitted over 1,000 of its volunteers in the past were known or suspected child molesters. In early 2002, the Catholic Church faced up to the now public and very unsettling problem that a large number of its priests have been child molesters. Many times, these molesters will first work to gain the parents' confidence and then convince the parents to leave them alone with their children, often by setting up outings for the children. Molesters have even been known to provide activities (basketball tickets, dinner gift certificates, etc.) for the parents and then offer to baby-sit for them. This is a terrible reflection on our society, but sex offense investigators warn that when a person wants to relieve parents of their duties, and that person seems almost too good to be true, the person usually is.

While in the past, child molesters usually worked on contacting and seducing one child at a time, a new innovation in our society, the Internet, has now allowed molesters to reach out and make contact with thousands of possible victims, breaking the old pattern of getting close to family first before seducing the child. Child molesters now haunt Internet chat rooms, looking for possible victims. A study conducted by the Crimes Against Children Research Center at the University of New Hampshire found that 1 in 5 children who have gone online regularly have received a solicitation for sex, while 1 in 33 have received an aggressive sexual solicitation in which the youngster was sent mail or asked to meet somewhere. Unfortunately, only 10 percent of these victims reported the solicitations to the police.

Two recent incidents demonstrate just how dangerous Internet solicitations can be. In late December 2001, police in Irvine, California, arrested a 20-year-old man who had corresponded with a 15-year-old girl on the Internet. After convincing the girl to meet him, he allegedly sexually assaulted her and carved swastikas on her face. In January 2002, the FBI forced entry into a Virginia home and freed a 13-year-old girl who was tied up inside. The FBI later arrested the 38-year-old owner of the home who, they said, met her on the Internet. Federal authorities charged the 38-year-old man with illegal transportation of a minor for the purpose of engaging in illegal sexual conduct.

Child Sexual Abuse Investigation

The investigation of child sexual abuse is different from most other police investigations because the crime is a very emotionally explosive one. Parents are often hysterical when they find out that their child has been molested. They are often enraged and want to kill the molester, or conversely, just as often are disgusted and disbelieving. But even worse than this, often an investigation of child sexual abuse will be blocked. Many times, unfortunately, people have an interest in having it decided that the crime actually didn't happen after all, whether it did or not. Sometimes it is the parents, who simply cannot accept that a close friend or relative would do such a thing or believe that the family will be shamed if it is found out what happened. When the molestation occurs in a school or other institution, often it is the administrators who, to protect the institution's reputation, will try to block a child molestation investigation. And quite often, when the molester has high stature in the community, he has highly connected friends who will try to have the investigation blocked, most because they simply refuse to believe the accusations are true.

Often, however, the most difficult part of a child molestation investigation is obtaining the necessary information from the victim. Many times the victim is an infant or still so young that he or she can't verbalize what happened. Many child molesters will also purposely pick victims who, while older, still can't tell, such as handicapped or retarded children. But often the children have been so traumatized by what has happened, so threatened by the molester, or are so afraid of what their parents will think that they simply won't talk to the investigator about the crime.

To be a good child molestation investigator an officer must be able to empathize with children and talk with them on their level. The investigator must be able to make children feel that they can trust and tell him or her anything. But also, a good child molestation investigator must be able to talk to child molesters. The detective must question them and persuade them to give a statement without showing the disgust he or she feels for them.

Therefore, a good child molestation investigator must be able to assume a number of roles. I have watched my wife (who was a top child molestation detective) talk to young victims. She is able to assume a very friendly and nonthreatening appearance, and usually can persuade the children to tell her what happened. I have also watched her question child molesters and she has a technique that seems to make them want to open up and tell her everything. Although a very sophisticated woman, if need be she is able to put on the facade of a downhome country girl who knows the molester didn't mean to hurt anyone. Within just a few minutes of talking to them she has molesters crying and telling her everything about what they did. For some reason, when she puts on the country girl facade, child molesters don't seem to mind when she turns on the tape recorder and advises them of their rights. They just start talking. To them she is someone who understands, someone they can pour out their heart to, and do. And if needed, she can also be as sophisticated as the molester believes he or she is. It's a rare talent that many police officers, including me, envy.

With the above exceptions, much of the rest of child sexual abuse investigation is similar to rape investigation. The detective must gather all of the physical evidence he or she can, obtain statements from everyone who knows anything about the case, and question the suspects. As with a rape victim, the child is usually taken to the hospital for an examination, and is asked to identify the molester, both during questioning and in court if necessary.

But usually, if the police have built a good case, the case won't go to court. Few child molesters want to have their actions exposed to the public. Many first-time molesters plead guilty and agree to take part in some type of counseling, while repeat offenders often settle for the minimum jail time they can get. But much, much too often, when the cases do go to court, both judges and juries simply refuse to believe that "pillar of the community"- type molesters would do such a thing and don't convict them. Much more often, unfortunately, the family, once they realize what a child molestation trial will do to them and to the child, either refuse to cooperate any longer with the investigation or send the child out of state. All of this, of course, only encourages child molesters, who begin to see themselves as untouchable. To stop a child molester there must be no hiding of what happened, and particularly no hiding of who the molester is. Child molesters thrive on secrecy.

Child Molestation Prevention

Many times the realization that a trusted family member or friend is a child molester happens only after the tragedy of child molestation has already occurred. And just as often, a parent doesn't know that a child has been molested until after it has been happening for a long time. There are, however, certain signs parents can look for that will alert them to the possibility of child molestation:

- Listen to your children. Child molestation detectives often find that children have tried to tell their parents about a molestation but were scared or embarrassed, and the parents just didn't have time for children who can't come out and say what is on their mind. It is for this reason that many children tell someone other than their parents about being molested. Only in open, loving relationships, in relationships where the children feel they can talk to their parents about anything, can parents expect children to tell them about being molested.
- Monitor your child's Internet use. Know what sites your child is visiting and whom he or she is talking to.
- Abrupt, radical changes in children's behavior, and sudden fear of someone they shouldn't be afraid of, are both signs of possible child molestation, and should be investigated.
- Don't be judgmental or show horror, shock, anger, or disgust when a child tells about his or her molestation. This is just what the molester very likely warned the child would happen if you were told. A child needs understanding, and needs to be assured that it was not his or her fault.
- Never insist that any story is too outrageous or that there is no way a certain person could be a child molester. Even after 33 years as a police officer, I still hear stories that are unbelievable and shocking, but true. Also, don't begin immediately accusing people. Listen to the child's story with an understanding ear and look into what he or she has told you. Child molestation detectives can attest that molesters usually come in the guise of the least expected person and that they will do outrageous and seemingly out-of-character things. Child molesters have been fathers, uncles, priests, bank presidents, and police officers. But also be warned that there is an occa-

sional, though rare, case in which for various reasons a child will make up a story of being molested. It is best simply to investigate without accusing anyone until the truth is known.

- Notify the police of any molestation. Many families are reluctant to do this because they fear the publicity will hurt the family and further traumatize the child. But secrecy is what allows child molesters to thrive.
- Be suspicious of any person who wants to spend a lot of time alone with your children, and who always tries to get you out of the way. Be suspicious of anyone who always wants to buy your children presents. He may simply be a nice person who likes children, but far too often he is not.
- Be suspicious of any person or house that all of the neighborhood children like to hang around. Often molesters, in order to attract victims, will try to make their home inviting and seemingly friendly to children.
- Children must be taught that they have the right to say no to any adult who wants to touch them in a way they don't like, and that if they are touched in a way they don't like, they must tell someone about it.
- While all of the above tips are useful, it is more important to prevent a molestation before it happens.

According to the American Medical Association, at least 20 percent of child molestation victims develop serious, long-term psychological problems because of the abuse. But since many victims of child sexual abuse never tell anyone about it, this is probably a low estimate. According to Dr. Don M. Hartsough, a clinical psychologist, "The long-term psychological effect of child sexual abuse is a bigger problem than people realize. In clinical practice we run into this problem frequently." In support of this, an article in the *Psychological Bulletin*, entitled "Impact of Sexual Abuse on Children," stated that sexual abuse in childhood often results in severe psychopathology. In addition, a number of studies have also found that sexually abused children are much more likely to be arrested later in life than are nonabused children.

Child Molesters in Disguise

Child abuse investigators say that child molesters often come in the guise of the least likely, least expected person. My own experience with child molesters substantiates this.

One afternoon when working as a uniformed district officer, I came across a car parked in the part of a railroad yard where derelicts usually slept. The flurry of clothing and bare skin told me I had happened onto a couple of lovers. After giving the pair time to get dressed, I walked up to the car to tell them that where they were parked was a dangerous spot. The man in the car was 52 years old. The other person was his 13-year-old niece.

After I arrested him, and while I was taking the young girl to the hospital, she told me the story of two years of sexual abuse. The girl's mother (the arrested man's sister) was an invalid whose livelihood was totally dependent on her brother. The molestation began through threats to throw the mother out of her house if the niece didn't submit.

Since I registered the girl as a rape victim, and she was only 13, the hospital needed a relative to come and okay the examination, and the arrested man's wife arrived shortly afterward. The woman's first words to me were: "It's impossible. She couldn't have been raped. She was with my husband."

I sat her down and told her the story of what I had found out so far. She didn't believe a word of it. Not a word. Her husband was a deacon of the church, she said, a loving father of four children and vice-president of a local heating oil company. There was just no way.

However, when they wheeled the young girl past us on the way to the examination room, the look on the young girl's face was enough. I then began to fear for the arrested man's life.

The best way to prevent child molesting from happening is to know where your children are at all times, whom they are with, and what they are doing. Quite often child abuse detectives find that the parents of molestation victims didn't know where their children were or what they were doing when the molestation occurred.

Myths About Sex Crimes

Along with the myth that all child molesters are degenerates who hang around schoolyards, there are a number of myths about sex crimes that have been around for years. For example, a defense often given by sex offenders and, amazingly, often even believed by the public, is that women and children many times bring rape or molestation onto themselves by their actions, their style of dress, etc. This is not true, and it is particularly difficult to understand how anyone could believe this about a child and thereby partly or wholly absolve the molester of any guilt. As evidence against this myth, in the FBI's study of serial rapists, only 15 percent of the rapists said that a woman's clothing had anything at all to do with selecting her as a victim; her accessibility was the much more important factor.

Another myth that has been accepted for many years by the public, and often even believed by many police departments, is that minor sex offenders, such as flashers or window peepers, are relatively harmless nuisances. This too is simply not true. As was shown in the FBI study, many hardcore rapists also admitted to being flashers and window peepers. For example, one of the serial rapists in the FBI's study was arrested for window peeping in the same neighborhood where a rape and murder had been committed less than a week before, but was not questioned about the crime because he was "just a peeper." Several years later, he tried to confess to the crime, but was not believed by the police because they still said he was just a window peeper. He eventually was believed, though, when he gave details of the crime that only the murderer could have known. Also, it should be noted that occasionally rapists will peep in windows not only to look but also to scout a possible rape victim, and to plan their attack. Any incidents of window peeping, along with flashing or obscene telephone calls, should be reported. Hang up immediately on any obscene phone call and get away quickly from a flasher. Always contact the police about these incidents.

Other myths about sex offenses include the beliefs that all child molesters are homosexual men and that most sex offenders are loners. These are also not true. Child molesters, while predominantly men, can also occasionally be women; and sex offenders, it has been found, are usually able to meet people easily, and are often far from loners. Many child molesters are married or involved in a consensual sexual relationship with a woman, and will molest their own or the woman's children. Lastly, as for the myth that most or all child molesters are homosexuals, to pedophiles the sex of the victim is usually not important. Often the only important thing is that the victim is a child. They want a child because children are not judgmental about sexual performance, but more often they want a child because the molester himself is very sexually and emotionally immature.

Best Advice

The best advice the police can offer about sex crimes is that it is much easier, and in all cases much safer, to use the tips presented earlier in this chapter to prevent sex crimes from occurring than it is to stop them once they have begun, or to deal with the consequences of them after they have occurred. Should a child be sexually molested, it is imperative that the criminal not be given the benefit of secrecy. He or she must be exposed.

4

ROBBERY

TYPES OF ROBBERY

Robbery is the taking of something of value by force or violence or by putting someone in fear. While partly a property crime, robbery is also a crime of violence, a crime in which the victim stands a very good chance of being injured or killed.

The truth is that, contrary to the myth of the "gentleman bandit," no type of robbery is safe. Most robbery detectives, however, agree that of the four major types of robbery—bank robbery (2.1 percent of the total); commercial robbery, which is the robbery of convenience stores, filling stations, restaurants, and the like (23.2 percent of the total); street robbery (46.0 percent of the total); and residence robbery (12.2 percent of the total)—the greatest threat to victims occurs in residence and street robberies.

Residence robberies, detectives believe, often result in violence because these robberies, unlike the other types, are unhindered by the need to get away from the robbery scene as soon as possible. But they are also dangerous because, regardless of what the robbers believed when they planned the robbery, they seldom find the money, valuables, or drugs they had hoped for, and often become violent when they think the victims are holding out on them.

Street robberies, on the other hand, present a high level of danger to the victims because they are usually spontaneous, unplanned crimes by very desperate people, and therefore, many things can go wrong. Street robberies include armed robberies in which, demanding money or valuables, the robber produces a gun, knife, or other weapon. They also include unarmed robberies in which the robber physically assaults the victims and takes their valuables, using no weapon other than physical strength.

Bank robberies are a bit different in that, though occasionally amateurs will kill during bank robberies, they are usually perpetrated by career criminals who simply want to get the money and escape, so these robberies traditionally present the lowest threat to victims. Commercial robberies lie somewhere in between so far as danger to the victims is concerned. But regardless of which type of robbery is more or less dangerous than the other, the truth is that thousands of victims are injured and killed in each type every year. Remember, all robberies have the potential for both violent and tragic consequences.

A new type of robbery that has grown in popularity is carjacking. During a carjack, a weapon-wielding criminal confronts a victim and takes his or her car. Like all other types of robbery, carjacking can be dangerous to its victims. A five-year study by the U.S. Department of Justice found that 16 percent of all carjackings during this period ended in injury to the victim.

Two major factors that give all types of robbery the potential for violence are, first, that perpetrators know they face very stiff penalties if caught, and, second, they also know the longer they stay in a bank, a business, or hold a person on the street, the more likely it is that someone will see them and call the police. During a robbery most perpetrators are counting the seconds, and this puts them under high stress, which can quickly erupt into violence if they believe their victims are stalling. Robbers, incidentally, are also viewed as being extremely dangerous to police. A police officer, it has been found, is more likely to be killed by a robber than by any other type of criminal. A police officer is also more likely to shoot a robber than any other type of criminal.

There is a particularly dangerous type of robber, though, who can commit any of the above types of robbery, a robber who is akin to a rapist. It's not the valuables (like sex to the rapist) this robber is really after; it's the power the robber feels while holding

The Dangers of Robbery

Every robbery detective I have ever spoken with agrees on one thing: being the victim of a robbery can be life-threatening.

"Any armed robber is a potential killer," says one veteran robbery detective.

"Anything can happen during a robbery because it's just as stressful for the robber as it is for the victim," claims a 20-year robbery detective.

The FBI's national statistics on robbery bear out what these detectives are saying. Over 1,000 people died in 2000 as a result of the over 400,000 robberies reported to the police (one reported for every 1.3 minutes of the year—but probably less than half the actual number), and many thousands of people were injured. Statistics show that 1 in every 3 robbery victims is injured, 1 in 10 seriously enough to need attention in a hospital emergency room. Statistics also show that 60 percent of the robberies committed in this country are committed by armed criminals, two-thirds of them armed with firearms, making each robbery a possible tragedy. These robbers, incidentally, often carry stolen guns and don't know how they work. Afterward, robbers often tell the police that they didn't know the gun had a hair trigger or that it was defective. It just went off.

the victims in fear. These robbers are extremely dangerous because they will often hurt, and occasionally even kill, their victims in an attempt to show their power. Like certain rapists, some of these robbers are sadists who enjoy inflicting pain on their victims. Fortunately, this group makes up only a very small percentage of all robbers, but still presents a real danger.

We had a case a number of years ago of just such a group of robbers. The young men robbed a convenience store and all of the customers in it. They then took the young female clerk and the customers into a back room and made the customers watch as one of the robbers raped the clerk. There was also a gang operating for a while that forced the male and female victims to engage in various sex acts with each other. This type of behavior is extremely dangerous because a refusal to do what the robbers demand will very likely be met with violence or even death.

Also extremely dangerous, of course, is being robbed by a street gang, because street gang members are very status conscious and want the other gang members to think of them as macho. Some gang members will therefore commit brutal robberies in which the victim is shot or beaten so that other gang members will think they are tough. Also, some gangs require a robbery as initiation for new members. This often translates into injury for the victims.

Motivations for Robbery

But why do people commit robbery if it can be so stressful and bring such stiff penalties?

Occasionally, the robbery of a young person for sneakers or a designer jacket that the robber wants for himself makes the news, but these robberies are in the minority. Most robbers rob to get money. But why do these people need money so desperately? Are most robbers simply out-of-work people who are down on their luck and in need of money to feed their families?

While this definition may fit a few cases, it doesn't fit the huge majority of robbers. The majority of robbers need money for one thing: to buy drugs. According to a study by the Interdisciplinary Research Center, 75 percent or more of all robbers are young drug addicts who resort to crime because the very high cost of supporting a daily drug habit won't allow them to pay for it out of legitimate income sources. These youths, it has been found, however, gain only an average of $80 per robbery, yet need many thousands of dollars yearly to support their drug habit, which means they must commit dozens and dozens of robberies each year. Testifying to this high percentage of drug abusers involved in crime, the federal government, under its Drug Use Forecasting program, has been testing new arrestees for drugs in major metropolitan areas for several years now. The percentage of arrestees who were either under the influence of an illegal drug or had recently taken one shocked many people, running as high as 92 percent in one large metropolitan area, which means that practically everyone arrested there was a drug abuser.

These frightening statistics become even more frightening when one considers how very desperate these young robbers are. A recent study of state prison inmates found that more than 40 percent of those incarcerated for robbery admitted they were under the influence of drugs when they committed the robbery, and that an even larger percentage admitted to using illegal drugs regularly before their incarceration. Considering how confused the mind is under the influence of drugs, this puts the victim of a robbery in extreme danger. And as I've noted before, since these are self-reports, the truth is that the percentage is probably closer to twice what is reported. However, robbery by addicts also has the added danger that, rather than being under the influence of drugs, they may instead be desperately in need of a drug fix or money to pay off a drug debt. If they owe money for a drug debt and don't come up with it, their dealer will likely shoot them in the kneecaps or kill them. While this sounds like a Hollywood invention, it isn't; it happens on a regular basis. When I worked as a uniformed district officer in a high-drug-trade area of Indianapolis, we would often be sent on calls to people shot in the knees or legs. Of course, when we talked to them the people claimed they had no idea who shot them or why.

But there is yet another feature of these robbers that makes them even more dangerous. That is the fear most drug addicts have of being forced to go through painful and dangerous drug withdrawal in jail, and of being forced to face life for a long time without the escape drugs give. This intense fear of imprisonment steamrolls them into doing almost anything, including killing their victims, to keep from being arrested. Because of this high level of danger, almost every robbery detective advises victims never to physically resist a robber, and never to refuse to give up whatever valuables are demanded.

"The only thing that money you don't want to give up will do is buy a nice set of clothes to bury you in," said Robbery Detective Alonzo Watford.

Methods Used by Robbers

While some robbers (a small percentage actually) are professionals who plan their robberies thoroughly by casing a location, watching for when traffic is the lightest, when the most money is there, what escape routes are available, and what security measures a location has, most aren't. Most robbers are opportunistic criminals. Often, robbers will simply walk into a business, look around for a second, and then pull out a gun and announce a robbery, without knowing anything about the business. For example, several years ago we had a robbery case at a credit union located in a high-crime area of Indianapolis. So high is the crime level that the business always has an off-duty uniformed police officer working as security, which would have been apparent with even the most casual casing of the location. However, two robbers walked into the credit union one morning and, not seeing anything to stop them, announced a robbery. The officer, in the back room on a break, stepped out, and after exchanging a few shots, arrested them both. Late in 2001, we had a similar robbery at the same location, but this time the uniformed officer was sitting at a desk in the lobby. The robbers didn't notice him until after they had pulled out guns and announced a robbery. Another case that demonstrates even more this lack of planning by robbers was one we had several years ago in which three ski-masked robbers charged into a bank annex and announced a robbery, only to find that the department they were in handled only canceled checks.

Residence robberies are particularly dangerous because they are also seldom planned, beyond hearing a rumor of large amounts of money and valuables kept there. The robbers break into a home and demand the money or valuables, but since the rumors are often just that, no valuables can be produced. The robbers then believe the victims are holding out and may injure or kill them. Street robberies are also highly dangerous because they are usually committed as the opportunity presents itself, with no planning at all.

The truth is that the lack of planning for most robberies is what makes them so dangerous. The robber has likely not even thought about what to do should the unexpected occur, which, without a doubt, it will. And when the unexpected does occur, the robber panics.

Many times, though, whether a robbery is planned or not, police officers find that the victims of robbery make it very easy for the robber. One of the newer kinds of robbery, that is quickly gaining popularity throughout the country, for example is robbery at automated bank machines. People using automated bank machines unfortunately often make it very easy for robbers by not paying any attention to their surroundings, by not paying any attention to the fact that there is a person not using, or in line to use, the automated bank machine, but just sitting in a car or loitering close by.

This inattention at automated bank machines is just one of the many ways that citizens make it easy for robbers. For instance, even though it is well-known that most government and pension checks come on the first or the fifteenth of the month, many elderly people, rather than using direct deposit, still insist on taking the checks to the bank themselves and then leave with sizable amounts of cash, becoming easy targets for robbers.

But one of the worst things that individuals, both young and old, can do to set themselves up for robbery is to pick up hitchhikers. Many Good Samaritans have ended up being robbed, raped, shot, or even killed by doing this. And this includes drivers who pick up young, pretty, and seemingly harmless female hitchhikers. Often they are not harmless, or not even really female. Other drivers, while not voluntarily picking up hitchhikers, have been known to be robbed of their valuables when someone jumped into their car while they were waiting at traffic lights with unlocked doors. And, as I noted earlier, one of the latest trends in robbery is carjacking, in which owners are robbed of their vehicles while getting into their cars, stopped at traffic signals, or parked on the street.

Most carjackers use one of several methods. Some will simply jump into a car while it's stopped at a traffic signal, others will jump in as people enter their car in a parking lot or on the street, and some will use the "bump method." With this last ploy, a car (often stolen) bumps another car in the rear and when the driver gets out to examine the damage, the carjackers steal the victim's vehicle. Carjackers, though, have become even more inventive. When publicity about bumping began to lessen its effectiveness, carjackers began a new ploy of pulling in front of a prospective victim and then slamming on the brakes, making the victim bump into the carjacker's vehicle. Most people are reluctant not to stop when they have hit another car.

Like all types of robbery, carjacking can be extremely danger-ous. There have been a number of cases, for example, in which victims have been shot to death, run over, or, as happened to a young mother in Savage, Maryland, dragged to their death during a carjacking (the woman's young daughter, still strapped into her child car seat, was simply tossed out by the carjackers, but luckily escaped serious injury). For this reason it is important to always be on guard against the possibility of a carjacking. Precautions include (particularly when passing through bad areas) driving with the doors locked, windows rolled up, and sun roof closed. Also, when you're involved in any type of minor traffic accident in an area of town you wouldn't walk through, don't get out of your car. Simply signal to the driver of the other car to follow you to a well-lit, busy location to exchange driver and insurance infor-mation. While it is always possible that you may have just been involved in a minor accident after all, don't take the chance of set-ting yourself up for robbery.

In addition, robbers are on the watch for any situation where a woman is working alone at night. The reason for this is that lone women are easy to scare, will usually not resist a robbery, and are often too frightened to identify the robber even if he or she is later caught by the police. And unfortunately, since the woman is alone and terrorized, the robber will also often take sexual liberties with her, a consideration that should be given serious thought by any woman thinking about taking such a job.

Finally, there are robbers who work in pairs. One will divert a victim's attention while the other sneaks up behind him or her, usually with a weapon. I had a recent encounter with just such a team. My brother (who is also a police officer) and I were walking to our car one evening after leaving a sports bar. Suddenly, a man came up to us waving his arms around and speaking very rapidly about needing $4 for a bus ticket. The man was jumping around and acting so wild that my brother and I both backed up against a wall and put our hands on our guns as we looked around. Although I'll never know if he was really part of the team or not, a man just up the street suddenly disappeared down an alley and the hyperactive panhandler decided it was also time to move on. My point is that the panhandler and his possible partner never saw our guns or knew that we were police officers, yet with just a bit of caution we were able to avoid a possibly dangerous confrontation. And while readers might think that our actions worked only because we tipped off the possible robbers that we were police officers, so what? If you are trapped in a similar situation, you can do the same. The worst that can happen is that the robber will call your bluff, and then you're no worse off than you were in the first place. If he demands to know what you were reaching for, tell him it was your wallet.

Robbery Investigation

In an attempt to solve the over 400,000 robberies reported each year, robbery detectives, like homicide detectives, follow a certain set of steps when conducting a robbery investigation, though, like homicide detectives, not all robbery detectives do them in the same order. Depending on the type of robbery, the amount of valuables taken, and whether the victims were injured or not, robbery detectives may or may not go to the robbery scene right away. If they don't go right away, the uniformed officers handle the initial investigation, collect any evidence, recover fingerprints, etc. When a robbery detective does go to the crime scene right away, however, he usually follows many of the same steps that a homicide detective does, such as having the crime scene videotaped and photographed, searching the scene for evidence, talking to witnesses, and so on.

But since most robberies are solved through victim identification of the robber, one of the first things many robbery detectives do, whether they go to the crime scene right away or not, is question the victims. Did the victim know the robber? (This happens more often than one would suspect—in about a fourth of all robberies.) If the victims were to later see the robber or robbers, could they identify him, her, or them? (A large percentage of the robberies committed involve multiple offenders, and though robbery is mainly a male crime, with 90 percent of the arrests made for robbery in 2000 being male, a number of females also commit it.) What did the robber or robbers say? What was he or she, or what were they, wearing? Was there anything unusual about the suspects? (Most large police departments now have automated mugshot systems that can electronically search through their files for birthmarks, tattoos, missing or gold teeth, etc.) How did the robbers get away? Is there a description of the getaway car or a license number? Did the suspects touch anything? (Through the new automated fingerprint technology available, a fingerprint left at the scene can very quickly identify the perpetrator.)

As the above would attest, robbery victims can be extremely helpful to the police by being observant during the crime. And if it is found that the victim was observant and can give a good description of the suspect, the robbery detective may have a composite drawing made of the robber (more often, though, detectives find that victims can describe the weapon in great detail, but not the

Not Your Typical Robber

While the majority of robbers share certain character-istics, it can be deadly to assume that a person who doesn't fit the stereotype isn't one. I had a case a number of years ago that demonstrates this.

One afternoon while working as a uniformed district officer, I heard over the police radio the report of a robbery in progress at the Bar-B-Que Heaven on North College Avenue. A moment of cold unreality rippled through me when I realized I was at that moment directly in front of the Bar-B-Que Heaven.

Although police officers may appear brave in books and movies, I felt my hands sweating rivers and my heart pal-pitating like a stamping machine as I burst into the Bar-B-Que Heaven with my .357 Magnum out, screaming for everyone to freeze. Inside I found the counter man stand-ing at the cash register with his hands up, and a scruffy-looking fellow with long shaggy hair and paint-spattered clothing facing me with a small revolver in his hand. Behind him stood a man wearing a new-looking suit, his expression one of shock.

"Drop it or I'm going to kill you!" I screamed at the scruffy-looking man, who immediately dropped the revolver onto the counter. "Hands on top of your head!"

For reasons I still can't explain, though I suspect it had something to do with an overdose of adrenaline, I turned to the man in the suit and ordered him to do the same. After a few seconds he brought his right hand up, which until this time he had held hidden from view, and also dropped a small revolver onto the counter.

As I found out a few moments later, the scruffy-looking man was actually the owner, who had been in the back room doing some painting. Hearing the man in the suit announce the robbery, the owner had called the police, then grabbed his own gun and come out to confront the robber.

robber). Many police departments now also use computer composite drawing, which is a computer program that begins with a basic face shape and then adds a mustache or beard, lengthens the nose, shortens hair, and so on, right on the computer screen.

After questioning the victims, many robbery detectives canvass the neighborhood around the crime scene for anyone who might have seen something that could be helpful. Often, witnesses will have seen something important that they didn't recognize at the time. For example, a robbery detective tells of a case he was investigating that involved the robbery and brutal beating of two elderly widows, whose eyesight, it was found, was so poor they couldn't even describe their assailants. However, upon canvassing the neighborhood, the detective found a witness who had seen a man in the neighborhood on the day of the robbery. The man wasn't doing anything suspicious; it was just that the witness knew the man and thought that he was supposed to be in prison. Upon being brought in for questioning, the suspect, not knowing anything about the victims' poor eyesight, immediately assumed that the two widows had identified him, and he quickly offered to turn state's evidence against the man who actually did the beating. He did this in exchange for not being charged as a habitual criminal, since he had just been released from prison the week before.

Lastly, in any robbery investigation, if there is no physical evidence, no usable description given by the victim, and no results from canvassing the neighborhood, most robbery detectives will turn to their informants. A very common, though self-destructive, trait found among criminals is the desire to brag about their crimes. All good robbery detectives have a number of informants who listen for this bragging and then report it back to them. Many of these informants are "fringe people," those who associate regularly with criminals and give information in exchange for money, people who know that the better and more accurate the information they give, the more money they receive. Some informants, on the other hand, are criminals themselves, who give the information in exchange for reduced charges or lowered sentences. Most experienced police officers, though, have learned through bitter experience never to rely totally on information from informants. While some informants are trustworthy and will regularly give good information, others will lie if they believe it will help them. For this reason, police officers always try to corroborate information from new informants.

In addition to using informants, experienced detectives know that certain locations contain good sources of information.

"If a person's a top investigator, he or she is always talking to people over in the jail," said Detective Lieutenant Vernon Pullings. "A lot of good information floats around that place."

Many of the people incarcerated in local jails, the police know, are there because they are unable to make bail, and so are simply passing the time waiting for their trials. Because of this, they have a lot of spare time for talking. In addition, there is a caste system within jails and prisons, with robbers being one of the upper castes. Many prisoners will therefore brag about their crimes in order to establish their position in this caste system. While some prisoners will, of course, exaggerate about their criminal deeds, they will still usually tell enough of the truth to let the police know what crimes they've been involved in. And within all jails, most detectives find, there are always people who are willing to report what they have heard if they believe it will help them with their own case.

Additionally, robbery detectives find it is often helpful to talk among themselves about the robberies they are investigating, and to compare descriptions of suspects, vehicles, and modes of operation. Occasionally, they will find similarities that lead them to believe they may be working on separate robberies that were perpetrated by the same individual or gang. Robbers tend to establish a pattern, and similar patterns often indicate either the same robber or the same gang of robbers. By comparing and pooling their information, detectives are often able to come up with the name of a suspect or at least a better description of him. And since the penalties for robbery are so stiff, detectives find that with any robbery gang, if they can identify just one member, he or she will usually, in return for a reduced sentence, inform on the others.

The truth is, regardless of what Hollywood would have the public believe, there is no honor among thieves. This is true even for large, tightly knit groups like organized crime. The reason why the FBI has been able to send so many organized crime members to prison in the last decade is the large number of informers they have inside these criminal organizations.

Likelihood of Robbery

In addition to the actions of victims discussed above, there are geographical and seasonal factors that can affect the likelihood of robbery. For example, a person living in the southern states has the largest chance of being robbed since 37.5 percent of the reported robberies in 2000 occurred there. The three other reporting regions of the country, the western, northeastern, and midwestern states, totaled 22, 20.5, and 20 percent respectively. Additionally, in all areas of the country robbery is 3 times more likely to occur in cities of over a million population as compared with smaller cities, 7 times more likely to occur in cities of over a million population as compared with the suburbs, and 28 times more likely to occur in urban than in rural areas. The time of year, it has been found, can also have an effect on the likelihood of robbery. In 2000, more robberies occurred during the months of October, November, and December than in any other three-month period (undoubtedly because of the large amount of cash around for holiday shopping), while the fewest robberies occurred during the months of February, March, and April. But regardless of the season or area of the country you happen to live in, you are always a potential victim of robbery. The Bureau of Justice Statistics has calculated that over a person's lifetime there is a one in three chance of being robbed at some time. Not fortuitous odds, but by using just a bit of caution and the tips below, you can lessen them considerably.

Avoiding Robbery

Since robbery is such a dangerous crime, citizens need to take whatever precautions they can to avoid becoming a robbery victim. Fortunately, there are a number of very simple things that can be done which will significantly lessen the chances:

- This one should be obvious: never flash large amounts of cash openly. This applies not only in bars and nightclubs, but also in restaurants and checkout lines. It is wiser to keep a small amount of money separate to pay with if you are carrying a large amount of cash. Also, don't wear flashy jewelry or expensive fad clothing if you must travel through bad areas of town. People have been killed for expensive tennis shoes or jackets. If you must be in or travel through a bad area of town, don't dress expensively; instead dress for freedom of movement.

- Use direct deposit for government and pension checks, or have someone accompany you to the bank.

- Don't use a bank machine if someone hanging around it appears to be simply waiting. Check out the area before going up to the machine. If possible, have a friend watch the surrounding area while you make a withdrawal. And most important, unless absolutely vital, if you're alone, never use self-service *anything* at night.

- Be observant when getting into a car in a parking lot or on the street. Are there suspicious people standing around? When traveling through undesirable neighborhoods, roll up the windows, close the sun roof, lock the car doors, and be observant when waiting at traffic lights. In addition to the possibility of a carjacking, there is another type of crime, called "smash and grab," that occurs in heavily traveled, congested areas where cars are forced to stop. A criminal walks up to the car and, using a rock or piece of metal pipe, smashes out a window and then reaches into the car, grabbing a purse, briefcase, or other valuable item. To be prepared for this type of crime, always allow enough space between your car and the car in front of you when stopped in traffic in case you have to maneuver your car to safety.

- If you're in fear of being robbed on the street, use the same defense as advised against a potential rapist. Immediately get away from the person you suspect. Cross the street, and if the person follows you, attempt to get to an open, populated area, into an open store, or make noise and try to draw attention to yourself.

- Be particularly concerned if a strange person seems to be violating your space. The person could be preparing to snatch a purse, necklace, or package. Or worse, he could be preparing to produce a weapon and demand your valuables. At a street corner, wait for this person to cross first. If he doesn't, go immediately to an open store or other place of safety. And particularly for women, watch for someone following you. Often purse or jewelry snatchers will follow a woman until she appears inattentive or distracted. If you think someone is following you, stop and glance into a store window. Does the person also stop? If so, go into an open store or other place of safety.

- Check out the surrounding area before going into a convenience store or filling station late at night. Are there people inside who could be dangerous? Are there people loitering around outside with no apparent business there? Be particularly cautious of the person all police officers watch for: the one wearing bulky clothing when the weather is too warm for it. Robbers do this to hide a sawed-off shotgun or other weapon.

- If you find yourself caught up in a robbery, either of yourself or of an establishment you happen to be in, there are certain things you should do. The first is, never resist unless you feel you are in imminent danger of being killed or seriously injured. Obey the robbers' instructions and give them whatever valuables they ask for. But also note the robbers' height (using your own for comparison), weight, hair, clothing, and anything distinctive, such as scars, tattoos, or glasses. Also note anything the robbers touch. When they leave, observe how the robbers get away, and if it can be done without endangering yourself, get the license number of any vehicles used. If you have found that your memory isn't what you'd like it to be, write down everything you observed immediately after the robbers leave. Save these notes for the police, but don't show them to the other victims since they can affect their memory of the events.

- Never admit strangers into your home. Recently, a large string of robberies was committed by a man and woman who would appear at the victim's door carrying an infant. The man would say that their car had broken down, and ask if they could please come in and use the telephone. A side note to this, however, is that a 12-year study of robbery showed that a third of all the robberies that occurred in the victim's home were committed by people who were, or had been, there legally, such as guests, relatives, or repair people.

- Don't keep your house keys with your money and identification. If you do, you'll likely find your home burglarized soon after you've been robbed.

- Remember, body language says a lot about your vulnerability. Robbers look for victims who appear to be inattentive or easily frightened.

Best Advice

The best advice the police can offer about robbery is that it is safest not to get into the position where a robbery can occur, but if one does occur, never physically resist a robber or refuse to give what is asked for. Money and valuables can always be replaced, but not a life.

5

TERRORISM AND HOSTAGE SITUATIONS

TERRORISM

When I wrote the first edition of this book, few Americans needed to worry about terrorism. Unless their jobs involved traveling to countries where unrest and revolution were the norm, most Americans could feel safe. Terrorist attacks were just stories on the news about faraway places. The last ten years, however, have now erased that feeling of safety. On February 26, 1993, terrorists exploded a bomb in the basement of the World Trade Center in New York City, killing six people and injuring over a thousand. Two years later, on April 19, 1995, a bomb destroyed the Alfred P. Murrah federal building in Oklahoma City, killing 168 people and injuring hundreds of others. Finally, on September 11, 2001, terrorists struck again, this time crashing aircraft full of jet fuel and innocent victims into the World Trade Center and the Pentagon, exacting a death toll in the thousands.

Because these three terrorist attacks ended in a huge loss of life and enormous property damage on United States soil, they not only shook Americans out of their lethargy about terrorism, but also forced them to focus on terrorism as a very real threat. Nationally, steps have already been taken to recruit American citizens in the fight to stop terrorism. In March 2002, Attorney General John Ashcroft, in order to bolster existing programs and start new ones, announced plans to funnel $2 million into the Neighborhood Watch program. The idea behind this infusion of money is that the Neighborhood Watch program, which for years has been the eyes and ears for the police about crime in America's neighborhoods, must now also be the eyes and ears for the police about terrorism. Americans must now, along with watching for car thieves and burglars, be on the lookout for possible terrorist activity.

"Through the Neighborhood Watch program," Ashcroft said, "we will weave a seamless web of prevention of terrorism."

Would the events of September 11 have occurred if Americans had then been actively on the lookout for terrorist activities? Probably not as easily as they did. Regardless, Americans must now be more vigilant about terrorism, as the change in the Neighborhood Watch program will promote. And while belonging to the Neighborhood Watch program is certainly a worthwhile undertaking for any citizen, and I support the program wholeheartedly, there is much more you can do to protect both yourself and your family from terrorism.

Though it might seem that terrorists strike unexpectedly and without any warning to their victims, as the three tragedies above would appear to indicate, this doesn't mean that Americans are defenseless against terrorism. By having just a little knowledge about how terrorists operate, individuals can greatly reduce both their and their family's chances of becoming victims of a terrorist attack.

The first thing readers must do in order to avoid becoming the victim of terrorism is to understand how terrorists think. To be effective, a terrorist incident must:

- **Be dramatic**
  In order to instill terror, an incident has to be dramatic enough to be newsworthy. Terrorist groups don't want to just terrorize those who personally witness an event, but also those who see it on the news. Consequently, terrorists often attack large public gatherings or high-profile locations that will give them lots of news coverage.
- **Be bloody**
  Bombing a vacant building, while perhaps dramatic, won't

terrorize many people. To really instill terror, an incident must be violent, bloody, and involve as many innocent victims as possible.

- **Hold some significance to the terrorist group**

    While terrorist groups may often seem to be just gangs of thugs who like to hurt innocent people, most terrorist organizations do espouse and hold some ideological position and beliefs. Consequently, terrorist groups often strike on dates that have special significance to them. (The Oklahoma City bombing took place on the second anniversary of the destruction of the Branch Davidian compound in Waco, Texas. Terrorists carried out the September 11 World Trade Center attack on the anniversary of the midpoint of the Camp David Accord negotiations, which occurred from September 5 to 17, 1978.) Also, terrorists often strike during important holidays, such as Christmas or Easter, so as not only to terrorize but demoralize as well. A number of years ago, for example, the Irish Republican Army exploded a car bomb in downtown London during peak Christmas shopping hours, in the apparent hope of not only killing and injuring large numbers of innocent people, but also ruining Christmas for all who saw the event on the news.

In addition, the targets of terrorist attacks are often symbolic, many times representing someone or something the terrorist group opposes. This explains why the World Trade Center, which represents Western capitalism, was the target of two terrorist attacks.

The first defense against terrorism is the same defense against almost all violent crime: being aware. Far too often, people become the victims of crime because they are so wrapped up in their lives or in doing some specific task that they don't pay attention to the things happening around them. As they can with many other crimes, observant individuals who do the following can greatly reduce their chances of becoming the victims of terrorism:

- Whenever you are in a location that could be a possible target for a terrorist attack, such as an international airport or a large international meeting, always know where at least two, and preferably all, of the exits are, and also know the best two or more ways to get out of the neighborhood as quickly as possible. Take note of, and stay away from, any heavy or easily breakable objects that could fall on you or shatter and cut you in the event of an explosion.
- Pay attention to and report any strange vehicles parked in or circling an area where terrorists might strike.
- Report any strange packages or briefcases left unattended.
- Be patient with and expect time-consuming security checks at airports and other locations where terrorist strikes are possible. Most airports now randomly re-search and recheck a small number of flight passengers even after they have already gone through an initial security check before entering the gate area. Keep in mind that these procedures are meant to protect you.
- Try to sit on the aisle if possible while traveling on an airplane, train, etc. This gives you much more mobility in the event you must take some action during a terrorist incident.
- Be observant of any seemingly nervous strangers in locations where terrorist attacks are possible. Terrorists know there is a good likelihood they will die and so are naturally very nervous.
- Be cognizant of specific dates. It would be wise to avoid traveling or attending large gatherings on dates important to terrorist groups.

If, however, you find yourself caught in what appears to be a terrorist attack, there are still actions you can take that will increase your odds of surviving it:

- If there is shooting nearby, immediately get low and, if possible, behind something thick and heavy. Terrorists often have no specific targets, but will simply shoot at anyone they see.

- If you see a person fall to the floor for no apparent reason, reacting as if he or she has had a stroke or heart attack, very likely the person has. If, on the other hand, you see several people doing this, it could mean poison gas (as occurred during the Tokyo subway terrorist attack in March 1995). Immediately get as far away as you can from these people. Without protective equipment and medical training you can't help them, and if you stay around you will likely be overcome by the same poison gas. If you are outside, your first warning of poison gas could be birds falling from the sky or other small animals overcome and collapsing. Again, get away from the area as quickly as you can. As soon as possible, remove your clothing and then rinse your skin with water (the sooner the better as clothing can become contaminated and hold hazardous material).

- Have at least two methods of quick exit from your place of business, and *never* depend on elevators. If you have only one exit in mind, remember that it could become blocked by an explosion or gun-toting terrorists. Know where the fire extinguishers are located and how to use them. Also, ask if your business has an emergency evacuation plan. If not, offer to help develop one. In addition, ask about what new security measures, such as photo ID badges or security checkpoints, could be taken to enhance the safety of employees.

- Since the September 11 attacks, several companies have been selling terrorist survival kits. A company named WorldPrep.com, for example, sells a "Personal Evacuation Kit" for under $35 that contains a disposable respirator, a small flashlight, a chemical light stick, a high-intensity whistle, eight ounces of drinking water, and a thermal blanket. All of these items are meant to help you survive, along with assisting rescuers in finding you, in the event you become trapped in a collapsed structure. A kit such as this, purchased or simply put together yourself, would be a wise precaution.

- Develop an emergency plan that your family can use in the event of a terrorist attack. Your children should be assured that you don't expect an imminent attack but that all families need to make plans in case of emergencies or disasters, which, besides terrorism, include tornadoes, floods, fires, etc. Both adults and children should have an alternate location to go in the event an emergency makes going home impossible. Also, plans should be made concerning how to contact each other during an emergency. A good idea is to have all family members contact a relative who lives out of town, but make sure the relative lives far enough away so as not to be affected by the same emergency. In addition, a wise precaution would be to assemble a disaster kit that contains items that would be needed in the event your family must vacate your home for several days (changes of clothing, toiletries, credit cards or cash, etc.). Be certain you also have a battery-operated radio with fresh batteries so that you can hear warnings and updates from government officials and emergency agencies.

- To prepare for the possibility that chemical agents could be dispersed by terrorists, show family members how to close the house up. All windows and doors should be shut and all outside air sources, such as the air-conditioning and heating system, fans, and fireplace ducts, should be turned off or closed. Also, families should be prepared to stay for several days inside the closed house, and therefore need to have a stockpile of basic survival items, such as bottled water, sufficient toilet paper, nonperishable food, first aid equipment, and battery-powered lighting and radio.

Unfortunately, as has been shown by a number of alarming incidents around the country in the last several years, schools often become targets for individuals who want to make a statement by either taking hostages or killing innocent victims. While everyone knows about the killings at Columbine High School, students have also been murdered at schools in Santee, California; Gary, Indiana; Baltimore, Maryland; and Deming, New Mexico, to name just a few. Consequently, parents need to confirm that their local police departments have developed emergency plans for handling such incidents. If they haven't, parents should begin at the police department and, if necessary, work their way up through the city council to the mayor, insisting that such plans be developed.

In addition, parents need to ensure that any schools their children attend also have emergency plans for terrorist-type incidents. The schools, however, not only should have these plans, but all members of the staff must be intimately acquainted with them.

As an article titled "Back-to-School Security" in the September 2000 issue of *Law Enforcement Technology* stated: "Sadly many schools remain unsecure and unprepared for violence." Curt Lavarello, executive director of the National Association of School Resource Officers, stated in this article: "There are still police departments that cannot produce a blueprint of the schools in their jurisdiction. That's alarming when you think about the tragedies we've seen across the country."

Bioterrorism

Of course, terrorism can take forms other than bombs, shootings, and chemical weapons. As we have recently seen with the U.S. postal system, it can also take the form of bioterrorism. Our mail system is obviously very vulnerable to such assaults, and, as a result, bioterrorism attacks through the U.S. mail resulted in several anthrax deaths in 2001.

"We're telling people that there is a threat—that right now the threat is in the mail," said Postmaster General John E. Potter a little more than a month after the September 11 attacks. "There are no guarantees that the mail is safe."

While this statement from the Postmaster General confirms that the threat of bioterrorism has become very much a reality in America, once again knowledgeable individuals can greatly reduce their chances of becoming victims of this type of terrorism. Like the previous advice, the best way to avoid becoming the victim of bioterrorism is to be aware and observant. Experts advise that you should be suspicious of a possible threat if:

- You receive strange mail unexpectedly or from someone you don't know.
- You receive a package that is addressed to someone no longer at your address.
- You receive unexpected mail that's handwritten and contains no return address or has one you can't confirm as legitimate. If there is a return address, check to see if it matches the cancellation mark.
- You receive a package that's lopsided, lumpy, or has stains as though it has been leaking. Be alert to strange powders on or odors coming from your mail.
- You receive mail that's sealed with excessive tape.
- You receive strange, unexpected mail marked with restrictive endorsements such as "personal" or "confidential."
- You receive a package that contains excessive postage (a sender of anthrax or some other bioterrorism substance can't risk having a mail clerk examine the package while weighing it for postage).
- If you should encounter mail that meets any of the conditions above, treat it as if it might explode. Don't handle it, turn it over, or shake it (you don't want to release possible spores). Cover it with a newspaper or a towel and immediately wash with lots of soap and water (which is good advice whenever you handle mail, as it could always have been inadvertently contaminated), then call the police.

Finally, the above warnings also apply to any packages you find simply left somewhere or apparently abandoned.

Hostage-Taking Incidents

During the last few decades the United States has seen an alarming growth in the number of hostage-taking incidents, alarming not only because these incidents create a huge drain on a police department's manpower—and consequently leave large areas of a community unprotected until they are resolved—but more because they present a very high level of danger to their victims. At the mention of hostage taking, though, many readers will undoubtedly think of a terrorist incident such as the Munich Olympics, but in truth most hostage situations don't involve terrorists at all. Many are perpetrated every year by criminals caught in the act of committing a crime, a scenario that was used, though considerably overdramatized, in the movie *Dog Day Afternoon*. Disgruntled employees who have been fired or disciplined also perpetrate a growing number of hostage-taking incidents each year. But the truth is that most hostage incidents are not initiated by any of the above, but instead by people who appear ordinary but are actually emotionally disturbed and reacting to some sort of stress in their domestic life, people whom no one would suspect of being a hostage taker. Every day, it seems, newspapers contain accounts of someone holding an ex-spouse, his own children, fellow employees, or simply innocent citizens hostage for some reason, and far too many times these incidents end in tragedy.

Readers should keep in mind, however, that while up to this time few terrorist organizations have held groups of Americans hostage, this doesn't mean it can't happen. Although the largest terrorist incidents on U.S. soil have involved bombs and aircraft, that could change. Terrorist groups know that United States authorities have become vigilant and watchful for terrorist incidents involving bombs and aircraft, and they consequently may want to strike at America in a new way. Large-scale hostage taking would be very newsworthy for terrorists looking to make a statement.

Types of Hostage Takers

While the chances of being taken hostage by a terrorist group are certainly lower than for most other crimes, these incidents do occur. A person might also think that the chances of having lightning strike one's house are small, especially after one has already been hit by a tornado several years before, but it does happen. (I know because it happened to me.) And terrorist activities also happen.

"The distressing fact is that over the past five years terrorism has increased," stated former secretary of state George Schultz to a conference on terrorism held in Washington, D.C., a number of years ago. Unfortunately, incidents during the last few years, such as in Oklahoma City and at the World Trade Center, demonstrate that terrorism shows absolutely no signs of slowing down.

Also supporting the idea that terrorism continues to be a threat is that there are now dozens of terrorist groups that have been known to be involved in hostage-taking, groups with such recognizable names as the Popular Front for the Liberation of Palestine, the Tupamaros of Uruguay, and the Italian Red Brigade. But there are also groups involved in hostage takingwhose names are not quite so recognizable, such as the Armenian Secret Army for the Liberation of Armenia and the Turkish Revolutionary Youth Federation. While the chances of being taken hostage by one of these groups—particularly for people who don't travel abroad—is small, the dangers if taken hostage by them are not. You have only to recall the fate of Leon Klinghoffer, a wheelchair-bound man who was shoved overboard during the terrorist takeover of the cruise ship *Achille Lauro*. Members of these terrorist groups are often idealistic, self-appointed crusaders who are so thoroughly indoctrinated that they are willing to die and become martyrs to "the cause." Unfortunately, these terrorists often also want to take hostages with them.

Rather than being taken hostage by a terrorist group, though, citizens have a much better chance of just happening to be in a bank, a department store, or some other commercial outlet when

Hostage Taking by Mail

There are many ways people can find themselves taken hostage besides those mentioned at the beginning of this chapter. For one young woman it began by becoming pen pals with a prison inmate. The two apparently corresponded until the young woman found out that her pen pal had been imprisoned for murdering his fiancée, and then she broke off their relationship and thought that was that.

It wasn't.

The prison inmate, accompanied by two guards to a doctor's office outside of the prison, escaped with the help of an accomplice. He immediately went to his former pen pal's home with his accomplice and took her and her two small children hostage. After two days of negotiation, the police felt the situation was deteriorating when the hostage-takers began repeatedly telling the negotiators that they were going to have to kill one of the children. The police finally decided to make a bold move and stormed the house, killing the escaped convict, arresting his accomplice, and freeing the hostages unharmed.

a robbery or other crime is bungled and the criminals know they'll be facing the police any second. Confronted with imminent capture and incarceration, criminals have increasingly resorted to taking hostages in order to buy time. Although the taking of hostages is not a good tactical move since it only complicates the criminals' position and increases their punishment when arrested, it is usually an impulsive act done under desperate circumstances with little thought of the possible consequences. These individuals, unlike terrorists, have no desire to die for a cause. Trapped criminals simply want to escape, and are hoping to use hostages as bargaining tools for this purpose. Unfortunately, the results are often deadly.

An increase has also been seen in the number of hostages taken by disgruntled employees who have been fired or reprimanded. These enraged former employees return to the workplace with a weapon, shoot the place up, and take hostages. Such events are usually impulsive actions by very angry people, and the incidents are at their best poorly planned, since the person has nothing to gain by doing this and much to lose. But because most of these hostage takers soon realize what the consequences of their impulsiveness will be, feelings of depression and hopelessness set in, causing these incidents often to end in tragedy.

Much more likely than being taken hostage by terrorists, trapped criminals, or even disgruntled employees, though, is the possibility of being taken hostage by an emotionally disturbed individual, quite often a family member or close acquaintance. These hostage takers, it has been found in most cases, are usually undergoing some sort of stress in their domestic lives, such as a divorce, loss of their children, or simply the end of a romantic relationship, and take hostages in an attempt to emphasize real or imagined injustices, or in the hope of forcing a change in their circumstances.

These hostage situations are also usually impulsive, unplanned actions that may have started out as only an argument. But because many of these hostage takers have been drinking or are under the influence of drugs, an argument, when it shows no sign of resolution to their liking, can suddenly snowball into a hostage incident. And while these situations are usually the most dangerous to people closely involved in the stress-inducing domestic incident, still, a person with no involvement in the domestic matter, and who may not even know the hostage taker, also may be taken hostage simply by having the misfortune of being in proximity when the hostage situation occurs.

In addition to all of these types of hostage takers, occasionally a severely psychotic person will take hostages for bizarre reasons. There was a case, for example, where the hostage taker's demand was that the letter "W" be taken out of the alphabet. But the most dangerous type of hostage taker is those who are suicidal but who don't have the courage to kill themselves and want the police to do it for them. This is what is known in law enforcement circles as "suicide by cop." These people are particularly dangerous to others because, after taking hostages in order to bring the police, they often do something threatening, such as shoot at the police or at the hostages in order to force the police to kill them.

There was a case, for example, in Rochester, New York, in which a man took eight hostages in a bank and demanded that the police kill him. Of course, the police both legally and morally can't do this, and so the man shot and killed a teller and then walked over and stood in front of a window, purposely making himself a target for the police snipers, who then did shoot and kill him.

A veteran police officer who has helped resolve many hostage situations warns: "The most important thing for any person who is taken hostage to remember is that seldom are hostage takers rational, clear-thinking individuals with a plan. Most have no plan at all. Most have gotten themselves into a really bad situation and now don't know how to get themselves out of it."

In psychiatric terms many hostage takers are what are called "inadequate personalities." According to the American Psychiatric Association, an inadequate personality is a person whose life has been characterized by ineffectual responses to emotional, social, intellectual, and physical demands. The inadequate personality manifests ineptness, unadaptability, poor judgment, social instability, and lack of physical and emotional stamina. Often this type of hostage taker is so insecure and unsure of himself that he actually has the hostages do the negotiating with the authorities for him. This type of hostage taker, it should be cautioned, is always a danger because he is a suicide threat. But because of his inadequate personality, he is seldom able to do it himself, and may try to force the police to do it by killing the hostages. A number of mental health professionals believe that almost all people who take hostages are probably inadequate personalities since hostage-taking is not an appropriate response or effective maneuver under almost any circumstances. Hostage-taking is simply not worth the high risk of the additional, and very serious, penalties when compared with the very small possibility of actually getting away with it.

Even in terrorist groups, who at least often have a plan and purpose for their hostage-taking, the members who actually do the hostage-taking, while perhaps not inadequate personalities, are still "throwaway" people. Although they may often be well trained and indoctrinated, these people are still usually considered expendable by the terrorist group leaders, since being a hostage taker is very risky and hazardous. But the most important fact to a hostage is that, with the exception of terrorists, most hostage takers are losers, desperate individuals with no idea how to resolve the situation they have gotten themselves into, and their lack of confidence can be either helpful or dangerous, depending on the action they finally decide to take. Hostage incidents, it must never be forgotten, always have the potential to end in death.

There is a final group of hostage takers: career criminals who kidnap for ransom. Rather than being emotionally disturbed individuals who may ask for money only as a side thought to the actual reason for the hostage-taking, they have no political agenda, no debts to settle with loved ones. They just want the money. These people can also be dangerous, however, because the ransom money is of no value to them if they are caught, and live hostages can identify them. And for anyone who thinks that this type of hostage-taking affects only wealthy people, remember the celebrated kidnapping for ransom of 26 schoolchildren a number of years ago in Chowchilla, California.

Police Response to Hostage Incidents

In the hope of avoiding many of these unnecessary tragedies, police departments across the United States have during the last few decades built upon each other's experiences and consequently become very sophisticated in their ability to handle hostage situations and resolve them peacefully. Almost every large jurisdiction now has hostage negotiators and a special weapons and tactics (SWAT) team on call to respond to and resolve hostage situations, peacefully if possible, but with force if necessary. Fortunately, however, most incidents are resolved without violence, using procedures that have proven effective in the past.

"The approach we use can best be compared to the eagle that carries an olive branch in one claw and an arrow in the other," said Captain James E. Campbell, formerly in charge of a large-city SWAT team. "Our first approach is to resolve the incident without violence, but we are capable of and willing to use whatever force is necessary to prevent injury to innocent victims."

Upon arrival at a typical hostage-taking situation, the SWAT team usually immediately establishes an inner perimeter around the hostage scene, a perimeter that encloses the area of greatest danger, and its members then take up strategic positions within this perimeter in order to prevent the hostage taker's escape. While they are doing this, regular uniformed police officers usually set up an outer perimeter, a boundary beyond which the danger is minimal. Once these perimeters have been established, information must be gathered on such things as: Who has been taken hostage? By whom? For what reasons? Information must also be gained on the armament of the hostage taker, his or her mental stability, the layout of the building or area where the hostages are being held, and any other item that may prove helpful in bringing about a peaceful resolution of the incident.

While this information is being gathered, the SWAT team commander usually deploys snipers at key points in order to gather ongoing intelligence and to kill the hostage takers if it becomes necessary. The SWAT team commander also quickly formulates a preliminary assault plan in case it becomes apparent that the hostages are in imminent danger of being harmed or killed. Throughout the hostage incident, while the hostage negotiators are talking with the hostage takers, the SWAT team commander, as each new piece of intelligence arrives, constantly refines and updates the assault plan, along with developing alternate plans, always ready at any moment to take over if negotiations break down and the hostages appear in danger of being harmed or killed. So long as the hostage takers are talking and not harming anyone the hostage negotiators handle the incident, but once it is felt that the hostages are in imminent danger, the SWAT team takes over.

While SWAT team members and hostage negotiators both work toward the same end—the safe release of the hostages—they require individuals with very different talents. Where a SWAT team member must be firm, decisive, and forceful, a hostage negotiator must be more flexible. It is the hostage negotiator's job to contact and talk with the hostage taker, keep him or her talking, establish rapport if possible, and let the hostage taker vent his or her anger and frustration (which in itself can often defuse the situation). A good hostage negotiator must be able to negotiate without arguing, must be able to direct the negotiations toward the avenues necessary for the safe release of the hostages, and, very important, must be able to distract the hostage taker if he or she begins showing anger or aggression toward the hostages. Most important, a good hostage negotiator must be able to find a way for the hostage taker to end the incident peacefully yet still save face. A good hostage negotiator must be a person who is flexible and able to change attitudes and directions as needed.

"I don't want someone as a hostage negotiator who has to win at everything," said Frank Connolly, a clinical psychologist and former head of the hostage negotiations team for a major police department. "I want a person who can lose the little battles in order to win the big war."

Other desirable traits of a good hostage negotiator, according to Connolly, are the ability to be a persuasive talker, to empathize without becoming emotional, and to play whatever

role is needed. He or she must also be a patient listener, knowledgeable about the psychology of hostage takers, and, most
important, perceptive of any subtle changes in the mood and
thinking of a hostage taker.

Most negotiations with hostage takers are conducted over a
telephone or some other communications device instead of face-
to-face. If at all possible, communications are done on a secure
telephone line that allows the hostage taker to talk with only the
police, while also not allowing others to listen in or contact the
hostage taker. The news media, in its zeal to get the scoop, often
wants to talk to the hostage taker while the incident is still going
on. Hostage negotiators have found, however, that this often
gives the hostage taker a feeling of power and makes a surren-
der much more difficult to obtain. This is very possibly what
made the standoff in Waco, Texas, between members of the
Branch Davidian cult and federal authorities last so long.

Communicating by telephone also denies the hostage takers
an opportunity to take the negotiator hostage (the danger of
which was clearly demonstrated in the Terry Waite case in
Beirut). The negotiator, after setting up contact by telephone or
other electronic device, must listen to the hostage taker's
demands and then decide what can and cannot be done. There
are certain items that, through some very unfortunate incidents,
have been shown to be totally nonnegotiable, such as weapons,
drugs, and additional hostages. There are other items, though,
that are negotiable, such as food, cigarettes, the opportunity to
make a statement to the news media, and so on. Yet still, no
demands, even those made for non-negotiable items, should be
simply dismissed out-of-hand without first talking about it.

"A good hostage negotiator never simply dismisses an impossible or even ridiculous demand," said Sergeant Don Wright, a
former police hostage negotiator who successfully resolved
many hostage situations. "Instead, a good hostage negotiator
always looks for alternatives or compromises."

A tenet of most good hostage negotiators is that for each item
given to the hostage takers there is a price; for everything given

something must be given back. Hostage takers have been known to trade hostages for as little as a ham sandwich.

Readers may wonder why, rather than having to trade hostages for items such as food, cigarettes, and so on, the hostage takers wouldn't instead simply threaten to kill or harm the hostages if the items are not delivered. The reason most hostage takers aren't successful in doing this is because at the first contact hostage negotiators make it very clear, either implicitly or explicitly, that negotiations will continue only so long as no harm comes to the hostages, and that any harm to the hostages will bring an end to the negotiations and very likely an assault on the hostage takers, which traditionally has been extremely dangerous, and often fatal, for them. The same reasoning applies to accepting deadlines for action from hostage takers. Whenever hostage takers set deadlines, they are usually ignored by the negotiators unless it is believed the hostage takers will actually do harm to the hostages, in which case the building or area will likely be stormed.

Through the experiences of negotiators who have successfully resolved many hostage situations, it has been shown that, while verbal and listening skills are essential, negotiators have an even more potent weapon. The most effective weapon that hostage negotiators have is time.

"The best philosophy we've found is to keep the hostage takers talking and wait them out," said Police Officer Shirley Purvitis, a police hostage negotiator. "Time, we've found, is almost always on our side."

When a hostage situation is new, the hostage takers are often running on pure adrenaline, their demands are firm, and they seem fully in control. However, as time wears on and the negotiations continue for hours, both the energy and resolve of hostage takers start to wane, and they finally begin to see the futility and hopelessness of their situation. While the hostage negotiators have been working in shifts and relieving each other, the hostage takers, usually too nervous to rest, are often worn down and exhausted by the hours of constant stress and danger, and after enough time are usually ready to give up if they can do so and still save face. The Los Angeles County Sheriff's Department did a study a number of years ago of 29 hostage incidents. They found that the average incident lasted 12 hours. And of course, though some have been shorter, there have also been incidents that lasted for days.

The Stockholm Syndrome

While hostage negotiators usually attempt to extend the negotiations in order to wear down the resolve of the hostage takers, during the time these lengthy negotiations are going on an interesting psychological phenomenon often occurs between the hostages and hostage takers. Called the Stockholm Syndrome, this phenomenon is named after a hostage incident that took place in 1973 at the Sveriges Kreditbank in Stockholm, Sweden. During the incident, it was found that as time wore on, the hostages became very emotionally attached to the hostage takers (a female hostage later even became engaged to one of the hostage takers). It was also discovered that as the hours passed, the hostages began fearing the police more than the hostage takers, and one of the hostages, in a telephone call to the Swedish prime minister, claimed that their abductors were not holding them hostage, but rather were protecting them from the police.

This syndrome, which appears to be an unconscious, long-term reaction, is caused by a combination of factors, and has been seen many times in hostage situations, with Patty Hearst probably being the most celebrated case. During a hostage situation a hostage's life is in the hands of the hostage taker, and hostages are often so thankful when they aren't killed that they begin feeling indebted to the hostage takers, and therfore develop a close personal and emotional relationship with them. Interestingly, hostages have been known to continue this emotional attachment long after the incident has been resolved and the danger is gone, with former hostages often visiting the hostage takers in prison, and even setting up defense funds for them. Many authorities believe that the Stockholm Syndrome is like a knee-jerk reflex, a reaction beyond the control of the people involved.

There are certain factors, though, that must be present before the Stockholm Syndrome will develop. There must, for example, be positive contact between the hostages and hostage takers, and while this positive contact can be simply the absence of expected negative contacts such as beatings, rape, torture, or murder, any negative contacts that do occur can block the development of the syndrome. The hostages and hostage takers must also have more than just minimal contact, and must both face danger and be under stress together. In addition, they must see each other as human beings with feelings, needs, and problems. The Stockholm Syndrome, incidentally, also works in reverse, with the hostage takers often developing close, personal relationships with their hostages.

In most hostage situations the authorities are glad to see the Stockholm Syndrome developing since hostage takers are usually reluctant to harm hostages they have developed a close relationship with. This was demonstrated during the South Moluccan hostage situation in the Netherlands a number of years ago, when a hostage who had been selected for execution was spared because he and the hostage takers had gotten to know each other and had unconsciously allowed the Stockholm Syndrome to develop.

Of course, the Stockholm Syndrome, while usually positive from the police point of view, can also occasionally be detrimental since the hostages will often become antagonistic toward, and distrustful of, the police, who they feel are unnecessarily endangering the lives of them and the hostage takers. A hostage negotiator, for example, told of an incident in which the hostages were being held in a room at one end of a building while the hostage takers were negotiating with the police over a telephone at the other end. The hostage negotiator, able to persuade the hostage takers to allow him to speak with one of the hostages, warned the hostage to take cover because in a few

---

Strength of the Stockholm Syndrome

While the strength of the Stockholm Syndrome can vary depending on the circumstances of the hostage incident, at times it can be very great indeed. Many people who have been held hostage for long periods of time report that because of the Stockholm Syndrome they found themselves cooperating with the hostage taker much more than they would have ever thought possible, and many have developed an affection for the hostage taker. But sometimes it's even stronger than that. But just how strong?

A SWAT team member who was present during a lengthy hostage situation in a high-rise office building reported: "We had, of course, set up surveillance and snipers on the rooftop across the street. After we had been there for a long time, the hostage taker finally told the negotiator to give him a few minutes and he'd come out and give himself up. He and the hostage obviously didn't realize that we were across the street watching with binoculars because they both stripped naked and then fell to the floor and made love."

---

minutes the police were planning to crash through the building with a bulldozer. The hostage immediately dropped the telephone and warned the hostage takers of what the police were planning.

Not all hostage situations, however, are totally susceptible to the Stockholm Syndrome. There have been a number of hostage incidents, for example, in which the hostages have developed the Stockholm Syndrome for only some of the hostage takers, the ones who treated them decently, but not for all of them. There have also been a number of hostage incidents in which the syndrome has not occurred at all. Any negative contacts between the hostages and hostage takers can block development of the syndrome, and the more negative contacts, the less likely the syndrome will develop. There have been extreme cases, however, in which the hostages, even though injured by the hostage takers, rationalized that the hostage takers had no choice but to injure them, and developed the syndrome anyway.

Often, to ensure the safety of hostages, negotiators will try to induce the Stockholm Syndrome by asking the hostage takers to check on the medical condition of the hostages, to check whether the hostages need anything, or anything to make the hostage takers see the hostages as people, not objects. Of course, if successful, the police must be prepared for later hostility from the hostages, which was very openly displayed in the Stockholm incident and in many hostage incidents since.

Surviving a Hostage Situation

In most situations, if the hostages are able to show that they are sensitive, feeling human beings who care about the hostage taker's plight, the aggression of the hostage taker can often be lessened, but not always. The truth is that much also depends on the personality of the hostage taker. He or she must be capable of having positive feelings toward another person. Some criminal hostage takers, though, it has been found, have antisocial personalities, and these individuals are usually unable to develop emotional attachments. These people are grossly selfish, callous, irresponsible, impulsive, and unable to feel guilt or learn from experience or punishment. Fortunately, however, people with antisocial personalities are also very self-centered and usually realize that harming hostages is not in their own best interests. Still, in incidents with hostage takers who display antisocial personalities, often the police have no choice but to resort to drastic action.

As a last resort for resolving incidents involving hostage takers with antisocial personalities, and in cases where the Stockholm Syndrome has not developed and the hostage negotiators feel they can no longer ensure the safety of the hostages, an assault by the SWAT team may be ordered. To cover their assault, which must be swift and decisive, SWAT team members often use devices such as smoke grenades, tear gas, or concussion grenades, also known as "flash-bang" devices, which are grenades that explode with a large amount of light and noise, disorienting those close by, yet doing little damage.

During an assault, the SWAT team members, prepared for armed resistance, usually carry, in addition to their regular sidearms, some type of rapid-fire automatic weapon. SWAT teams also often carry weapons with sound suppressors (silencers). These have proven to be very effective for storming multistory buildings. Terrorists or hostage takers on one floor can be neutralized without those on another floor being aware of it. But regardless of their armament, the SWAT team members assault the hostage area under the plan developed by the SWAT team commander, usually by violently bursting through windows and doors with the intent of surprising and then neutralizing the hostage takers by whatever means necessary. This can be a very terrifying and dangerous time for the hostages. Any resistance from the hostage takers will likely be met by gunfire from the police. At the first sign of a police assault, hostages should immediately fall to the floor and stay there until the assault is over. Although there are no national statistics on how many hostages are accidentally wounded or killed by SWAT team members, it does occur. Readers have only to remember the Attica prison incident in which a number of guards who had been forced to trade uniforms with the prisoners were mistakenly killed. Therefore, it is important to show by falling to the floor and offering no resistance that you are not one of the hostage takers.

But regardless of how the police end a hostage situation, through negotiations or an armed assault, the most significant thing to a hostage is to be alive when the incident is resolved. Fortunately, there are a number of survival behaviors that have been shown to work for hostages in the past, behaviors that have allowed them to live long enough to be rescued. SWAT team members and hostage negotiators recommend the following:

- The first half-hour of any hostage situation is the most dangerous. The hostage taker is extremely tense and apprehensive during this time, and may be prone to violence if provoked or frightened. Do not make any sudden moves or struggle with the hostage taker unless you're in imminent danger. Until a hostage incident stabilizes into the negotiations phase, physical danger to the hostages is very possible.
- Remain as calm as possible during the incident. Hostage takers are usually very nervous, and therefore easily aroused to anger or frustration. A hysterical hostage can often cause the hostage taker to do something violent.
- Do exactly as the hostage taker orders. Being belligerent or uncooperative can be dangerous, and perhaps even fatal.
- Particularly during the initial stages of a hostage incident, don't speak to the hostage taker unless spoken to, and under no circumstances argue about the wisdom of his actions or point out mistakes or shortcomings. Nothing upsets a hostage taker quite as much as a hostage telling him how stupid he is. A hostage taker wants to feel he is in control. However, if later the hostage taker appears to want to talk, do so, but talk about positive and future things. Show concern for the hostage taker's plight.
- If you're ill or in need of medicine, tell the hostage takers. Most hostage takers don't want to be responsible for sick hostages or for the effects of a hostage incident on an ill person. In addition, ill hostages are often released first. Although one might fear that the hostage takers would just shoot ill hostages, this very seldom happens. Doing so wouldn't be in the hostage takers' best interests since they are warned immediately by hostage negotiators that any aggressive actions toward the hostages will likely force a

SWAT assault, which has historically been extremely hazardous to hostage takers.

- Be observant of the area you are being held in, its fortifica-
tion and defenses, and of the hostage takers, their appearance, weapons, etc. This information can be vital in successfully rescuing remaining hostages in the event you are
released before the others. However, don't stare at the
hostage takers; most are extremely tense and nervous, and
this will often intimidate them and cause them to act aggressively toward you.

- If you are being held hostage at a location unknown to the
police, or being transported in a car, try to leave your fingerprints where the hostage takers won't think of wiping them
off, or leave behind personal items such as earrings or tie
tacks. Be sensitive to smells (the ocean, factories, etc.),
sounds (railroads, boats, etc.), and sights (when being taken
in, when doors are opened, etc.) so that you can lead the
police back to the site in the event you are released before
the other hostages.

- Stay away from windows and doors through which the
police may enter or shoot during an assault, and once a
police assault does begin, drop to the floor and stay there.

- Don't lose faith in the likelihood of rescue. The police in the
last few decades have become very sophisticated in their ability to resolve hostage situations without violence. Although
occasionally an armed assault is necessary, the large majority
of these incidents are peacefully resolved with the hostages
unharmed.

Because of the extreme danger involved, I have not included
in the information above any advice about a hostage escaping on
his or her own. There are undoubtedly situations in which a
hostage must try to escape, especially when death or serious
injury is imminent. But a person must make the decision based
totally on the circumstances of the situation, and on whether or

not the opportunity has an excellent chance of success (failure will very likely result in serious, and perhaps fatal, consequences). In addition, a hostage should also consider whether escaping will endanger any hostages left behind.

People knowledgeable about hostage situations disagree over whether a person should attempt to escape or not. Some point out that, particularly in hostage situations over two or three hours old, the chances are much better of being freed unharmed by the police than of escaping unharmed. Others warn, however, that any hostage not escaping when the opportunity presents itself is simply leaving him-or herself at the mercy and whim of a usually unstable, and undoubtedly dangerous, person. The events of September 11 also underscore the extreme danger of passively allowing hostage takers to control the fate of the hostages. The decision, therefore, to attempt to escape or not must be up to the individual hostage based on the prevailing circumstances of the situation.

Avoiding Becoming a Hostage

While all the tips in the preceding section are valuable for increasing the chances of surviving a hostage incident unharmed, it would naturally be much safer simply not to be taken hostage at all. Yet some hostage incidents, particularly those that stem from a domestic fight, happen so quickly and unexpectedly that no one could have seen them coming, not even the hostage taker.

"I really didn't go there to take her hostage," said a former boyfriend who kidnapped and held his ex-girlfriend hostage for 11 hours in a high-rise office building. "I really didn't. It was just one of those spur-of-the-moment things that got out of control."

But still, there are a number of commonsense precautions that can prevent you from becoming a hostage, particularly to a professional hostage taker:

- Before traveling to any foreign country learn about the political conditions there. Take seriously any government travel advisories.

A Loved One Taken Hostage

For many people there is a situation probably even worse than being taken hostage themselves, and that is for a loved one to be taken hostage. The anxiety and distress of not knowing what is happening to a loved one can be heart-wrenching. However, there are some things you can do that will help ensure the eventual safe return of the loved one:

- If you receive a call from the hostage or a hostage taker, write down everything that was said, and note the time. Be sensitive to any accents or voice peculiarities of the caller, and listen carefully for any background noises that will tell you where the person is calling from. No matter what the hostage taker tells you, notify the police immediately.
- Handle any written correspondence from a hostage or hostage taker as little as possible. Fingerprints can be recovered from paper.
- Inform the police of any medical conditions or problems the hostage may have so they can relay this information to the hostage taker.
- Provide the police with a recent picture of the hostage. This can be a lifesaver because if the police must storm the area where the loved one is being held, they won't mistake him or her for a hostage taker.

- If you must travel to a volatile foreign country, pay attention to the dates of your travel. Don't plan to be there on a national holiday since terrorists often plan their activities for these dates.
- Avoid international flights that make many stops. Each one is an opportunity for terrorists to board.
- Wearing flashy jewelry or traveling first class marks you as a member of the class most terrorists oppose.

- When in a foreign country, don't meet people in lonely or deserted spots unless you know them well. You wouldn't do this, I hope, even in your own country.

Best Advice

The best advice the police can offer for anyone taken hostage is to remain calm, be cooperative, and at every opportunity show concern and humanity. But above all else, don't lose faith in the likelihood of a rescue.

For readers wanting more detailed information about hostage situations, I recommend they read my book, *SWAT Teams* (Perseus Books, 1999).

6

RESIDENCE BURGLARY

THE REALITY OF BURGLARY

One of a police officer's least favorite jobs is to take the report at a home where there has been a burglary. Technically, burglary is the unlawful entry into a structure to commit a felony, usually theft. The victims are always upset, often enraged, and occasionally deeply despondent to find that their personal items have been ransacked and their valuables stolen. It is a feeling, victims say, similar to being violated, and an event that runs contrary to the popularly held belief that a person's home is sacred territory, a place where the owners are safe from the outside world. In 2000, however, almost 3.5 million households in the United States lost over $5 billion in property to burglars. In the process, they also found out that this belief in the sanctity of the home is only a myth. Every year millions of people discover that they can no longer feel secure, even inside their own homes.

Further evidence against the myth of the sanctity of the home comes from national statistics showing that, because of the huge number of burglaries each year, over the next 20 years, 72 percent of the homes in the United States will be burglarized, 37 percent two or more times. Even more evidence comes from a recent national poll that found that over 60 percent of the respondents said they now worry regularly about the possibility of being burglarized. The truth is that no one should feel safe from being burglarized.

The above figure of 3.5 million burglaries, incidentally, is only an estimate. The actual number could be higher, since even though burglaries in 2000 accounted for almost a fifth of all property crimes reported to the police, it is believed that less than 50 percent of victims actually report the crime. There is a direct relationship, the police have found, between the amount of property stolen and the likelihood of reporting a burglary. In addition, it is also believed that the actual number of burglaries committed in our country could be higher because for many years there were more burglars in the nation's state prisons than any other type of criminal. Only in the last decade has this ranking been surpassed by people convicted of drug offenses. Also, burglars have one of the highest recidivism (repeat offender) rates of all criminals.

The chronic recidivism of burglars was dramatically demonstrated to me by a gentleman I have encountered twice so far in my career as a police officer. As a rookie officer I was working one day in an unfamiliar part of Indianapolis and received a radio run on a burglary in progress. Unsure how to get to the address, I accidentally turned down the wrong street and almost immediately pulled up behind a car with a large console television hanging out of the trunk. As it turned out, I was several blocks from the site of the crime but I had stumbled onto the burglars trying to get away. I arrested the driver of the car and his partner. They were soon released on bail, however, and then arrested again for burglary (by another officer) the day before they were to go to trial on my arrest. They were both eventually convicted of burglary and sentenced to 10-to 25-year terms in the state prison.

A little over 10 years later, I was a district uniformed sergeant and heard a radio call on a burglary in progress less than a block away. Slipping up the alley behind the address, I caught the burglar coming out of the back door carrying a small portable television set. Although I didn't recognize him, he recognized me. It was the driver of the car from the burglary 10 years before. He had been out of prison for that crime less than two weeks.

Types of Burglars

The mental picture many people have of a burglar is a masked, middle-aged man who stealthily slips into a home in the middle of the night to steal the family silver. But like many popularly held beliefs, this is not a totally accurate picture. Even though more than half of the burglars seen each year by the victims are strangers, a full third are acquaintances or family members, and while 87 percent of the burglars arrested by the police are men, almost two-thirds are under 25.

Almost all burglars, detectives say, fall into one of four groups:

1. Professional Burglars.   Only a very small percentage of burglars actually belong to this group. Professional burglars are career criminals who often have extensive knowledge of alarm and security systems, and support themselves through burglary. At one time there were a number of burglars who were expert at slipping into businesses undetected and opening safes. However, since few businesses keep large amounts of money or valuables in safes any longer, there has been a dramatic decrease in the number of safe burglars. The professional burglar of today, rather than safe-cracking, instead often steals items on order for fences (criminals who specialize in buying and then reselling stolen property), and, except for certain homes in exclusive areas, these burglars usually focus their criminal activities on businesses that carry easily disposed-of merchandise, particularly electronic equipment. Most professional burglars are of little threat to the homes of average citizens.

While there are many burglars, both professional and not, who prey mainly on businesses, I will concentrate here on residence burglary since businesses often face unique problems whose resolution is beyond the scope of this book. Businesses, as opposed to homes, are many times secluded behind large parking lots, often have many more entry possibilities, and are susceptible to such high losses that the services of professional security consultants are recommended. Still, many of the security tips given at the end of this chapter can also apply to businesses.

2. Drug-Habit Burglars.   Most burglary detectives say that addicts in need of money for drugs make up about 85 to 90 percent of all the burglars they deal with. The truth is that, along

with being the most common type of burglar, drug-habit burglars, because they are many times primarily residence burglars,
are also the biggest threat to the homes of average citizens. In
addition, because of the possibility of being desperately in need
of drugs at the time of the burglary, and the very high probability of being in terror of having to go through drug withdrawal in
jail, drug-habit burglars are extremely dangerous when confronted. Because of their fear of arrest they will usually pick
homes that have the lowest level of risk for them. The methods
of entry for drug-habit burglars are often crude, and, if they
can't find an unlocked door or window, they will many times
simply kick in a door or smash out a window.

3. Thrill Burglars. Economic gain is seldom the main
incentive for these individuals, who instead break into homes
for the thrill. Rather than stealing, they often do things such as
trash a house, defecate on the living room floor, watch a woman
as she sleeps, or rummage through her underwear drawer.
Street gangs that require a burglary as part of gang initiation also
fall into this category. It should be remembered, however, that
while many of these burglars are voyeurs, a confrontation with
one can just as easily turn into rape.

4. Opportunistic Burglars. These are quite often juveniles
who burglarize a home simply because the opportunity presents
itself. They usually don't need the money, and often keep the
items taken in the burglary rather than trying to sell them.

Signs Burglars Look For

Many burglars, it has been discovered, like to concentrate their
crimes in large apartment areas or buildings. They like these
locations because apartment dwellers seldom know each other
and are not suspicious of a strange face. Often the burglars will
strike during the day when most apartment dwellers are at
work, or if it is early evening they will select their victims by

checking which apartments are darkened. Other burglars like to victimize single-family homes in residential areas, and often have specific criteria for picking their victims.

"I always look for the house that's got the nicest yard," a burglar I arrested once told me. "You know that any house really kept up nice outside is probably owned by people who've got some nice stuff inside." The sad commentary on this, since other burglars have said the same thing, is that the more attention people pay to their property, the more likely they are to become a target for burglary.

A large number of burglars looking for victims will also knock on doors in a residential area and, if answered, ask for fictitious people, for directions, or perhaps to use the telephone. Through the open door, or if they are able to get inside, these burglars can quickly size up how easy a house will be to break into and what is inside that is worth taking. Another indication of a good burglary prospect is the house with a television satellite dish. Burglars know that anyone with a dish will also have a nice television and VCR or DVD player (items easily disposed of by burglars). Some burglars, using the same reasoning, look for homes with cable television hookups.

A general lack of concern about security can also mark a home as a good burglary prospect. Lower-level windows left open at night or garage doors left open during the day indicate to a burglar that there is a low risk of getting caught. There have also been a number of cases in recent years in which the computer printouts of stop-service notices for local newspapers—a list of people who have requested that their service be temporarily stopped because they will be out of town—have fallen into the hands of burglars. Homeowners would have to assume that the same thing could possibly happen with stop-mail notices. The information in these documents is very valuable to burglars since it lists homes that are easy targets with a low level of risk of confrontation with the victims.

Although the police, when taking a burglary report, are often told by the victims that the burglars must have "picked" the lock since there were no signs of forced entry, this usually means the victims left a window or door unlocked and are afraid their insurance company won't pay if they admit their negligence. In my career as a police officer, I know of only one case in which it was verified that a burglar actually picked locks. Most of the burglary detectives I have spoken with tell me they have never seen a case of this. Most burglars, if they can't find a window or door unlocked, simply select a door or a window out of view and then kick it in or smash it out. Many of today's burglars don't even carry tools, other than an occasional screwdriver.

Discouraging Burglars

The really unfortunate aspect of being a burglary victim, though, besides having a window or door smashed and personal possessions stolen, is that most burglars dispose of items the victims have worked very hard for at a small fraction of their real value. The average profit per crime to a burglar in 2000, for example, was only about $100, even though it cost the victims $1,381 to replace the items stolen and repair the damage done by the burglars.

While burglars could possibly receive more for the stolen property if they were to attempt to peddle the items themselves, this is risky and most burglars prefer to sell them at a lower profit to fences, or trade them to fences for drugs. This easy and quick disposal of stolen items by burglars could be greatly discouraged, however, if homeowners would simply engrave their initials or some other identifying mark in an inconspicuous place (the bottom of a VCR, DVD player, or portable television, inside the air cleaner cover of a lawn mower, and so forth) on all valuable property. Few fences (who often operate legitimate businesses through which they resell stolen property) will buy engraved items since most police departments have officers who regularly visit pawnshops and secondhand stores looking for stolen property that can be identified. Homeowners should also keep in a secure place somewhere away from the home a list of the serial numbers of all valuable items.

"People could really do a lot to discourage prospective burglars by simply engraving all of their valuable items," said Detective Lieutenant Thom Greene. "But after doing it, homeowners have to let burglars know about it by using Operation Identification window decals. Burglars who see these decals will usually move on." Despite this advice, though, every year our police department has an auction at which we sell thousands and thousands of dollars' worth of recovered stolen property that cannot be positively identified by the owners.

Dangers of Burglary

A brutal truth that everyone needs to know is that while the crime of burglary is usually perpetrated in order to get money to buy drugs, it can often escalate into something much more serious. According to the Bureau of Justice Statistics, burglars commit three-fifths of all rapes and robberies in the home, and a third of all household assaults. A study of crime over a 10-year period, for example, found that 2.8 million violent crimes occurred during burglaries, and while as many burglaries are committed during the day as in the night, 13 percent of all burglaries are committed when someone is home, with 30 percent of these ending in violence. Because many are drug addicts who dread the thought of incarceration, burglars will often panic when confronted, and have been known to seriously injure, or even kill, the homeowner. The biggest danger, however, when confronting burglars is not just that they might be heavy drug users, but that 50 percent of them, by self-report, are either under the influence of drugs or very drunk when they commit the crime, making many burglars prone to violence and other irrational behavior. A study of jail inmates by the Bureau of Justice Statistics found that burglars, more than any other type of criminal with the exception of those arrested for drug charges, reported using an illegal drug regularly in the month prior to the offense they were incarcerated for. Because of this, you should never intentionally confront burglars, and if you unintentionally confront them, you should allow the burglars to take whatever they want. Most items can be replaced, and are not worth risking your life for.

A bizarre case a number of years ago demonstrates the violence and irrationality of some burglars. Marjorie Jackson, an eccentric grocery chain heiress who didn't trust banks, kept her entire fortune, over $9 million in $100 bills, hidden in her home. Burglarized at least once by criminals who found only a couple of hundred thousand dollars, she refused to call the police or prosecute; however, when she confronted more burglars, who were believed to have known about the previous burglary and her refusal to prosecute, they murdered her, even though doing so certainly wasn't in their best interests, since her death then made the state responsible for prosecuting them not just for burglary but also for murder.

Burglary Investigation

Because incidents such as the Marjorie Jackson case are in the minority, and because 87 percent of all burglaries occur when no one is home (and are therefore seldom witnessed), the crime of burglary has the lowest clearance rate of all major crimes, with only 13.4 percent of the over 2 million burglaries reported to the police in 2000 being solved. But part of the reason for this low clearance rate is the actions taken by the victims. Quite often, burglars will ransack a home looking for valuables, and the homeowners, embarrassed by the mess, will straighten it up before calling the police, but in doing so destroy any chance of finding evidence or recovering usable fingerprints.

In the past the recovery of fingerprints was of little value to the police unless they had a suspect to match them against, since police files often contain millions of individual fingerprints. This is no longer true. With the advent of the Automated Fingerprint Identification System (AFIS), fingerprint recovery has now taken on a new importance. These computerized systems can match a recovered fingerprint against the millions in its memory in just minutes, a task that would take years if done manually, making these new systems the biggest advance in criminal identification since the recognition of the value of finger-prints. Therefore, it is imperative in the solving of a burglary (or any other crime) that the victim not touch or disturb any-thing, or even go into a house if a burglary is detected before entering. (This is also much safer, since the burglar may still be inside.) It can make the difference in whether the case is solved or not. I must point out, however, that a brutal truth about police work today is that if no one is injured and noth-ing extraordinarily valuable is stolen (old paintings, antiques, very expensive jewelry, and so forth), burglaries have a low priority in many large police departments. This includes not just the amount of time an investigator gives to a case, but also the waiting time to put a set of fingerprints from a bur-glary case on the AFIS computer. This is because every day a burglary detective has more new cases on his or her desk, and old ones to close out. Therefore, it is critical that you assist the detective as much as possible by following the suggestions outlined above.

To solve burglary cases, detectives use many of the same tech-niques that are used to solve most other crimes. The detective will usually first interview the victim, and then canvass the neighborhood for witnesses. If a victim has engraved the stolen items, has a list of their serial numbers, or if the stolen items are unique, the detective will put out an alert for the items on the local and national police computers. If no clues are forthcoming through these methods, burglary detectives will many times talk to their informants and talk among themselves, comparing cases and suspects.

Often, however, a burglary detective will not visit the crime scene until several days afterward, and instead allow the initial investigation to be handled by uniformed officers, who are many times rushed because of their heavy workload. The truth is, because of this time crunch, uniformed officers will sometimes not even attempt to recover fingerprints or search for physical evidence, but will simply want to take the report and then go on to their next call. Victims, however, should not allow uniformed officers to leave without searching for and recovering fingerprints, and without collecting any physical evidence left behind by the burglar. Few uniformed officers will refuse to do this if the victims insist. This, however, can make the difference having irreplaceable property returned or lost forever and apprehending a burglar or allowing a criminal to go free. However, whether this is done or not often also depends on whether the uniformed police officers in your community have been trained to recover fingerprints. A number of cities have made this a standard part of training in recent years in order to expedite the collection of evidence. If not, you may be required to wait several hours to several days before an evidence technician arrives, and few people could blame you if you cleaned up the mess in the interval.

Burglary Prevention

Burglary, though often difficult to solve, is actually one of the easiest crimes to prevent. Most residence burglars are not professionals, most don't carry tools other than a screwdriver, most don't know how to disarm security devices, and none want to get caught. Therefore, in order to discourage burglars, all homeowners have to do is simply make access to their homes appear both difficult and risky.

"All crimes have a certain level of risk attached to them, and if you can increase the risk level, you can lower the chances of crime," said Burglary Detective Charlie Kaiser. "Rather than gambling on trying to break into a difficult and high-risk home, it's been my experience that most burglars will simply move on to a home that has a lower risk level."

While most security experts believe that it is probably not possible to make a home completely burglarproof and still livable, particularly for a family, the following steps can increase the difficulty of burglary to an unacceptable level. These tips are for

Homeowner's Insurance

Most readers would probably not consider police officers to be authorities on the topic of homeowner's insurance. However, having had a house destroyed by a tornado, and a few years later having a home hit by lightning, gives me, I believe, some serious experience in the intricacies of obtaining the proper homeowner's insurance policy. Readers can benefit from what I've experienced because it can also apply to losses brought on by a burglary.

The most essential thing about homeowner's insurance, besides obtaining your policy through a reputable agent and a company that has a reputation for dealing fairly with claims, is to have a policy that guarantees *full replacement value* for your property. This costs only a few dollars more per year than the standard policy that depreciates the value of your belongings and pays only their present worth. With a standard policy, for a $600 television set several years old you may be paid only $100 or less, its present worth, while with a full-replacement-value policy you are paid whatever it costs to replace your television set with one of comparable value. This becomes very important when many items need to be replaced.

When my home was destroyed by a tornado, I was just one of a dozen homeowners in the area who suffered serious damage to their homes, and all 12 of us had different insurance companies, most of them large and well-known. The difference in payout and customer treatment philosophies among the companies was huge. Some of the companies were compassionate and paid off without quibbling, while others wanted to argue about every item and squeeze the homeowners for every penny they could, which is anxiety you can do without at such a time.

To find the company you should buy insurance from, talk to people who have filed large claims, because after a burglary is not the time to discover that your insurance company isn't nearly as nice now as they were when they were trying to sell you the policy.

average homes in average neighborhoods. If you live, however, in a high-crime area, included are some additional tips following these.

- Have dead-bolt locks, keyed on both sides, with at least one-inch bolts (if local fire codes allow) on solid-core doors (good locks on flimsy doors are useless). Dead-bolt locks are difficult to pry or force and will discourage many burglars because they know the longer it takes for them to get inside, the more likely it is they will be spotted. Also, don't leave the key in the lock on the inside or hanging on a nail nearby (but do have the key easily accessible to all family members in case they must get out in a hurry). With a double-keyed lock, even if burglars gain entry into your home through some way other than the door, such as a basement window, without a key they won't be able to carry out large items. If hinges are on the outside of the door, replace them with non-removable hinges. Finally, install additional locks on poorly secured windows and sliding glass doors. But locks, of course, are of no value if not used. A fourth of all burglars, it has been found, gain entry to homes through unlocked windows or doors. Many burglars, incidentally, look for bathroom windows, since they are often left open to let the moisture out of the room. Also, many times air conditioners simply sit in the window frame. Secure them.
- "Be cautious of who you allow to come into your home," warns retired detective sergeant Elizabeth Robinson. "They could be casing it for a burglary. Also, watch who your children bring home with them."
- Form or join a neighborhood block club. Once neighbors begin making it a common practice to look out for each other, they become more alert to the suspicious car prowling the neighborhood or to the stranger on a neighbor's property. Draw a diagram of the neighborhood with the owners' names and telephone numbers on it. Distribute copies to all members of the block club.

- Don't make access easy for burglars. Lock up your ladder and avoid putting trellises and drainpipes where they can be used to gain access to second-story windows (which are often left unlocked or open at night). If you have a utility pole close enough for a burglar to use, smear it with axle grease.
- Don't have a name or license tag attached to your key chain. If you do and your keys are lost or stolen, you will likely have an unwelcome visitor at your home. Also, if you regularly have your car valet-parked, keep your house keys separate from your car keys.
- Make entry to your garage as difficult as entry to your house. Far too many garage doors are made out of flimsy fiberglass. Remember, once a burglar gets into your garage, he is hidden from view and now has a large selection of tools, *your tools*, to use to force his way into your house.
- Basement windows offer easy access to a house. Secure them, but have a way to release the security device from the inside in case you have to get out in a hurry.
- High, solid hedges and privacy fences, while attractive, make it much easier for burglars to break in without being seen.
- Since half of all burglaries occur at night, outside lighting around windows and doors can be helpful in discouraging burglars.
- Take a serious look at your property, but look at it from a different perspective than that of a homeowner. Look at your property as if you were a burglar. How would you get in? How easy would it be? Any faults you can find in your security will be seen by a burglar.
- Whenever you move to a new address, have all of the locks rekeyed. The previous owner may have been a saint, but you don't know who's had access to the keys in times past.
- Leave a light on when away at night. A quiet, darkened house early in the evening is a sure sign no one is home. A good idea is to have the lights on a timer so they will turn on and off while you are away, but have different lights on different timers so that all of the lights don't go on and off at the

same time. Also, if there is a second car, park it in the driveway when you're away from home, or have a neighbor park his car in your driveway. Some might worry that if they do this, after a criminal has finished burglarizing their home he would also steal the car. The idea behind parking the car in the driveway is to make a burglar believe someone is home. If a burglar does steal your car, it means he has gone further than most burglars and has somehow confirmed there's no one home. It is likely then that it doesn't make any difference where you parked your second car because if he is bold enough to steal your car from your driveway, he would also have stolen it if it had been parked in the garage since he already had access to your house while burglarizing it. This is why it is important to have a strong block club who watches out for each other, and who will notice and report anyone tampering with your car or house.

- Don't advertise that you're out of town. Have a neighbor pick up your mail and newspaper rather than having delivery stopped. The few dollars saved on discontinuing the newspaper is not worth the damage that could be done by a burglar. Also, have your neighbors pick up the supermarket flyers that always seem to be attached to your mailbox. In addition, grass not mowed and snow not shoveled are also signs no one is home. Putting out for trash pickup the boxes from expensive purchases simply advertises what you have inside your home. Instead, tear up the boxes and put them in trash bags. Also, be cautious when wedding or funeral announcements involving your family are printed in the newspaper. Burglars will read these and plan their burglaries for when you're away. Use a house sitter.

- When you're away from home for an extended period, turn the telephone and answering machine down or off. An unanswered, ringing telephone, or the message on an answering machine, tells a prospective burglar no one is home. Make sure no one can hear the telephone or answering machine from outside of your home.

• Write down the serial numbers of all valuable items in your home, and to really discourage burglars engrave your initials or another identifying mark on the bottom or back of these items. Photograph expensive jewelry with a card containing your name and address. This way it can be identified in the event it is stolen and recovered. Mark fur coats with invisible ink on the inside of the fur. Burglars will often remove the tags. Neighborhood Watch programs often have marking devices to loan and decals for the windows, which will notify prospective burglars that all items inside the home have been marked for identification.

As a final note, 589 convicts were polled for *The Figgie Report Part IV—The Business of Crime: The Criminal Perspective.* They were asked what they felt was the best way a person could protect a home from burglary. The largest number recommended an alarm system that rang at the local police department, and many of these career criminals also said that they would get a dog. But homeowners need to be warned that dogs left outside can easily be neutralized, while a dog kept inside can warn the homeowner of a possible intruder.

While the list above may seem extensive and perhaps even a bit troublesome, home security is definitely an area in which you must keep up with the Joneses. Most burglars, when they are sizing up a neighborhood, look for the easiest target. Of the convicts polled for *The Figgie Report,* 41.1 percent said that if the risk at one home was too high, they would simply find another house in the same neighborhood to burglarize. And so the key here is that if everyone's house but yours is well secured, expect a burglary at your house.

High-Risk Homes

If your home is located in a high-crime area, then there are several additional precautions you should take:

- To avoid being awakened by a burglar, who could also be a rapist or perhaps just a thug who likes to hurt people, consider installing steel gates across halls or stairways to prevent access to parts of your home. But you must also have a quick method of exit from the secured part of your home that won't force you to pass by the burglar, and will also allow you to escape in case of a fire. A folding rope and wooden ladder that can be hung out of a second-story window is a good method.

- When leaving your home vacant in the evening, keep the television on and set an opened can of soda and a half bowl of popcorn or bag of potato chips nearby. In addition to the television, an opened magazine next to the soda and chips will work. Or you might want to tune the radio to a talk station and turn it down low enough so that the voices can be heard from the outside, but not what is being said. These things will make anyone scouting your home for a burglary believe someone is there.

- Add auxiliary locking devices to all windows and access doors. Standard window and door locks will not deter a determined burglar.

- Burglars, when they enter a home, will often remove a telephone receiver from the cradle, thereby disabling all of the telephones in the home, or will have cut the lines outside. Consider keeping a cellular telephone in your bedroom. We had a case recently in Indianapolis in which three young burglars, who surprised and beat an 89-year-old woman to death, had cut the phone lines before entering her home.

- If you live in an apartment building with a security buzzer, always know whom you are giving access to. Tell anyone who says they're calling on a neighbor to buzz that neighbor.

- If you live in an apartment building where the hinges on the entry doors face the outside, have them replaced with non-removable hinges.

- In order for apartment dwellers to have real security, an active tenants' association is a must. The association should insist on good locks on all entry, basement, and roof doors. They should also insist on good lighting in hallways, stairwells, laundry rooms, and elevators.

- Have a safe room in your home with a solid wood door that opens out, with protected hinges and a dead-bolt lock. Inside the room should be a device for calling for help, such as a cellular telephone. There should also be an easy exit from the room to the outside. It will take an aggressive burglar time to force his way into this room, and you can use this time to summon help or escape.

- A last problem for many people who live in high-crime areas, especially on hot summer (and busy) weekend nights, is getting the police to come to your address. If you are certain you are in a life-threatening situation—and I don't mean just hearing a creaking sound—but are absolutely sure an intruder is in your house trying to get to you and the police can't get help to you right away, you might want to consider hanging up the phone and then calling back and reporting a fire. This should be done only in desperate situations since there will likely be some legal consequences later because of calling in a false fire run, and there is the possibility that you could be drawing the fire department away from a real fire. But if you have absolutely no doubt there is an intruder who knows you're in the home and is trying to get in anyway, there's a very good chance you will be raped, beaten, and/or murdered. There have been cases in which the police dispatchers have listened as a caller was murdered before the police could get there. At a time like this you really can't worry about legal niceties.

In addition to the above security measures, there are many other things homeowners can do, depending on the peculiarities and features of their home. Many police departments sponsor programs through which police officers will come out and inspect the security of a home and then advise the occupants about problems. This is an excellent idea for any home since police officers, through their experience, can often see weaknesses not apparent to the homeowners, and can also give tips on how to easily and inexpensively correct these weaknesses.

The length of the two lists above may lead readers to think that I am going a bit overboard. But I'm not. There is an army of people in America who either do not want to hold down a regular job, have selected the occupation of being a thief, or are so addicted to drugs that they can't work. These people survive by ripping off people like you, people who have worked hard to accumulate a home full of nice things. And the brutal truth is that the police offer very little, or no, protection to your property. There are just too many homes, too many burglars, and too few police. You are the person who must protect your home. And remember, if you don't do at least as much as your neighbor does to protect your home, you will likely be the target of the next burglary in your neighborhood.

Home Security Devices and Systems

Because of the huge amount of burglaries committed every year in our country, 25 percent of the respondents in a survey conducted for the National Victim Center said they had installed a home security system. This is a popular development that has sent the sales of home security devices and systems running into the billions of dollars annually. But a person doesn't have to live in a mansion or spend tens of thousands of dollars for home security. Home security devices and systems can range from under $20 to several thousand dollars for the latest technology.

At the low end, for a person on a very tight budget, alarm system window decals can be purchased for only a few dollars. It is even possible to augment the decals with a battery-powered device that looks like a key-operated alarm switch, blinking lights and all, that can be mounted by the front door. These devices are an inexpensive way to create uncertainty in a prospective burglar's mind about the risk of burglarizing your home.

For people who want more protection than this but don't have much more money, there are "doorstop" alarms. These alarms, shaped like a doorstop, can be purchased for under $20 each. In

An Impregnable Home

A question often asked of police officers is whether it is possible to make a home completely burglarproof, yet still livable. Many experts will say no. But I'm not sure.

One afternoon when I was working as a district uniformed sergeant, I was called to assist one of my officers who needed to force a door open. When I arrived, I spoke with a man waiting there with the officer, who said he had called the police because he had spoken on the telephone earlier that day with his brother, who had a heart condition and said he was having chest pains. Now he wouldn't answer the door.

The single-story brick home, clean and well kept, was obviously owned by a man who was very security conscious. The doors were reinforced steel, the windows covered with huge bars bolted into the frame. The officer told me he had tried looking in the windows but the shades were pulled, and while the complainant said his brother had given him an extra key several years before, he had misplaced it.

I really wasn't eager to destroy a person's property without being certain that there was a sick person inside, but the man who had called us was insistent, so we gave the door our best drug warrant kick, but only embarrassed ourselves. After ten minutes more of kicking and shoving on both the front and rear door, we called for the fire department. I then watched in horror as their fire axes smashed into the steel door, only to fly off and gouge out huge chunks of the brick on either side, but hardly dent the door.

The fire department was about to call for the Jaws of Life (a device used for extricating people from wrecked cars) when the wife of the man who had called us pulled up with the missing key. Considering the damage we had done to the house, I hoped that the man's brother was inside (he was—dead). But still, the house had resisted probably a half-hour of our best efforts and would have undoubtedly stopped any burglar.

addition to wedging a door shut, these devices set off a loud alarm if someone tries to open the door. They have a number of drawbacks, however. For example, there is no warning about anyone who comes in through a window or some other way that is not protected by these alarms, and they are of real value only when you're home. However, they are an inexpensive and functional security device for people who live in high-rise buildings and are only concerned about safety while someone is home (for example, a wife home while her husband works nights) or a person who is not as worried about a burglar as he is about being surprised inside his house or apartment by someone who may have a key, such as an ex-spouse, ex-lover, or former tenant. These devices are also useful for hotel rooms.

For systems beyond the simple options described above you must be prepared to pay increasing prices because you will have to invest in a system that contains many components, each of which will be expensive. To detect a burglar before he gets into your home, "perimeter alarm systems" use a number of devices. Some have magnetic switches mounted on doors and windows that set off the alarm after they are separated and the circuit interrupted when the door or window is opened. Others use vibration detectors that are attached to various entry points and are activated by breaking glass or a burglar trying to smash his way into your house. Another method is an audio system that picks up sounds around your house and relays them to a central monitoring station, where workers determine whether the noise is someone breaking into your house or simply something nothreatening, such as the wind.

To detect a burglar already inside your home, "inside alarm systems" use other devices, such as pressure switches hidden under the carpeting, photoelectric beams across stairways, infrared beams, and motion detectors that are sensitive to movement in the room. All of these devices are particularly good for detecting intruders who have managed to gain entry to your house without activating the perimeter alarms, such as through a basement window without an alarm.

The prices for the systems above range from several hundred dollars for an install-it-yourself alarm to several thousand dollars for a professionally installed system. For people with more money to spend there are systems that not only detect an intrusion into your home but that can also be hooked up to a fire alarm system, can monitor and adjust your home's temperature, and can even monitor the operation of a sump pump or freezer. Some even have an "ambush alarm," a special code that when punched into the control panel will shut off an alarm system but alert the alarm company that someone has forced you to shut off the system. A new security system on the market, a very expensive one, instantly sends pictures to a central monitoring station of the spot in your house where the alarm has been activated. The people at the monitoring station can then see what is happening and report it to the police as it is occurring. However, when you begin adding all of these special features onto a security system, you are likely to run the price up to prohibitive levels. Rather than these elaborate, expensive systems, most people find that $1,000 to $3,000 will cover the installation of a quality alarm system.

Be forewarned, however, that after you pay for the alarm system and its installation, you will probably also then be charged a monthly fee, usually at least $25, for a company to monitor your system and call the police for you if they believe an alarm going off at your home is valid. You will likely need this service because while in years past an alarm system could be set up to ring directly into the local police headquarters, the high false alarm rate of most home alarm systems (over 95 percent nationwide) has forced many cities to end this practice, and now most alarms must ring into a monitoring station first. This is unfortunate because, as I stated earlier, the convicts questioned for *The Figgie Report* said that by far the best thing a homeowner could do to discourage a burglar was to install an alarm system wired directly to the local police department.

Some alarm systems, to beat the high cost of this monitoring, are set up so that when the alarm goes off, an automatic telephone dialer calls the local police department and a taped message alerts the police to a possible burglary at your address. However, because of the high false alarm rate and the fact that with a taped message there is no one the police can talk to or request additional information from, some communities have banned these types of alarms. Check your local ordinances before purchasing such a system.

The Best Alarm Systems

What kind of alarm system should you buy?

If money was tight and I couldn't afford a monthly monitoring fee, but still wanted good protection against break-ins, I would install either an inside motion detection system or a perimeter magnetic and vibration system, all hooked up to a loud outside bell or siren. Homeowners can install either of these systems for several hundred dollars, or more if installed professionally. With this kind of system, monitoring is not necessary. Even though when the alarm is activated no one automatically calls the police for you, few burglars will continue trying to break into a home with a loud alarm going off. If you have this kind of system, though, it is advisable to either give a trusted neighbor a key to turn the system off or have the alarm on a timer that resets itself after 10 or 15 minutes in the event it goes off while you're away from home (some local ordinances require this).

If I had more money to spend, the next step up would be to have a monitored system with motion detection devices inside and vibration or magnetic devices on the perimeter windows and doors. This would likely cost a couple of thousand dollars, since to be monitored it would probably have to be installed professionally. And if I had a home with a lot of valuable possessions and I felt money was not really a consideration, I would have an audio alarm system installed. When I used to run a beat car as a patrolman, I knew most of the bad alarms in my district because they were always going off, and they were almost always false alarms. So, if another officer and I were having coffee and one of these alarms went off, we usually finished our coffee first before responding. But whenever we heard that a public school alarm was going off we dropped whatever we were doing and raced to the school. The school board in Indianapolis had audio alarms installed in all of the schools, and we knew that if we responded quickly enough, we would catch a burglar. Unlike other alarms, which are 95 percent false, the school board's audio system was probably 95 percent correct.

Drawbacks of Alarm Systems

Having an alarm system, even an expensive one, does not absolutely guarantee that you will not have an undetected break-in. Any system can be bypassed by someone with enough knowledge about alarms. For example, almost all alarm systems are monitored through telephone lines, and so if your outside telephone lines are cut or out of service, your alarm system is useless. To counter this problem, most alarm companies are now offering cellular telephone technology for monitoring, and this is an important extra since with this a burglar can't disable your alarm from outside your house. Also, to bypass a perimeter alarm system some burglars will enter your home through a way that is not monitored by your system, such as by cutting a hole in your roof or wall (aluminum-sided houses are unbelievably easy to cut through).

The most important thing to remember about any alarm system is that you should never allow it to give you such a sense of security that other protection measures are forgotten. All systems are made by humans and can fail. Just because you come home and your alarm system shows that everything is okay, never assume that this means no one is inside. Such a mistake could be fatal.

In addition, having an alarm system requires a change of lifestyle. If your alarm is to be effective, you must constantly be aware of the system whenever you are entering or leaving your home. You usually have only 30 to 45 seconds after arming the system to leave your home. Any longer and the system sends in a false alarm. In addition, you must always remember to disarm the system when you come home. If you have a motion detection system you can no longer, for example, just go downstairs in the middle of the night to raid the refrigerator. You must remember to turn off the alarm first. And if you have children living at home, you must show them how the alarm system works, particularly older children who may come home after you've gone to bed. Pets, on the other hand, unlike children, can seldom coexist with a motion detection system. While some systems claim to compensate for pets by measuring movement only three or four feet above the floor, my family has had several cats who loved to jump up to high places.

Another important drawback you need to consider before purchasing an alarm system is false alarms. Actually, "false alarm" is not always a true description because occasionally high winds will shake a window or rattle a door, or sometimes a mouse will run across the room. The alarm system senses something it was built to sense and sets off the alarm, which is what it is supposed to do. But in many more cases the alarm system was not installed properly and regularly sends in false signals for no apparent reason, or in just as many cases the owners or their children have forgotten the alarm when entering or leaving. The police arrive and of course find nothing wrong. This can be extremely dangerous for you because after enough false alarms, the police no longer rush to your home when the alarm goes off, and there may come a time when you really need them.

Also, with the huge growth in the number of home security systems installed over the last few years, false alarms have begun using up more and more of police departments' time and resources. As a consequence, a number of communities have begun assessing fines against the owners of alarms that are constantly going off with no break-in. This can add up to quite an expense before you find the problem in your system.

Before You Purchase an Alarm System

A friend of mine, a retired police captain who now works for an alarm company, was kind enough to give me the benefit of his experience working in the alarm industry. He said there are a number of things that homeowners should consider and be aware of before having an alarm system installed:

- Be certain that the company you're dealing with is reputable, and not just the most inexpensive dealer you can find. All alarm systems and alarm companies are not equal. Ask for references and check them out. Because of the rapid growth in the home security business, many companies are now involved in alarm installation, and there are some companies that will promise you a top-of-the-line system, but install junk. Once this happens, you are then stuck either with a system that doesn't work or with one that constantly sends in false alarms. Select a company that will come back and fix any problems until the system works as advertised.

- Be certain the alarm system company does the monitoring locally. Some companies will charge a monthly monitoring fee, usually at least $25, but then sell your monitoring contract to another company, some of which advertise their services in alarm industry trade magazines for as little as $10 a month. The company that installed your alarm then pockets the extra $15 a month. The problem with this is that the person monitoring your alarm system may now be in another city, perhaps a thousand miles away, and won't be of much help if the police in your town are confused about an address or want more information.

- There was a case, for example, of a person with an alarm system who lived on Meridian Street in Indianapolis, which is one of the main thoroughfares; few people in Indianapolis haven't heard of it. The person's alarm system, however, was being monitored by a company hundreds of miles away.

A burglar broke into the home, but when the alarm monitor called the Indianapolis Police Department, he said they had a break-in alarm at an address on "Mary Dan" street, then hung up. No police car was sent because there is no "Mary Dan" street in Indianapolis, a pronunciation mistake that wouldn't have occurred if the system had been monitored locally. Ask to tour the company's monitoring facility before you buy.

- Be certain your alarm has a backup power system in case of a main power failure.
- Ask whether the company will assume at least partial responsibility for false alarm fines if they have installed your alarm system improperly.
- Be certain that your warranty covers all of the work necessary to get your system working properly, and that it doesn't require you to pay for all or part of this work.

Best Advice

The best advice the police can offer to citizens who want to avoid having their homes burglarized is simply to increase the difficulty level for burglars to unacceptable levels. Burglars know that the harder it is to get into a home, the more likely it is they will be seen, or that if a home is alarmed the police could be there in minutes. Therefore, if you make breaking into your home look like a very risky venture to the burglar, he will likely move on to one of the millions of less protected homes.

7

LARCENY AND VEHICLE THEFT

LARCENY STATISTICS

According to predictions from the Bureau of Justice Statistics, 99 percent of all the people alive today will be the victim of a larceny sometime during their lives, and 87 percent of these people will be a victim three or more times. A larceny is theft without forced building entry or violence. A larceny is when someone who has a right to be where he or she is steals something without threatening the victim. Actually, in most larcenies the victim doesn't even know until later that the theft has occurred—for example, when someone steals money out of a purse sitting on a desk or steals a bicycle off the sidewalk in front of someone's home.

Substantiating this prediction of almost universal victimization, during 2000 in the United States almost 7 million larcenies were reported to the police, for a total loss to the victims of over $5.1 billion. And while this may sound like a huge number of crimes, actually the majority of larcenies in our country, particularly those with small losses, are not reported to the police at all, making larceny by far the most commonly committed crime, with a total likely nearer 20 million. It is estimated that less than 10 percent of all thefts under $10, less than 15 percent of those from $10 to $50, 35 percent of those from $50 to $250, and only 65 percent of those over $250 are reported to the police. Still, those larcenies that are reported to the police each year make up over half of all the major crimes reported. In 2000, for example, out of the over 11 million crimes reported to the police, about 60 percent were larcenies, and this does not even include the larceny of automobiles (which is so common the FBI, in its *Crime In The United States,* gives auto theft its own category), embezzlement, bad checks, and con games (which I will discuss in the next chapter).

The truth is that the crime of larceny has become so common in America that many police departments no longer even assign detectives to investigate larceny cases unless there are suspects, witnesses, perpetrator vehicle information, or identifiable property. It is a sad truth, but with one reported larceny occurring every four and a half seconds, the crime is just so common and widespread in the United States that if a detective was assigned to every case, police departments would not have time to investigate any other crimes.

"People, it seems, will steal anything you aren't watching," said Detective Lieutenant Sheryl Turk. "They steal so much, though, that we just simply don't have enough detectives to assign one to every case."

Motivations for Larceny

Occasionally, criminals commit larcenies simply to have whatever it is they steal, and occasionally because they are down on their luck and in need of money (as is the case of thefts by some street people), but more often criminals commit larcenies in order to buy drugs. A recent study found that almost half of all persons convicted of larceny had used an illegal drug daily during the month before they were arrested. In addition, 37 percent of these people also reported being either under the influence of drugs or very drunk when they committed the larceny.

To protect against larceny, the almost universal warning by larceny detectives is never to leave valuable property exposed and unprotected, yet victims far too often do just that. And so, as expected, larceny is much more likely in the summer (when people leave bicycles, lawn furniture, and so on outside) than in the winter. Larceny, incidentally, is often very lucrative to the criminal, considering its small risk. Criminals convicted of larceny traditionally receive light sentences compared with those convicted of other crimes, even though in 2001 the average value of property lost in a larceny reported to the police was $735, an amount that would sting most people.

From over 30 years' experience as a police officer, I can attest that until a thief has amassed a huge record of arrests or steals something of great value, no serious jail or prison time is ever meted out. Many people convicted of larceny are instead put on probation, and then go right back to stealing.

But in fairness to our judicial system, even if judges wanted to imprison all of the thieves the police arrested, they couldn't do so. There would be no place to put them. Most jails and prisons are already operating at 100+ percent capacity, and putting more thieves in jail would mean having to let violent criminals go.

Many people might believe there is no solution to this seemingly catch 22 other than continuing the present system of letting most thieves go. But actually there are two solutions. The first is to lessen (but not stop, which probably is impossible) America's drug problem, which is the root cause of most crime, and which I will discuss later. The second is to build more minimum-and medium-security prisons for this type of criminal and leave the maximum-security prisons for violent criminals. The immediate argument against this is, of course, the cost. But the billions saved every year through reduced thefts and insurance premiums would make the slight tax increase certainly worth it. Clearing this type of criminal, incidentally, out of maximum-security prisons would also give additional room for more violent criminals, which some states have been forced to release early because of overcrowding.

A study was conducted by reporter Eugene Methvin of the criminal situation in two states, California and Texas, and his findings support my solution. California spent almost $4 billion on prison construction in the 1980s, and by 1990 had seen a 24 to 37 percent drop in its murder, rape, and burglary rates. In

Texas, on the other hand, little money was spent on prisons during the 1980s, and they actually began releasing prisoners as soon as they could. During the 1980s, Texas saw a 29 percent increase in its crime rate.

And while some people, instead of advocating more prisons, might say that setting up programs to train these people in useful and productive skills would be a better solution, the people who work regularly with thieves know this really isn't a workable solution. Since most of the people who would be committed to the new prisons I'm advocating are hard-core addicts, they couldn't hold a job for long anyway, particularly since addicts so often return to drug use as soon as they are released from prison. In addition, there are already dozens of job training programs available, but career criminals who specialize in larceny are seldom interested. I realize that my suggestion is a simplistic solution to a complex problem, but the "solution" we're using now is not working and we must look for other ones that will work.

Types of Larceny

One of the most common types of larceny in America is shoplifting. The losses each year from this type of larceny are staggering and, while not seeming to affect the average citizen, the truth is they actually do because unfortunately the effects are usually passed along to the consumer in the form of higher prices. As with business burglaries, because of the size and scope of the problem, and because most large stores have their own trained security staffs to combat shoplifting, I will concentrate on other areas of the larceny problem.

Shoplifting aside, most detectives believe that the majority of larcenies that victimize the average citizen occur not so much through the craftiness of criminals as through the carelessness of victims. This is particularly true for the most common type of larceny reported to the police, which is theft from motor vehicles. Larceny detectives often shake their heads at the naivete of many victims who have left purses, cameras, portable CD players, and other valuables lying out in plain sight inside cars. In addition, at locations such as swimming pools and beaches, where people usually don't take their wallets or valuables with them, thieves frequently cruise parking lots looking for (and much too often finding) these valuables either exposed or slipped under the front seat. The same is true for the parking lots of shopping centers, where people will often park vehicles filled with bags of purchases made at other locations.

Many victims, though, detectives find, tend to develop a false sense of security about leaving valuables exposed in cars if they have a vehicle alarm. Car alarms, however, are not foolproof. They can be bypassed, made inoperable by spraying the mechanism with freon, or even simply ignored. A larceny detective told the story of a man who had parked his package-loaded car in the parking lot of a major shopping center and then returned to find not just the packages but the car gone. Livid when talking to the uniformed officer called to make the report, he told him how he had just paid to have a siren-type alarm system installed. The officer became red-faced when he realized he had seen the car going in the opposite direction as he was en route to the shopping center. He and the other cars had pulled over because they thought, since it had a wailing, police-like siren, that it was an unmarked detective unit on an emergency run.

Another common type of larceny, the theft of automobile accessories, such as radios, CD players and tape decks, T-tops, and tires, is also a crime that could be made more difficult for thieves by owners not parking their cars in dark, unguarded areas for lengthy periods of time. Of course, the theft of automobile accessories can also (and often does) take place in other, less likely locations, such as in large shopping center parking lots, and even on the street in front of the victim's house. Because the likelihood of serious punishment is low, this type of thief has become very bold. But, as I will explain at the end of this chapter, the possibility of all types of larceny can be greatly reduced with just a few simple precautions.

After larcenies from motor vehicles, the police are called most often for larcenies in businesses and homes, where a purse, loose money, portable CD players, and other easily carried-away items have disappeared. Many times, particularly in the home, the owners have allowed someone to enter whom they shouldn't have, such as strangers who ask to use the telephone; while in businesses the thefts have often taken place out of purses sitting out exposed or off desktops easily accessible to the public.

"People are just too trusting and unaware," said a veteran larceny detective. "They leave way too much stuff out where people can grab it."

The theft of bicycles is a type of larceny so common in some areas of large cities that the police assume that many of the youths pedaling by are on a stolen bicycle. Last year, for example, 4.5 percent of all reported larcenies, or over 300,000 cases, were stolen bicycles, and this is very likely only a small percentage of the actual number.

Purse snatching and necklace snatching, depending on how they are committed, are another common type of larceny. It is larceny if the purse or gold chain is simply snatched out of a woman's hand or off her neck. It is robbery if the woman resists and the purse or necklace is taken by force. Purse snatchers, in particular, are usually youths who many times like to target the elderly, often outside of banks, where the victims have just cashed their monthly pension checks. Thieves also like to grab purses and packages from people who leave them sitting on the seat next to them while riding on a bus or subway. The thief will walk by, then grab the items, and run off the bus or subway just as the door opens, or will reach in through an open window and grab them. These thieves occasionally work in teams, one distracting the victim while the other snatches a purse or package.

Pickpockets also often work in teams. One member of the team will distract the victim, while the other actually picks the pocket or purse (some pickpockets like to take the billfold from a purse as it hangs on a woman's arm). Many times the stolen item is quickly passed to a third member of the team, so that

Thieves Prey on Habit

Thieves, the police find, often prey on the predictable habits many people have about protecting their property. I had a case once that illustrates this fact very well.

One wintry morning when I worked as a district uniformed sergeant, I was pulling down an alley in a business district when I noticed a man wearing a large overcoat with something obviously bulging underneath come out the rear door of an office building. When he spotted me he stopped for a moment and then began walking rapidly away from me. Since being a good police officer means always being suspicious, I stopped and got out of my car. The moment I yelled for the man to hold on for a second, he started to run, but slipped on a patch of ice and fell, a half-dozen purses dropping out from under his coat.

Placing him under arrest since it was obvious the purses were stolen, I asked him how he had managed to take so many purses without anyone spotting him. He said he had simply walked along the hallways of the office building and took the purses off desks and countertops when the people weren't looking or were distracted. He also said that whenever he found an office empty he would always look in either the bottom drawer of the file cabinet or the bottom drawers of a desk, and often found purses there.

even if the victim realizes what has happened and grabs the pickpocket or identifies the thief to a nearby police officer, that person will not be carrying any evidence of the crime. This type of thief likes to work large events where there are a lot of people bumping into each other, such as parades, concerts, street fairs, etc. For the best protection, women should keep their purses closed and held close to the body, with the opening away from passersby. Of course, there is always the possibility that if the purse is held too securely, a woman will be knocked down if a purse snatcher tries to grab it. But more likely, a purse snatch-er will move on to an easier target if it is apparent the woman will be a difficult target. Men, on the other hand, should keep their wallets in either a front or inside pocket, and not the back pocket, or "sucker pocket," as pickpockets call it.

A final type of theft that is becoming more and more com-mon is that of credit cards. Often, thieves will steal only a sin-gle credit card out of a purse they find sitting around unpro-tected, so that it can be days before the victim misses it. Many credit cards are also stolen out of mailboxes. In addition, it is wise to check your credit card when it is returned to you after a sale. Occasionally, thieves who have a "hot" credit card they can't use any longer will switch it for your card. Also, check your credit card statement closely every month since thieves that somehow find out your credit card numbers can use them to purchase items under your name. Also, it is even possible to simply manufacture a false credit card under your name, and only through examining your credit card statement each month can you detect these crimes.

Larceny Investigation

Over half of all the arrests for major crimes in the United States in 2000 were made for larceny. And even though many of the larcenies reported to the police in 2000 were not assigned to a detective, still over 18 percent of the almost 7 million reported larcenies were solved. Many of these larcenies were solved by store security staffs, many through stolen property recovered, and many through information gathered in other investiga-tions.

The statistics for larceny show it is a crime different from the many other types reported to the police. For example, more women, it has been found, are arrested for larceny than for any other major crime. In 2000, while women represented only 22 percent of all the arrests made nationwide, they made up over 36 percent of the arrests for larceny. In addition, almost half of all those arrested for larceny, both male and female, were under 21, and a third under 18. In 2000, incidentally, over 30,000 of the arrests made nationwide for larceny, or 4 percent of the total larceny arrests made, were of juveniles 12 and younger, and over 4,500 of those arrested were under the age of 10.

But the brutal truth about larceny is that if a case is to be assigned to a detective, the victim must have one of the following: suspects, a vehicle description, a license plate number, the stolen items engraved, their serial numbers recorded, or the stolen items must be unique. Otherwise, there will likely be no investigation of the theft, just a report taken for insurance purposes. Even fingerprints are many times of little value for larcenies because, by definition, larceny is often committed by people who have a right to be where the crime occurred and can thereby justify the police finding their fingerprints there. The simple truth is there are just so many larceny cases reported to the police every year that without substantial information from the victim about possible suspects or the stolen property, the chances of solving the case are simply too slim to justify expending a detective's time. While victims may or may not know anything about the suspects, anyone who wishes to increase the chances of having valuable property returned can at least mark the property or record its serial numbers. Often, property stolen in one case will turn up in another, but unless you can positively prove this property belongs to you there is no way you can get it back.

Vehicle Theft

There is one type of larceny so common and so widespread in the United States that the FBI, in its national crime statistics report (*Crime in the United States*), gives the offense its own category, and that is vehicle theft. It includes not just the theft of automobiles but also the theft of trucks, motorcycles, snowmobiles, etc. Last year alone, thieves stole over 1.1 million vehicles, or 1 out of every 180 registered vehicles in the United States; a vehicle was stolen every 27 seconds. Due to the large economic loss to its victims, though, vehicle theft is the most highly reported of all property crimes (over 90 percent), and, like most other thefts, is more a summer crime, but not overwhelmingly so. Vehicle theft represents an almost $8 billion loss to its victims each year. More than 80 percent of a car owner's comprehensive insurance premium goes for losses insurance companies suffer due to vehicle theft.

"Car theft is a very popular crime not only because it is so lucrative, but also because it involves very little risk," said Detective Sergeant Oliver Jackson. "Even when we arrest them, the courts are usually pretty lenient in sentencing car thieves compared to other criminals."

In the poll of 589 convicts taken for *The Figgie Report,* of those who admitted to at least one vehicle theft in the year preceding their present incarceration, 50 percent said that they felt the crime of auto theft was worth the risk (as compared to 25 percent who felt that burglary or robbery was worth the risk). Thirty-seven percent of these criminals said that they felt auto theft would be worth the risk of arrest even if the risk was doubled. This undoubtedly reflects their knowledge of the lenient sentences for those convicted of vehicle theft.

Still, even though serious punishment is seldom imposed, to escape arrest by the police some car thieves purposely drive stolen cars to other states, knowing that most jurisdictions will not pay to have car thieves extradited, and that the federal authorities will usually not prosecute them. The problem of vehicle theft, though, is finally becoming recognized as widespread and serious enough that in a number of states, organizations have been formed that offer cash rewards and guarantees of anonymity for callers with information about vehicle theft.

But even though it is lucrative and often lightly punished, the crime of vehicle theft, statistics show, is still basically a young person's crime. In 2000, over 66 percent of those arrested for vehicle theft were under 25, and almost 35 percent were under 18. In addition, over 8,600 arrests made for vehicle theft nationwide in 2000, or almost 9 percent of the total arrests made for vehicle theft, were of children aged 14 or younger, and in over 1,100 cases the thief was 12 or younger.

Motivations for Vehicle Theft

While occasionally car thieves steal because they need parts for their own cars, and sometimes because they are youths who just want to go for a ride, more often, as with most other property crimes, criminals steal cars in order to sell them to buy drugs. Forty-six percent of the persons convicted for vehicle theft, it was found in a recent study, had used an illegal drug daily during the month before the crime, and, by self-report, almost 45 percent were either under the influence of drugs or very drunk when they committed the crime. Vehicle theft is such a drug-related crime that many of the people who regularly buy stolen cars from thieves now pay for the stolen vehicles with illegal drugs rather than cash.

As might be expected, some vehicles are more popular targets for vehicle theft, either because they are the type of cars youths like to steal for a joyride (sports cars like Corvettes, Camaros, etc.) or, more often, because they are easy to steal and in high demand by those who buy stolen cars and car parts. In 2001, a few of the more popular brands among car thieves who steal for profit were Toyota Camrys, Honda Civics and Accords, Jeep Grand Cherokees, and the Chevrolet Silverado. Some vehicle types are so popular and in such high demand by car thieves that they are never safe from vehicle theft. One auto theft detective told the story of coming into his office on a Monday morning to find his next-door neighbor there reporting his Corvette stolen. The police recovered the car and returned it to the owner on Wednesday. On Friday morning the detective found his neighbor there again, once more reporting his Corvette stolen.

Methods Used by Car Thieves

"A good car thief can be in a locked car and driving it away in less than 30 seconds," said Auto Theft Detective Paul Oler. But unfortunately, it is usually much quicker than that because 40 percent of all stolen cars had the keys left in the ignition. But for those 60 percent of cars left locked and without keys, Detective Oler reported, a car thief uses a screwdriver (often his only tool) to pop out a window. Then, after reaching inside and unlocking the door, the car thief uses the screwdriver to pry off the plastic steering column collar and, with it removed, then has access to the mechanisms operating both the steering wheel and ignition lock. In cars with metal steering-column collars, car thieves often use a "dent-puller" (a tool used by auto body shops to straighten out dents) to pull the ignition lock completely out of the column; then they are able to start the car with a screwdriver.

Car alarms will often deter young or amateur car thieves, but these can be made inoperable by professionals who, for example, spray the mechanism with freon or unhook the alarm once they have gained access to the car. Steering wheel locking devices will also usually deter amateur car thieves, but present only a minor obstacle to professionals, some of whom have been known to drive wreckers (called "gypsy wreckers") and simply hook up and tow away the cars they want. Every year, though, it seems, car manufacturers come up with new security devices, such as adding computer chips to ignition keys or making transmissions that lock up along with the steering wheel. The plus side is that these devices do deter many thieves. The minus side is that a number of thieves, not sophisticated enough to get around these security devices, have, rather than simply given up stealing cars, resorted to such brutal tactics as carjacking in order to steal cars.

There are several things car thieves do with stolen vehicles. If a car is stolen by youths out for a joyride, once they are through with it they often drop the car off close to where they live or where they have another means of transportation. The same thing happens when a car is stolen to be used in a crime. In 2000, over half of all the cars stolen in the United States were recovered, even though only 14 percent of the cases were solved by arrest.

Cars stolen for profit, however, are usually driven to a safe location where the valuable and easily salable items (tires, radios, tape decks and CD players, T-tops, etc.) are stripped off, and then the car is taken to a drop spot. Stolen cars are also often taken or sold to "chop shops," which strip a car completely into pieces and then sell it as parts, which collectively sell for more than the complete car. Until recently, parts taken from cars were not identifiable. In the last few years, however, large car manufacturers have begun putting identifying numbers on major car parts. It is still advisable, though, to put your initials or other identifiable marks in some inconspicuous area of key car parts. A vehicle theft detective told the story of a car owner who had engraved his initials in a hard-to-see spot on his custom rims. When his car was stolen and then recovered, minus wheels and rims, the car owner went with his insurance check to what he thought was a reputable dealer who, as it turned out, attempted to sell him back his own stolen rims.

Criminals who deal in selling complete stolen cars, rather than car parts, will often visit junkyards looking for a wrecked car of the same type they have stolen or plan to steal. After they purchase the wrecked car in order to have a valid car title, the vehicle identification number plate is removed from the wreck and placed on the stolen car. The criminals then have a stolen car with an identification number that matches the one on the legal title, and with the title they can sell the stolen car to an unsuspecting citizen. Because of this problem, a number of states will not allow junkyards to sell whole cars, and so these thieves have begun buying wrecked cars from private citizens, usually telling them that they have a similar car and want the wrecked car for parts. To save yourself a huge expense, never buy a car with an identification plate (located on the driver's side dashboard and visible through the windshield) that appears to have been tampered with. If you do, you run the risk of having the car seized by the police, and any money spent purchasing the car will be lost.

Auto Theft Investigation

Compared with other types of larceny, vehicle thefts are much more likely to be investigated since vehicle identification numbers are usually recorded at state motor vehicle bureaus and are therefore easily obtained by the police. Once a vehicle has been confirmed by the police as stolen, its license plate number, vehicle identification number, and description are usually put on a "hot sheet," which is distributed to all uniformed officers and detectives, who then know what type of car to watch for. While uniformed officers make most vehicle recoveries, vehicle theft detectives also often recover vehicles through raiding chop shops and serving search warrants on locations known to sell stolen vehicles.

One of the more rewarding parts of police work is to recover a stolen vehicle before the owner even knows it is missing. What happens quite often is that the police chase and catch a speeding car thief or stop a stolen car for some other reason. The thief cannot, of course, produce proof of ownership or explain why the car has been started with a screwdriver. But since the owner is unaware of what has happened and the car has not officially been listed yet as stolen, police officers will have the dispatcher call the victim (often late at night) and ask him if he knows where his car is. The sleepy-voiced answer is usually "Sure, it's out in the driveway." The dispatcher then politely asks the owner to go check, waiting for the often stunned and out-of-breath owner to come running back to the phone. The officer feels good when he or she can reassure the owner that the car is safe and sound.

Previously, I recommended that you should leave a second car parked in the driveway when you're away from home for long periods of time, and it would seem that thefts like those described above would contradict this advice. But the idea of leaving a car parked in the driveway is to fool a prospective *burglar* into believing someone is home, and therefore make him want to look for another location to burglarize. Car thieves, on the other hand, don't care if anyone's home or not. They will often steal cars when they know for certain the owner is close by but not aware of what they're doing. Cars are many times stolen, for example, while people have run into a drugstore for just a moment. The advice I gave earlier about leaving a car parked in the driveway is still good advice, because you have a much better chance of having a stolen car returned than you do of property taken in a burglary.

Larceny and Vehicle Theft Prevention

As with all crimes, the chances of both larcenies and vehicle thefts can be greatly reduced by following a few simple safeguards. To decrease the likelihood of larcenies:

- Engrave your initials or some other identifying mark in an inconspicuous spot on all valuable property.
- Don't leave valuables lying around visible in a car. Lock all valuables in the trunk, but do it before arriving at your destination. If you must leave packages visible inside your car, visit the most expensive shop last. Also, leaving cassette tapes or CDs on a car seat simply advertises that the car has a tape or CD player, which are common items stolen by thieves.
- When parking at malls or other spots away from home, cars with valuable accessories should be parked in a lighted or heavily traveled area if at all possible. Although it is not foolproof, consider installing a loud alarm system.
- Be cautious of whom you allow into your home, and if you work in a business with access to the public, don't leave valuables out where they can be simply picked up and taken. *Lock* purses in a file cabinet or desk.
- In order not to let thieves know what valuables you have at your home, keep the garage door shut except when entering or leaving. If you store skis, golf clubs, or other expensive sporting equipment in your garage, build or purchase a security locker so they will be both secure and out of sight. Be sure the locks on the garage door and yard barn are sturdy and secure. Don't leave lawn mowers, tractors, snow blowers, etc. outside unguarded.
- If something of value must be left outside, don't leave it where it is visible from the street, but instead where it is

visible to a neighbor. Any expensive items left parked on trailers outside should be protected when not in use by removing a wheel from the trailer.

- Be cautious of what you leave lying out unguarded when you have private contractor work done. While the contractor may be scrupulously honest, his employees are usually seasonal and quite often have criminal records.
- Install hidden power switches on motorized equipment left parked outside. This will prevent a thief from starting up and driving the equipment away.
- Always lock up a bicycle when parking it, even if you're only going to be gone for a few minutes. Buy a good-quality lock and chain. Register the bicycle with the police and keep a record of the serial number. Some of the better bicycles have front wheels that can be removed easily. This can be both good and bad. It can be good in that you can make it impossible for someone to ride away on your bicycle if you take the wheel off, but bad in that it is easy for someone to steal your bicycle wheel if you don't take it off.
- Don't leave keys or valuables in coats left on racks in businesses, and don't set purses on the floor when using the rest room.

To protect against vehicle theft:

- When parking a car, lock it and take the keys. Don't hide a spare key in the car. Thieves know all of the hiding spots.
- Park in a well-lighted and, if possible, guarded area. Leaving the car parked in the same location every day at the same time lets a car thief know that stealing it is a low-risk venture. If you must park your car in a bad neighborhood, put a note under the wiper that says "Won't start—have gone for help" or "Out of gas—will return soon." In parking lots, park away from the ends of the row. Parking at the end only makes it easier for thieves to hook up your car and tow it away.
- Replace knob-style door lock buttons with tapered ones that can't be pulled up with a coat hanger or butter knife.

The Best Auto Security Devices

Many auto security devices, including reinforced steering-column collars and steering-wheel brace locks, offer increased protection against thieves (at least against amateurs). According to many vehicle theft detectives, however, the most effective device against car theft, even though not totally foolproof, is a loud alarm system combined with a "kill switch" that, when activated, allows power to go to the starter but not the spark plugs. A car thief will quickly abandon a car that has a loud alarm going off and won't start.

However, a security device offered by several companies will ensure that, even if a car is stolen, the police will quickly recover it. The device, hidden in the car, emits a signal that can be picked up and tracked by the police. When tested in several communities, these devices worked exceptionally well, allowing the police to locate stolen cars within a very short time of receiving the signal. And time, it has been found, can often make the difference between getting back an undamaged automobile and getting back just a stripped-down shell. Unfortunately, these devices are currently only offered in certain areas because they are of no value unless the police have the equipment necessary to track the cars.

A recent addition to automobile accessories is also helping the police locate stolen cars and catch car thieves. Many new cars now come equipped with OnStar, a device that uses a Global Positioning System to assist drivers in finding their present location and then mapping the way to their desired destination. However, it can also be used to pinpoint the location of a stolen car. Recently, the police have recovered a number of vehicles taken during carjackings after activating the stolen cars' OnStar system and finding their location.

"More people are interested in the security features (of OnStar) than the mapping capabilities," Rich Kissling, who sells the systems, told a reporter for *The Indianapolis Star* in an article that appeared on December 6, 2001.

- Install a reinforced security collar on the steering column. Even though this won't stop all thieves, it will stop many.
- Disable vehicles that are parked for long periods of time without being used.
- The best protection available against both larcenies and auto thefts is having neighbors who watch out for each other and report suspicious people and activities to the police.

Best Advice

The best information the police can offer about decreasing the chances of a larceny or vehicle theft is that most larcenies and vehicle thefts occur not so much through the craftiness of thieves as through the carelessness of victims.

8

FRAUDS, CONS, AND SCAMS

THE CON

Recently in a central Illinois city, a 72-year-old widow eagerly handed over her life's savings, $11,230 in cash, to two women in the parking garage of a downtown office building. Earlier that day, while waiting for an elevator in the local Sears store, she had been approached by one of the women and asked if she had heard about the person who found the bag of money in the parking lot. As the two women stepped onto the elevator, they were joined by a third. The first woman seemed surprised and whispered to the widow that the woman who had just joined them was the one who had found the money. The newly arrived woman overheard them and admitted she was the person, pulling a bulging manila envelope out from under her coat and saying in an exhausted voice how tired she was of everyone watching her. The first woman suggested she come with them as the three women exited the elevator and walked to the women's lounge.

Plopping down onto one of the brown leather settees and letting out a loud breath, the women with the manila envelope hefted it several times and told them that it contained over $50,000 in cash. She showed them a name written on the outside of the envelope. It was, she said, the name of a local gambler. The money, she added, was probably the receipts of illegal gambling, and she wasn't sure what to do with it. Although the elderly widow suggested calling the police, the first woman spoke up and said she worked for a tax accountant and would call him for advice.

Returning a few minutes later, she told them that her boss had said the woman was legally entitled to keep the money, but it would take a little time for him to fix up the tax end of it, and that government regulations required she be able to prove she could support herself during this time without spending any of the $50,000. The woman with the envelope seemed pleased and said that since the widow and other woman had been so kind and considerate to her she wanted to split the money with them. The three of them then left and drove to two banks, where, as the widow waited in her car, the two women went in to withdraw sizable amounts from their accounts to use as proof they could support themselves. They then drove to the widow's bank, where she withdrew her life's savings.

At a downtown parking garage the woman who claimed to have found the money asked the widow to hold the manila envelope while she and the other woman took the widow's $11,230 and their own withdrawals to the tax accountant's office for verification. When they didn't return after almost an hour, the widow became suspicious and opened the envelope, finding only cut-up newspaper.

A common con game ("pigeon drop" in police jargon), the above case is typical of the many thousands of schemes perpetrated every year on gullible and trusting people, representing the loss of millions of dollars. The perpetrators are usually seasoned professionals who nearly always appear clean-cut and always speak pleasantly. They never seem to be "criminal types," and often don't live in the area where they pull their scams, but will travel across the United States several times each year, setting up and stealing from anyone who will fall for their con.

"Most con artists look just like ordinary people," said former Fraud Detective R. C. Davidson. "They seldom look like the kind of person who would cheat you."

Selecting Victims

The victims of most cons, police investigators have found, are the elderly, usually retired people between the ages of 60 and

90, many living on small, fixed incomes, but who often have substantial bank accounts containing their life's savings. There are a number of reasons why con artists select the elderly as victims:

- With advanced age, the con artist believes, comes a lessening of the power to make well-thought-out judgments. Con artists are smooth talkers who rely on their ability to either convince victims of their honesty or confuse them.
- With the decrease in visual acuity that often comes with advanced age, elderly victims will not, con artists hope, be able to identify them in the event they are ultimately arrested.
- "They're trusting souls," fraud detectives say of most elderly victims. "They were raised during a time when a person could leave the windows open and the doors unlocked. They were brought up to help people in need, and this blind trust and desire to help are often used against them."
- Many elderly people are lonely and receptive to talking with strangers at length. This is exactly what the con artist wants.
- Con artists also feel that they can rely on the reluctance of elderly victims to report cons and scams because of fear of family embarrassment. This reluctance, incidentally, also keeps the police from knowing the actual number of fraud cases every year, but many experts believe it is probably several times the reported number.

Picking the elderly as victims, however, is not an unbreakable rule of con artists. Although many prefer to victimize the elderly, they will play their con on anyone they believe will fall for it. Some scams, for example, target victims who are often thought to be shrewd investors or who are at least people with good judgment, which means no one is really safe from con artists.

Common Scams

Even though there is often a reluctance to report many scams, still detectives receive reports of thousands of frauds, cons, and scams perpetrated every year across the United States. Most victims, detectives find, usually fall for a variation of one of the following scams:

Pigeon Drop.   Most of these are similar to the case of the elderly widow outlined above. They are easy to spot because in each variation the victim is asked to hand over "good-faith" money to strangers, usually as cash, but occasionally con artists will accept jewelry, other valuables, or a check made out to cash, which they then have the victim cash for them.

Home Improvement.   One variation of this scam involves a phony gas company serviceman who knocks on the door and claims he is checking on a reported gas leak in the neighborhood and needs to inspect the victim's furnace, always finding it in dangerous condition and in need of immediate repair. Soon after the phony serviceman leaves, a representative of a fraudulent repair service calls, talks the homeowner into unnecessary and often sloppy repairs, and then charges an inflated price, either demanding the full amount immediately or insisting that the victim sign a contract.

Another variation is the representative of a bogus repair service or construction company who offers to check a chimney for cracks, a roof for leaks, or a crawl space for termites (often smuggling in a piece of termite-infested wood), and always reports the need for repairs. Yet another variation is phony painting contractors who charge inflated prices and use paint that washes off with the first rain.

Home improvement scam artists also follow natural disasters. The police find them many times canvassing for work in areas struck by tornadoes, floods, hurricanes, and so on. They will usually offer to fix damage to the home at very reasonable prices, but then disappear with the up-front money they say they need in order to purchase the materials necessary for the repairs.

The Bank Examiner Scam.   This con begins when a person claiming to be a bank official telephones the victim (often after

The Williamson Gang

When fraud investigators hear of a home improvement scam, the name Williamson usually comes to mind. The Williamson Gang has been bilking homeowners across the United States for over 80 years. Estimated to number several hundred members, many of whom can trace their ancestry to a group of Scottish and British immigrants that arrived in the United States around the turn of the century, this gang is one of the most elusive and well-organized groups of con artists in the country. Because many of the gang members are related by blood, the police have found it extremely difficult to infiltrate the Williamson Gang, which seems to have an uncanny knack of getting out of a community just ahead of the law.

The Williamson Gang, which still uses many of the same schemes today it has used for years, usually operates in older neighborhoods populated by elderly residents. Their scam begins when a clean-cut and pleasant-speaking young man knocks on the door and tells a homeowner that he and his daddy have just finished paving a driveway or waterproofing a roof nearby and have enough material left over to do the homeowner's if he or she likes. The young man then quotes a very reasonable price. After the unwary homeowner agrees, the driveway or roof is coated with some cheap substance such as crankcase oil, aluminum paint, or gasoline. The young man then collects the money and leaves before the homeowner realizes he or she has been swindled.

peering over the victim's shoulder in a bank and getting his or her name and bank account number). The caller says he is investigating a bank teller believed to be stealing money from the victim's account, and recites the victim's account number to establish credibility. The caller then asks the victim for assistance in catching the crooked teller, often offering a reward as incentive. In one variation of this swindle a second person calls soon after the first and identifies himself as a police officer and thanks the victim for his or her cooperation. Often the caller will use the name of a real local police officer (obtained from the local paper or television news) in case the victim is suspicious and calls the police department to verify that there is such an officer.

Soon after the victim agrees to help, the first caller arrives and accompanies the victim to the bank, where he or she is instructed to withdraw a substantial amount of money. Afterward, the con artist asks for the money so the amount can be verified and later checked against the amount the teller records. The money is then switched for cut-up newspaper and placed in a sealed envelope, or else the victim is given a receipt and told that the money will be redeposited after it is marked and fingerprinted.

The Inheritance Scheme.   In this con, a person claiming to be an attorney calls on the victims. The bogus attorney informs the victims that they are heirs to a huge inheritance, but must first pay inheritance tax before receiving the phony cashier's check they have "accidentally" been allowed to see.

C.O.D. Scam.   After obtaining a list of names and addresses from the city directory, the con artist canvasses a neighborhood to find someone not at home, then makes out a mailing label containing that person's name and address. The con artist, with package in hand, then knocks on nearby doors, inquiring if the people will accept a perishable C.O.D. delivery for their neighbor, collecting the C.O.D. charge, and leaving the victim with a box of old newspapers.

A variation on this scheme has the con artist showing up at the door soon after a funeral announcement to collect a supposed debt owed by the deceased or to collect for some highly overpriced gift that the con artist says the deceased had ordered as a surprise for the surviving spouse.

Telephone 900-Line Scams. Seeing the ability to get quick dollars from gullible people, a large number of con artists have set up scams using 900 numbers. A common example is offering free items to callers. Unfortunately, the items are worth much less than the call since people are usually put on hold or stalled for a long time before their names and addresses are taken. These services offer anything the con artist knows people want and believe they can get cheap, or want but can't obtain anywhere else legitimately.

A few years ago, there was a very innovative scheme involving a 900-line fraud. The announcer on a television commercial instructed young children to hold the telephone receiver up to the television screen. The commercial then transmitted the computer dial tones for a 900 number.

Ponzi Schemes. This scheme, named after Charles Ponzi, a swindler who worked the scam in the Boston area around 1920, operates on the human desire to "get rich quick," but even more on the human desire to brag about success. The con man approaches a small number of people with an investment offer that is guaranteed to give big returns in a short time. And indeed it does. The con man will pay the investors a 50 or maybe 100 percent return on their money in just a few months. These investors, then, as most people will, brag incessantly to their friends about their investment savvy, and soon everyone wants in on the investment. The con man collects additional investments from the original investors and funds from many new people, and then absconds with the money. Sometimes, to pull in even more people, the con artist will pay off early investors several times with money taken in by later investors so that the original investors will continue to brag.

In December 2001, Republic New York Securities pleaded guilty to securities fraud and conspiracy, agreeing to repay $606 million to investors. Republic New York Securities, part of the huge international banking concern HSBC, admitted that some of its top executives helped run probably the largest Ponzi scheme ever. In a similar case in January 2002, Kenneth R. Payne, former president of Heartland Financial Services, pleaded guilty to mail fraud and money laundering. He admitted to swindling investors out of $10 to $20 million in a Ponzi scheme. On April 12, 2002, a judge sentenced him to 17 years in prison.

A little thought on the part of prospective investors ought to make this scheme difficult to pull off, but the draw of quick and easy money, along with the recommendation of other investors, is often too much to resist. But what people need to ask themselves is, why would a complete stranger want to offer such a great deal to them, instead of to his or her own family and friends? But still, the police believe, this scheme is pulled off many more times than it's reported since people who consider themselves shrewd investors seldom want to admit being fooled. A caution to remember is that the chances of a complete stranger wanting to bring you in on a one-in-a-million deal is far more than one in a million.

The Rental Scheme.   In this scam, the con artist finds a nice apartment or piece of property and leases it for a short period. He then advertises the apartment or property for lease at a very reasonable price. The con artist shows the property to many people, and tells them that it will be available in 30 to 60 days. Since the price is so reasonable, many people immediately hand over a deposit and the first and last month's rents, which the con artist pockets. The first defense against this scam is to be suspicious of any rental property that looks too good to be true. If you are suspicious, ask to see proof that the person has the right to lease it. If he balks, it's time for you to leave.

Work-at-Home Scams.   Everyone has seen these advertisements in the back of even very respectable magazines or posted on practically ever other light pole, advertisements that claim there are just dozens of businesses simply drooling to pay you huge sums of money to stuff envelopes (work they could get done very easily at minimum wage) or that a fortune waits to be made using your home computer. Most of the advertisements even say "Free Information." However, the free information is usually simply an offer to purchase a list of these purported companies or a list of the businesses you can start at home on your computer. Unless you can think of a really good reason why a company would want to pay you many times the minimum wage to do menial work, or why everyone isn't making a fortune off of their home computer, stay away from these deals.

With the rapidly increasing use of the Internet, cons and scams have naturally found their way there too. A very popular scheme is an offer over the Internet to fix bad credit, naturally for a price. "These credit repair con games are spreading like wildfire on the Internet and in unsolicited e-mail," said Jodie Bernstein, director of the Federal Trade Commission's Bureau of Consumer Protection. Usually, however, the only thing that happens is that people with bad credit still have bad credit, but now also have a little less cash. Another scam involves a phony e-mail notifying you that a sexually oriented company has charged a large sum to your credit card, with a telephone number to call if there are questions about the charge. The number, however, is not toll-free and the caller ends up with a huge phone charge. Just as con artists follow natural disasters, they also follow manmade ones. In December 2001, authorities began investigating an Internet site that claimed to be the official site of the Federal Emergency Management Agency (FEMA) and requested donations to help the survivors of the September 11 attack.

There are dozens of other schemes, such as three-card monte, which is just a form of the old shell game; fraudulent retirement estates; pyramid and airplane scams; fake oriental rugs; money-making machines that con men claim can duplicate large bills; jewelry hinted to be stolen but that is actually junk; announcements through the mail or over the Internet that you have won a prize but that require a call on a 900 line or a shipping and handling charge; fake medical cures; and many more. In the Midwest, a con artist pulled a scam in which he sold prepaid funerals, and then absconded with the money. Most of these schemes, however, have one thing in common: asking the victim to hand over large amounts of money or valuables to strangers. This is the clearest sign of a scam—and the best protection against it. The moment that someone you don't know well asks you to hand over money or valuables for some promised benefit that sounds too good to be true, it is time to say "No thank you" and leave. If it's such a fantastic deal, why is he or she offering it to a stranger?

Identity Theft

There is a type of fraud that, while around for decades, has grown dramatically in the last few years: identity theft. The FBI calls identity theft America's fastest growing white-collar crime. This crime starts when a con artist somehow obtains your personal information and then uses it to open bank accounts, get credit cards, apply for loans, set up cellular telephone accounts, etc. While you are usually not financially liable for the debts the con artist accrues using your name and personal information, you are responsible for the expense of clearing your name and credit rating. The California Public Interest Research Group found that victims of identity theft spend on the average over 175 hours and over $800 clearing their names. The police believe that over 700,000 people will be the victims of this crime in 2002.

How do these con artists get your personal information? In April 2002, sheriff's deputies in Marion County, Indiana, stopped a woman for a traffic violation. In the backseat of her car they found a large bag of mail. When they served a search warrant at her home, the deputies found an additional 236 pounds of mail. Police believe she was stealing these items from mailboxes and then using the information in them to fraudulently obtain money in the victims' names. In addition to stolen mail, however, con

The Jamaican Switch

This scam, so named because a number of its participants have been from Jamaica, begins when a person speaking heavily accented English approaches the intended victim and seems bewildered. The con artist says he has just arrived in the country and needs a place to stay. He then pulls what looks like a huge wad of money out of a bag to show that paying for a place to stay is no problem. The victim usually immediately warns the con man not to be flashing so much money in public. The con man then says he has to carry it on him because all the banks in his country are crooked and would steal his money. The victim usually assures the con man that American banks are honest, and is persuaded to go to his bank and demonstrate how easy it is to make a large withdrawal. The con man, seeming impressed, wants to put his money with the victims and places the victim's in the bag with his. The victim is then distracted and the bag is switched. The con artist, making some excuse to leave for a moment, absconds and leaves the victim holding a bag of cut-up newspaper.

To most readers this swindle probably seems almost too transparent for anyone to fall for, but a report came over my desk recently in which the victim lost not only $5,000 from his bank account but also an $8,000 Rolex watch that he was persuaded to put in the bag with his money. No scheme, it seems, is too transparent, and there is always some person gullible enough to go along with it.

artists many times obtain personal information on their victims from the Internet, where this information often floats around freely. At my bank recently, I saw a notice warning customers that someone was sending out e-mail claiming to be from the Internal Revenue Service. The e-mail, titled "e-audit," stated that the recipients had 48 hours to fill out an attached questionnaire or they would be subject to interest and penalties. The questionnaire asked for Social Security numbers, bank account numbers, and other confidential information. One can only imagine the damage that can be done with this information.

A few simple precautions will help reduce the chances of becoming the victim of identity theft:

- Your Social Security number is often the key con artists look for in order to obtain much more personal information about you. Guard this number and don't give it out unless legally required to do so.
- Shred old correspondence from utility companies, banks, credit card companies, etc. Con artists often go through a victim's trash in search of personal information and can use these documents to steal your identity.
- Never give out personal information over the telephone or the Internet unless you know the person receiving the information.
- Since many identity theft victims are unaware someone is using their name until they are turned down for some type of credit, check your credit report at least once a year.
- You can call 1-888-5OPTOUT to have your name removed from the mailing lists of credit card companies that send out credit card offers.
- The Federal Trade Commission has a toll-free number (1-877-438-4338) that victims of identity theft can use to report the crime.
- For readers interested in more information on protecting their personal information, please read *Stopping a Stalker* (Perseus Books, 1998) where I go into great detail about the topic.

Fraud Investigation

Fraud investigation follows most of the same procedures as other criminal investigations with, two very important exceptions. First, many con artists don't live in the community where they pull their cons, but travel across the country, stopping in each town just long enough to pull a con and leave before the police are notified. This makes identifying and apprehending con artists much more difficult than other criminals. And second, even in those cases where an arrest is made, it is usually days or weeks after the crime, which means seldom is any of the victim's money recovered. Therefore, from a victim's point of view, it is much better to prevent a con or scam from happening than it is to have the con artist arrested afterward.

However, fraud investigation also has several advantages over other criminal investigations. For example, con artists differ from other criminals in that they usually don't try to hide or disguise their features, but want to appear very open and honest. Therefore the victim is quite often able to give a good description and recognize the perpetrator if he or she is caught. In addition, since fraud has one of the highest recidivism rates of all crimes, the police know many of the con artists. Of course, if the victim is elderly and feeble, identification and testimony in court are not always possible, making fraud investigation very frustrating at times. In addition, often the police know a con artist has struck many times in a community, but because of embarrassment they can't get the other victims to come forward.

Defenses Against Frauds, Cons, and Scams

To avoid becoming the victim of a con or scam, the following precautions are recommended by detectives specializing in fraud investigation:

- Beware of any deal that requires the putting up of large amounts of money or valuables to show "good faith" or to prove that you really don't need the windfall promised. Be particularly cautious of any "now or never" deals.
- Don't be afraid to ask for identification from anyone claiming to be a police officer, bank official, or employee of a public

utility or other agency. Also, don't be afraid to verify badges or credentials with the agency the person claims to represent. These can be faked. In addition, verify with the agency that the person's actions are proper. This will not offend genuine employees.

- Be cautious of anyone offering to perform home improvements at a ridiculously low price, or anyone offering to check a furnace, chimney, crawl space, etc. Before dealing with any company doing home improvements, call the Better Business Bureau and check on whether any complaints have been lodged against the company. If they have no file on the company, check the Yellow Pages to see if the business the person claims to represent actually exists.

- Never give your credit card number to anyone unless you *know* the person is reputable. Often, con artists will call victims with various ruses in order to obtain their credit card number, and then use this information to order expensive items. Be cautious when giving credit card information over the Internet. Make certain the site is legitimate and secure. Also, keep the carbons from any charge slips. Some stores simply want to tear them in half and throw them away. A person going through the trash, however, can easily piece your slip together.

- Read any contract before signing. Be suspicious of any pressure to sign right away, or to sign a contract with blank spaces. Take time to think about it and to get others' advice before signing. Legitimate contractors will not mind this precaution.

- Never send money in any form blindly through the mail. Know exactly what you're ordering and that the company you're ordering it from is legitimate and reputable.

- If in doubt about any person or firm, call the local police department.

- A final warning: con artists who have defrauded many people in a community will often come back for one more hit. In this scheme, the victims of the con artist will receive a call from someone purporting to also be a victim of the con artist. The caller says that the con artist has been caught and apparently has sizable assets. The caller then claims that he is initiating a lawsuit against the con artist to recover his losses and invites the victim to join in the lawsuit, collects the victim's "share" of the attorney costs, and absconds.

Best Advice

A retired con artist and swindler warned: "Anytime people are promised something for nothing, they usually get just that—nothing." The best advice the police can add to this is that frauds, cons, and scams only work when victims willingly cooperate. And so, when a deal looks too good to be true, be careful: it probably is.

9

SUBSTANCE ABUSE

AMERICA'S SUBSTANCE ABUSE PROBLEM

Substance abuse, while seeming to have become a problem in America only during the last three or four decades, is actually not a new problem at all, but has been around the whole of the last century. And yet, while the substance abuse problem in America is not new, its magnitude and infiltration into almost every level of American society are a new development. In just the last few decades the use by young people of drugs such as marijuana and cocaine, along with widespread alcohol abuse, has found its way into the average American home, and has even become the accepted norm for many young people.

But many readers may still wonder if all of this concern and publicity about widespread substance abuse isn't really just a lot of media hype. Many may wonder if there really is a substance abuse problem in America, and, if so, whether it is really all that bad.

From a police officer's point of view, there is a very real substance abuse problem in America. It is ominous enough that every president since Ronald Reagan has felt the need to appoint a "Drug Czar." It is serious enough that almost all of America's major police departments and over 80 percent of the country's Fortune 500 firms now test for drugs. The drug problem in America is bleak, and the cost of this problem is staggering. The dollar cost of lost productivity due to substance abuse and the criminal justice system's expenditures in arresting, trying, and imprisoning drug abusers—plus social welfare needs and health care expenses due to substance abuse—have been estimated to be at least $65 billion yearly. But the problem goes much deeper than that. Substance abuse ruins families and weakens our nation's industries. A study, "Substance Abuse in the Work Place," interviewed 224 corporate heads. Of these, 79 percent said drugs and alcohol are a significant problem in their organization.

The problem of substance abuse is so ominous in the United States, the National Institute on Drug Abuse reports, that over 16 percent of America's 13-year-olds have tried marijuana, while the Institute for Social Research reports that over 17 percent of America's high school seniors have tried cocaine. Other studies have found that in large metropolitan areas 50 percent of all high school seniors report illicit drug use, while 6 percent of the nation's high school seniors report drinking alcohol daily. The National Center on Addiction and Substance Abuse at Columbia University released the results of a study in February 2002 that found that almost a third of high school students report binge drinking at least once a month, and that underage drinking accounts for 11.4 percent of America's total alcohol consumption. The U.S. Department of Education's *Schools Without Drugs* states that research shows drug abuse among young people is so serious it is actually 10 times more prevalent than parents suspect. Supporting this, a recent survey found that over 85 percent of high school seniors said that obtaining marijuana or hashish was fairly easy or very easy for them, while almost 65 percent said the same for amphetamines, over 50 percent for cocaine, and almost 30 percent for LSD (a drug that has recently made a comeback). And, of course, of all drugs, alcohol is probably the easiest for young people to obtain. But statistics aside, what these studies are really saying is that many illegal and very dangerous drugs are readily accessible to any young person who wants them.

Substance Abuse and Crime

But how does all of this substance abuse translate into crime? Very directly. Several long-term studies have shown that the best predictors of future criminality are a combination of the person's prior adult and juvenile criminal record, age, and *history of drug use*. According to the U.S. Justice Department's *Report to the Nation on Crime and Justice*, 78 percent of all prison inmates report having tried illegal drugs, while the same is true for only 37 percent of the general population. More recent studies have found an even higher percentage for inmates. But more important, 40 percent of these prison inmates reported that they were either under the influence of drugs or very drunk at the time they committed the offense they were incarcerated for. This percentage, incidentally, varies for individual crimes, with murderers reporting the lowest number being under the influence of drugs or very drunk (about 32 percent) and burglars reporting the largest (about 50 percent, with robbers close behind at 47 percent).

The figures above, however, are self-reports, which a long-term study by the National Institute of Justice (NIJ) has found are very conservative. In 1987, NIJ instituted the Drug Use Forecasting (DUF) program, which was designed to measure the extent of illegal drug use in America by constantly monitoring the drug use of arrestees in 39 major U.S. cities through interviews and urine testing. The results have been shocking indeed. While by self-report 40 percent of institutionalized prisoners admitted illegal drug use just prior to their arrest, DUF found that the percentage was much larger. The findings for 2000 showed that the percentage of adult males arrested who tested positive for illegal drugs ranged from 79 percent in New York City to 51 percent in Des Moines. Female arrestees, previous studies have shown, had percentages even higher, ranging from 85 percent in New York City, to 78 percent in Philadelphia, to 50 percent in Indianapolis, to 44 percent in San Antonio. Even more disturbing, though, was the finding in an earlier report that many juvenile arrestees also tested positive for illegal drugs, ranging from 44 percent in Washington, D.C., to 10 percent in St. Louis. But most disturbing of all is that past studies have shown illegal drug use as high as 92 percent among arrestees. What these figures are really saying is that a very large majority of the people committing crimes in America are drug abusers. This fact is often demonstrated when one of these addicts is finally caught and convicted, and then wants to make a cleanup statement to the police (an admission to other crimes he or she has committed on the understanding that he or she will not be charged with them). These statements will often clear up hundreds of cases.

Building on these frightening statistics, studies done in Baltimore, Harlem, and several cities in California show that a substance abuser's involvement in crime is three to five times what it was before the substance abuse began. The study in Baltimore also found that drug addicts, on the average, commit a crime every other day, and that the greater the drug use, the more criminal convictions the addict has. James A. Inciardi of the University of Delaware found in a study of 611 adolescent hard-core drug offenders (those addicted to drugs such as heroin, crack cocaine, and so on) that over a 12-month period they were involved in 429,136 crimes, including 6,269 robberies and 721 assaults. Researchers at Temple University in Philadelphia studied 243 heroin addicts in Baltimore. Over an 11-year period they committed over 500,000 crimes. Moreover, the researchers studied criminal activity during times the individuals were on and off drugs and found the subjects committed 84 percent fewer crimes when off drugs. More proof of the effect of substance abuse on the crime rate comes from Los Angeles, where the police estimate that up to 60 percent of that city's crime is drug-related. The mayor of East Orange, New Jersey, claims the amount is closer to 70 percent in that city. Citizens are now also beginning to see this connection. In 1981 only 13 percent of the people questioned in a nationwide Gallup poll thought that drug abuse was a cause of crime. By 2000 the percentage had risen to 60 percent.

But what do all of these figures really mean?

Reduced to one sentence, it is a little-known truth that many police officers have known for a long time, namely, that a small number of people in our country are committing an enormous percentage of the crime. A person with a serious heroin, cocaine, or other drug habit must raise a tremendous amount of cash each year to support their extremely expensive habit. And, since serious addicts can seldom hold jobs for long, many of them must raise the cash needed by robbing, stealing, and burglarizing. Researchers, for example, estimate that young drug abusers commit 75 percent of all the robberies in our country, a group that makes up only approximately 3 percent of all young people.

But what these statistics really mean to average citizens is that if they are mugged and robbed, if their car is stolen, or if their home is burglarized, the chances are very good that it was done by a person on drugs or in need of money to buy drugs. And, as all police officers know, these are very desperate and dangerous people whom both research and practical experience have shown are especially prone to violence. But just how violent are these people?

Dr. Steven L. Brody, former director of the Medical Intensive Care Unit of Grady Memorial Hospital in Atlanta, found in a study of his patients that an intense state of cocaine intoxication, for example, can result in a variety of violent and aggressive behaviors. Other drugs, the police find, can produce even more dangerous and aggressive actions. How aggressive? Serious abusers will come off a day long drug high during which they have had no food or sleep, and now find themselves suddenly sick and shaky, realizing that they are careening downward toward an excruciatingly painful cold-turkey withdrawal unless they can somehow get money for more drugs. In this state they have often sold or even killed their own children for the money they need. A long-term study published in the October 2000 issue of the *Archives of General Psychiatry* found elevated violence levels in young adults with three conditions: schizophrenia, alcohol dependence, and marijuana dependence.

"Our study suggests that a significant proportion of the violence that frightens and injures the general public may be attributed to young adults who are prone to [these disorders], many of whom have not been hospitalized or treated," stated the article.

When I was a street captain, my narcotics lieutenant related to me some of her experiences several years back when she was working deep undercover obtaining evidence on a doctor who was suspected of selling illegal drugs to heroin addicts. She said that for heroin addicts everything they think, say, or do during the day has only one purpose: to get more heroin. Absolutely nothing else matters.

What Can Be Done?

After reading all of these frightening statistics, many people may wonder if the problem is already too far out of hand for anything to be done, if the crisis of substance abuse in America hasn't already spiraled out of control.

Actually, quite a lot can be done, but the police alone simply can't stop the drug problem in America. Arrests nationally for drug users and sellers have increased dramatically, and in the last 10 years the incarceration of drug offenders has increased by 50 percent. Every day, it seems, the papers are filled with stories of some gigantic seizure of drugs, but still drugs are plentiful and available. The problem goes on and on, and it does so because it is caused by many social factors that the police can't control.

When I was a street captain, I attended a neighborhood meeting and listened to a number of the people there complain about drug sales in a specific area of their neighborhood. To see how bad it was I went along with a team of my narcotics detectives when they raided a "shooting gallery" (a location where addicts go to shoot up drugs), and caught three old-time heroin addicts there shooting up. These three men were all in their late forties, had been heroin addicts since their teens, and now supported their heroin addiction by selling cocaine. Separating the three addicts, we attempted to persuade one of the men to work as an informant for us, but he just shook his head and told us he had been a heroin addict all of his adult life and probably would be until he dies. He had no job, no home, no real life. With that future what could we really offer him? Nothing, apparently, because we couldn't convince him to help us.

To go into all of the social reasons why illegal drugs flourish in this country, reasons outside of police control, is beyond the scope of this book, but I can illustrate one of the major reasons. Several years ago, when I was the police department's executive officer, I was driving with the deputy chief of operations to a neighborhood meeting in a really seedy part of Indianapolis. The chief looked out the car window at the dilapidated homes, at the trash-strewn streets, and at empty hulks of junked cars and said, "Bob, you know, I think if I lived here and knew that this was all my future was ever going to be, I'd be stoned on drugs 24 hours a day."

Although this story says a lot about the cause of part of the drug abuse problem in America and the huge undertaking that would be necessary to eradicate it, there is something that individual neighborhoods can do about drugs. At present it may not be possible to totally stop the sale and use of illegal drugs in America since every day tons of drugs cross our borders. For every large seizure that makes the news, dozens slip by, and will continue to so long as there is a demand for drugs and people willing to pay for them. Nevertheless, it is possible to eradicate them in your neighborhood, but to do so the public must be willing to become involved. Several years ago, for example, the New York City Police Department reported that its Operation Pressure Point not only decreased drug sales on the Lower East Side of Manhattan, but also produced a significant reduction in serious crime in the area. This program involved some very aggressive action by the police against both drug users and pushers, including highly visible uniformed patrols in the worst drug areas (not only to keep drug dealers off the streets but also to discourage people from entering the area to buy drugs) and plainclothes detectives and police dogs that flushed drug dealers and users out of vacant buildings. But a large part of the program's success depended on community involvement, and on citizens who were willing to report drug law violations in their neighborhood and to work in cooperation with the police. To facilitate this, police distributed flyers in the most drug-prone neighborhoods explaining how to make anonymous reports of drug violations, which many citizens did.

Another antidrug program, called Quick Uniform Attack on Drugs (QUAD), located in Tampa, Florida, also showed great success in chasing drugs and drug dealers out of neighborhoods that many people had thought were lost. Aggressive, sweeping action by the police, in cooperation with residents who were willing to participate and provide the police with information, saved several Tampa neighborhoods that many had given up on. The measure of the program, designers decided, would not be the number of arrests or the amount of drugs seized, but the return of quiet, safe streets in the neighborhoods.

These programs, only two of the many police-citizen cooperative drug reduction programs across the country, illustrate very graphically that America's neighborhoods are not completely at the mercy of drugs and drug dealers. They demonstrate that neighborhoods, by working together and with the police, can defeat drugs, at least on a localized level.

Do programs like these run the drug dealers completely out of business? Does cleaning up a neighborhood mean there is now less demand for drugs? No. Programs like this will, if residents watch carefully for and report any attempts by drug dealers to return, keep a neighborhood clean, but will likely crowd these dealers and users into another drug-prone area. To completely eradicate America's drug problem, as I stated earlier, will take a very serious overhaul of our society.

Yet, while these type of programs can be successful at stopping present drug users and pushers locally, and should be embraced by any neighborhood experiencing drug problems, much of our nation's future drug problems could be stopped by simply keeping young people from abusing drugs or alcohol in the first

Signs of Neighborhood Drug Problems

In far too many neighborhoods in the United States illegal drugs are now no longer someone else's problem. But even in those neighborhoods as yet untouched, the residents worry that they will soon be overrun. The people living in these neighborhoods realize that to remain untouched they must be vigilant and watch for any signs of drugs, yet most aren't sure what these signs are. According to Captain Michael Sherman, former head of a large police department's narcotics branch, the following are good indicators that the problem of illegal drugs has invaded a neighborhood:

- A sudden increase of new faces in the area, strangers who appear to have no legitimate business in the neighborhood.
- A home or other location with a large amount of vehicular and foot traffic in and out, yet with few of the visitors staying long.
- Dilapidation of a piece of property (grass not cut, house not painted or repaired, etc.). When people become involved in drugs, drugs are all that matter.
- An unusual amount of police activity (assault and battery, disturbance runs, etc.) at one address. Drugs can often cause mood changes that erupt into violence.
- Evidence of drug use, sale, or manufacture, such as drug paraphernalia (plastic bags with corners cut off, small pieces of tin foil, large number of balloons, etc.) or the odor of ether or acetic acid (from drug manufacturing).
- A sudden increase in crime in the area, such as car break-ins, burglaries, etc.
- A final clue can come from your children, since even children who are not using drugs often know about drug activity in their neighborhood.

place. But to do this, the widespread apathy or lack of awareness of much of the general public regarding the problem of substance abuse must be replaced by knowledge, concern, and involvement.

There have been a number of locations across the country, for example, where knowledgeable, concerned, and involved citizens have helped local schools successfully stem the availability of drugs to their students. Communities have been able to do this by initiating aggressive, no-nonsense programs aimed at ridding the schools of both drug users and suppliers. The most famous example of this was Eastside High School in Paterson, New Jersey, with its principal, Joe Clark. One of the keys to the success of these programs is that the schools work in cooperation with the local police in both presenting drug prevention programs and arresting drug pushers, which include both students and outsiders. The programs also work because these schools tolerate no drug use by students, and use their power to suspend and, if necessary, permanently dismiss students for drug use. These students, then, if they demonstrate they are off drugs, can often attend evening adult classes to finish up their education. In order for such programs to really work, they must have the overwhelming and unqualified support and personal involvement of parents.

In addition to helping the schools rid themselves of drugs, parents can do something at home to reduce the chances that their own children will become substance abusers. "Communication is the key to preventing substance abuse," said Jackie Ginther, a retired police officer who has worked for many years with young substance abusers. "I'm shocked many times at the lack of communication between parents and children, especially in families where the children are involved with drugs or alcohol. When the parents come to me and say they think their children may be involved with drugs or alcohol, I usually ask them if they have spoken with their children about it, and far too often all I get is blank looks. Far too many parents and children simply don't sit down together and talk about the problems and pressures of growing up."

Signs of Drug Abuse

Many parents respond with growing trepidation to the almost daily flood of news stories about widespread drug abuse among the young. Could their child be using drugs? What signs should they look for?

Narcotics investigators advise parents worried about the possibility of their child abusing drugs to look for the signs below, and also warn that these signs do not prove a child is using drugs, but only indicate the possibility:

- Has your child's personality suddenly changed dramatically? Is he or she now moody, short-tempered, or hostile? Does he or she seem "spaced out"?
- Has your child become less responsive about chores, less enthusiastic about school work and extracurricular activities?
- Has your child suddenly changed friends?
- Does your child strongly defend a person's right to use drugs, or simply refuse to discuss the subject?
- Has your child suddenly become an obsessive liar?
- Has your child's relationship with other family members deteriorated, and does the child stay alone for long periods in his or her room?
- Are there any signs of drug use, such as dilated pupils, hyperactivity, sluggishness, slurred or incoherent speech?
- Are easily salable items or money suddenly missing from the home? Is your child always broke?
- Is the supply of liquor, diet pills, or other drugs in the home dwindling without apparent cause?
- Is there any drug paraphernalia in or around the house, such as clips to hold marijuana, pipes for smoking drugs, small pieces of tin foil, or injection equipment?

When concerned parents corner Ginther after a presentation, she also asks them: "What are your children's guidelines and rules at home? Who are your children's friends?" Often, though, she reports, the parents cannot answer these questions because they have set no guidelines for their children. And many times parents don't know who their children's friends are, or what they are doing, because they don't know their own children. This apathy of many parents toward their children, she finds, comes from being too concerned about their own careers and lives, from simply not caring, or occasionally from having to struggle 16 hours a day to meet the monthly bills (e.g., single parents raising kids on their own). The police find, however, that whatever the cause, this apathy often turns to panicky concern when the problem of substance abuse suddenly becomes apparent. But far too many times it is simply too late then to reverse the years of neglect.

Most police officers who work with young substance abusers agree that frequent and meaningful communication between parents and children is one of the keys to preventing substance abuse. In addition, most agree with Ginther that setting rules and guidelines for children, such as times to be home, doing homework before socializing, having certain duties around the home, and so on, along with knowing who your children's friends are and what your children do with their friends, are also important. But police officers and experts in the field of substance abuse are unanimous in their agreement that even more important than all of these is the setting of a good example. Children model themselves after their parents, and imitate weaknesses as well as strengths. It is difficult for parents who in times of stress resort to mood-altering substances to convince their children that this is the wrong thing for them to do.

Effective Programs

Substance abuse prevention programs and organizations exist in most large communities, some structured for adults, such as Mothers Against Drunk Driving (MADD), an organization that

Drug Legalization

For a number of years there has been an argument circulating that America's drug problem could be brought under control by simply legalizing drugs. Even President Clinton's Surgeon General once suggested that this should be considered. This idea, sponsors claim, would put drug pushers out of business, eliminate the present black market for drugs, and thereby drastically reduce the price of drugs. The result of legalization, they claim, would be a reduction in the crime rate, now at astronomical heights due to the need for money for drugs. Also, supporters argue, many of the people who use drugs could escape being labeled as criminals and instead could become productive members of society.

Besides the horrible example this would set for future generations as to what is an acceptable lifestyle, there are a number of disturbing questions and issues I have never heard addressed or answered by the proponents of this theory:

1. What about the really dangerous drugs that can cause irrational and often aggressive behavior, such as PCP, LSD, crack, or crystal methamphetamine? Will they be made available? If not, the drug pushers are back in business.
2. Who decides what dosage or strength the drugs will be? Unless the users can decide this, pushers will simply start selling larger dosages or concentrations.
3. At what age will people be allowed to buy drugs? Twenty-one? Will drug pushers simply move their market to the under-21 crowd?
4. The argument that legalization will make drug abusers productive members of society flies in the face of reason. Drug abusers want to escape from responsibility. Why would they want to *(continued)*

Drug Legalization (continued)

change if we provide them with a cheap and easy way to continue their lifestyle, particularly if we say this is an acceptable lifestyle? And worse, the expense of social programs to support these people and their families while they live a life of drug euphoria would cost everyone.

5. Finally, in my over 30-year career there haven't been more than a half-dozen out of the thousands of disturbances I've responded to in which someone hadn't been drinking or doing drugs. Making drugs easier to obtain would only increase the number of disturbances in a community and the amount of injuries and deaths that accompany them.

lobbies state legislatures for stiffer drunk driving laws, while promoting programs to increase an awareness of the dangers of drunk driving. Other programs and organizations target young people, such as Students Against Drunk Driving (SADD), Drug Abuse Resistance Education (DARE), Students Taught Awareness and Resistance (STAR), and others.

It is important to know that these and many other programs have value in that they make people more aware of a problem whose magnitude far too many adults either are unaware of or have chosen to ignore. They provide the vital information that parents should be, but often aren't, providing to their children. And even in those families in which the parents do talk with their children about substance abuse, these programs have value because they offer the technical and scientific information the parents usually don't have, and often have discussions and presentations by former substance abusers who can tell children what substance abuse is really like. Parents concerned about the problem of substance abuse should support these programs and organizations, and should also encourage their children to participate in any that are offered by schools, churches, or other groups.

Drunk and Drugged Drivers

There is a deadly side effect of America's substance abuse problem that we all need to be more aware of. According to the FBI's *Crime in the United States*, robbers, rapists, arsonists, and burglars killed almost 1,300 people in 2000, a seemingly large and alarming number of innocent victims. This number, however, is actually small when compared with the more than 16,500 victims who were killed in 2000 by drunk and drugged drivers, a side effect of America's substance abuse problem that has now become so widespread and serious that many people no longer feel safe driving at certain hours—and with good cause. The National Highway Traffic Safety Administration estimates that from 50 to 60 percent of all fatal traffic crashes are alcohol- or drug-related, and that at certain times of the day and week, particularly weekend evenings, 10 percent or more of all drivers are under the influence of drugs or have blood alcohol concentrations of at least 0.10 percent (as little as three drinks for some people), the most lenient legal level nationally for the offense of driving while intoxicated (DWI). Adding to this, every year over 500,000 people are injured in alcohol-related accidents. The estimated yearly cost of DWI deaths, injuries, and property damage ranges up to $24 billion.

No one is safe from the effects of this continuing tragedy. The National Highway Traffic Safety Administration, for example, estimates that two out of every five Americans alive today will be involved in an alcohol-related accident, and therefore has recommended that the legal limit for DWI nationally be reduced to 0.08 percent. Presently, 20 states still use 0.10 percent blood alcohol content as their definition of DWI. In addition to alcohol, however, a long-term study done in New York City found that one out of every four drivers from ages 16 to 45 who were killed in an automobile accident had used cocaine within two days of the accident. No statistics were reported on any of the other victims of these drivers, on others injured or killed in these accidents, though there were certainly many, but the latter are frightening statistics indeed.

Compounding these statistics is the further finding that DWI is not a once-a-year or once-in-a-lifetime offense for many people. Roadside surveys of drivers in several states suggest that the average DWI offender may commit the crime up to 80 times a year, and many of them while their licenses are suspended because of prior DWI convictions. In addition, a survey a number of years ago by *Psychology Today* magazine found that 41 percent of its readers said they occasionally "drove while drunk." I believe that part of the reason for this was revealed in a study by the AAA Foundation for Traffic Safety. The study found that it was 50 minutes after the last drink before a person's blood alcohol level reached its most dangerous level. This is the reason, I'm certain, that many people who have just finished drinking believe they can safely drive, though, as the people in the *Psychology Today* survey probably did, only realize after driving for a while that they are actually drunk.

An example of the rampant recidivism of DWI offenders was made clear to me one night when I noticed a vehicle veering from one curb to the other as it traveled probably less than 10 Mph down a major thoroughfare. Drunk drivers often slow their speed drastically when they realize they've had too much to drink, hoping that a slow speed will compensate for their impaired ability, though it doesn't seem to stop them from being involved in accidents. Naturally, I turned on my emergency lights and siren and stopped the vehicle. The driver tried to get out of the car, but instead fell out onto the pavement. He looked up at me through bloodshot, watery eyes. "Come on, give me a break, Officer," he slurred. "I'm on probation for drunk driving." (He didn't get a break.)

National columnist William Raspberry, with whom I seldom share opinions, made a very valid point in one of his columns that while Americans usually think of drug abusers as criminals who need to go to prison, we tend to think of drunk drivers as people who have a problem that we ought, as a society, to help them overcome. This is true, I find, even though drunk drivers kill and injure many more people each year than do the worst drug abusers. This casual acceptance by society of one of America's most deadly crimes makes DWI a major concern to police departments everywhere.

To combat this growing national problem, many police departments have begun aggressive programs of roving patrols, driver checkpoints, and weekend roadblocks. But while there were almost 1.5 million DWI arrests nationally in 2000, which was 10.5 percent of all the arrests made and the second largest number of arrests for any single crime (after drugs), this was only a very small percentage of the actual number of DWI violations, probably less than 1 in 2,000, according to the International Association of Chiefs of Police.

Spotting Drunk and Drugged Drivers

While these statistics are indeed frightening and seem to give credence to the fear that many people have of driving at certain hours, particularly in the evening, sober drivers are not totally defenseless and at the mercy of DWI offenders. Whenever sober drivers are alert enough to spot DWI offenders before a collision, they often have the critical time needed to take evasive, and perhaps life-saving, action.

The major drawback to this defense, however, is that intoxicated drivers are not always that easy to spot. Even though a person may often be considered legally DWI (0.08 percent blood alcohol concentration in the majority of states), that person is not necessarily drunk and, depending on the person's drinking history, age, physical condition, and other factors, may appear to be sober, even to veteran police officers, who also occasionally have problems spotting DWI offenders. However, at a blood alcohol concentration of 0.08 percent, or while under the influence of drugs, a person's driving skills, particularly reaction time and judgment, are impaired seriously enough to be deadly.

Researchers for the federal government have attempted to solve the problem of spotting some DWI offenders by developing a guide for identifying DWI offenders through predictable changes in their driving behavior brought on by intoxication. The National Highway Traffic Safety Administration has compiled a pamphlet entitled *Guide for Detecting Drunk Drivers at Night*. This guide, developed from the results of more than 4,600 patrol stops of DWI offenders, describes for police officers certain specific driving behaviors that can establish to various levels of probability that a person is DWI.

Even though the information in this guide was originally collected and developed exclusively for use by police officers, it can also be used as a driving survival guide by average citizens to give them the few seconds necessary to take evasive action when they spot what appears to be a DWI offender. In addition, if while using this information they should find themselves in a vehicle driven by a DWI offender, they have the chance to insist, before a collision takes place, that the driver either let someone else drive or stop and let them out. According to the National Highway Traffic Safety Administration, 21 percent of the people killed in DWI crashes each year are sober passengers riding with a DWI driver.

The *Guide for Detecting Drunk Drivers at Night* describes 20 driving behaviors. It also gives the probability in percentages that drivers who exhibit these behaviors are DWI. It is important to remember, though, that not everyone exhibiting these behaviors is necessarily DWI. There could be legitimate reasons besides DWI for their behavior. But still, you should view any of these drivers with caution.

1. Turning with a Wide Radius—65 percent. According to the National Highway Traffic Safety Administration, vehicles that

turn at night with a wider than normal radius (for example, into the oncoming lane of traffic) have intoxicated drivers in 65 out of 100 cases, or, in other words, the probability that a person exhibiting this driving behavior is DWI is 65 percent.

2. Straddling Lane Marker—65 percent. One of the most dangerous effects of intoxication is an inability to properly focus the eyes. Intoxicated drivers often compensate for this by lining up the center of the car's hood on the lane marker and then using it as a guide.

3. Appearing to Be Drunk—60 percent. The appearance of drivers can be an important clue to their condition. Eye fixation, face held close to the windshield, slouching in the seat, and tightly gripping the steering wheel are all signs of intoxication.

4. Almost Striking a Fixed Object—60 percent. A driver who nearly strikes a fixed object or other vehicle at night has been found to be a DWI offender in 60 cases out of 100.

5. Weaving—60 percent. Because of the sensory impairment brought on by intoxication, a DWI offender will often weave from one side of the road to the other in a zigzag pattern. Many times this pattern will appear very regular as the driver overcompensates for each weave, thereby causing the vehicle to weave in the opposite direction.

6. Swerving—55 percent. Different from weaving, swerving is a sudden, abrupt change in the direction of travel, usually after a period of drifting across lanes into oncoming traffic or after running onto the road shoulder.

7. Driving on Other Than Designated Roadway—55 percent. Intoxicated drivers will often operate their vehicles on the interstate breakdown lane, on the road shoulder, off the road entirely, or will drive straight through a turn-only lane.

8. Speed Slower Than 10 mph Below Limit—50 percent. Many DWI offenders realize that their ability to drive has been affected, and attempt to compensate by reducing their speed, many times drastically. Unfortunately, this doesn't decrease the chances of them hitting your car or running you down if you're a pedestrian.

9. Stopping Without Cause in a Traffic Lane—50 percent. Intoxicated drivers cannot rapidly interpret information and make decisions. This will often cause abrupt stops at locations where it is unnecessary, such as in the middle of an intersection or while turning. Half of the vehicles doing this at night have been found to have an intoxicated driver.

10. Following Too Closely—50 percent. Because of the impaired vision brought on by intoxication, DWI offenders will often follow other vehicles too closely at night.

11. Drifting—50 percent. Some intoxicated drivers, while able to keep their vehicles moving in a straight line, do so at an angle to the roadway, thereby causing their vehicles to drift over into the other lanes.

12. Tires on Lane Marker—45 percent. Similar to the DWI offenders who straddle a lane marker for guidance, some intoxicated drivers will keep one set of tires on a lane marker.

13. Braking Erratically—45 percent. Because of the reduced reaction time and coordination experienced by intoxicated drivers, they often ride the brake or stop in an uneven or jerky manner.

14. Driving into Opposing/Crossing Traffic—45 percent. The act of driving at night into the opposing lane of traffic, driving the wrong way on a one-way street, or failing to yield the right-of-way to crossing traffic indicates a DWI offender in 45 out of 100 cases.

15. Signaling Wrong for Driving Actions—40 percent. This behavior includes failure to signal when turning, signaling in the opposite direction for the turn or lane change completed, or signaling constantly with no turn or lane change.

16. Slow Response to Traffic Signals—40 percent. These DWI offenders will either fail to slow when a traffic light turns yellow, instead braking abruptly, or will sit for an abnormally long time after the traffic light has turned green.

17. Stopping Position Inappropriate—35 percent. Stopping a vehicle at night on a crosswalk, in a prohibited zone, far

back from the intersection, or for a yellow flashing light indicates an intoxicated driver in 35 cases out of 100.

18. Turning Abruptly or Illegally—35 percent. DWI offenders will often turn abruptly with excessive speed, turn from the wrong lane, or make an illegal turn.

19. Accelerating or Decelerating Rapidly—30 percent. This behavior includes any unusually rapid acceleration, rapid deceleration, or alternately accelerating and decelerating rapidly.

20. Headlights Not On—30 percent. Intoxicated drivers often forget to turn their headlights on at night, especially in well-lit areas.

Adding to the information above, several studies have shown that intoxicated drivers will many times exhibit more than just one of the listed driving behaviors. When two or more behaviors are observed, the guide instructs police officers to add 10 percent to the largest value among the behaviors seen, and this total will then provide the probability in percentage that the driver is intoxicated and dangerous.

Evasive Actions

Using the information above, any drivers spotting what appears to be an intoxicated driver either approaching or following them should take immediate evasive action. This includes pulling off onto the road shoulder or into a gas station or parking lot. Also, when approaching an intersection, it is not wise to insist on the right-of-way from a suspected DWI offender. But the most important action sober drivers should take when spotting what appears to be a DWI offender is to immediately call the police and report the type of car, color, license plate if available, and direction of travel. Most citizens would not hesitate to turn in a vicious criminal, and drunk or drugged drivers are more dangerous and deadly than America's most vicious criminals.

Best Advice

The best information the police can offer concerning America's substance abuse problem is that the only really effective weapon against it is a public who is knowledgeable, concerned, and willing to fight.

10

CHILDREN IN TROUBLE WITH THE LAW

KIDS IN TROUBLE

Several years ago, the advice columnist Ann Landers did a survey asking her readers, "If you had it to do over again, would you have children?" A surprisingly large number of the respondents said no, they wouldn't have children if they had it to do over again. Many of her readers gave vivid examples of the frustrating problems their children had caused them, graphic examples of how their children had proven to be much more of a burden than a blessing.

During my over 30 years as a police officer I have seen many families in which the parents certainly belong to the group who wouldn't have children again, parents are constantly in trouble with the law, abuse drugs and alcohol, and basically give them almost daily grief. But while the results of the Ann Landers survey were certainly startling, they gave no indication of the actual number of problem children, and many people may wonder just how many children in our country actually do get into trouble with the law each year.

According to the FBI's *Crime in the United States*, in 2000 the police took almost 2.4 million children under the age of 18 into custody. The same report also shows that nearly 16 percent of all those arrested for crimes of violence and almost 32 percent of all those arrested for property crimes in the United States were under the age of 18. Confirming the percentages above, the National Crime Victimization Survey found that victims of violent crime perceived their attackers to be under 18 in almost 20 percent of the incidents, while in 1998 (the latest date with records available for juvenile judicial proceedings), juvenile courts in this country processed over 1,750,000 delinquency cases. The number of delinquency cases, incidentally, increased 44 percent in the 10 years preceding 1998, while during the same time, juvenile drug cases increased 148 percent and violent juvenile crime cases increased 88 percent. And, of course, these numbers do not include the many millions of children whom police officers took home rather than into custody (thereby bypassing the juvenile court system), an option officers can use if they believe the parents are responsible individuals who will take the appropriate action needed.

Types of Families

Even though police officers naturally deal more often with the families who have children constantly in trouble with the law, they also occasionally see the other kind of families, those with children who mind their parents, do well in school, and make their parents glad they had them. But, unfortunately, police officers usually see this type of family only when one of the children has, almost always for the first time, gotten into some kind of trouble with the law. But even under these circumstances the differences between the two types of families are startlingly apparent. While any child can get into trouble, police officers find that the type of family a child comes from and the type of upbringing he or she has had are usually what makes the difference as to whether or not the child will return to proper behavior. What is offered below is not meant to be an exhaustive review of child rearing advice, but to include things that police officers see so many times in the two types of families they run into that the differences between them are startling.

One of the major differences between the two types of families, those with well-behaved children and those with children constantly in trouble, is how discipline is handled. In those families with children constantly in trouble with the law, the discipline is usually at one of two extremes: either there is no discipline at all or it is extremely harsh and often not in keeping with the level of the child's misbehavior.

"One of the biggest problems we see in the homes of problem children," said Police Captain Michael Sherman, "is that the parents are either too permissive with their children or just the opposite and are too harsh."

Both of these extremes in discipline have the same result: they push children into further misbehavior. At one extreme of discipline the children either believe that their parents condone their behavior by ignoring it, or that they simply don't care, and the children quickly realize they won't get into trouble at home by continuing their bad behavior. At the other extreme, children are often pushed into further misbehavior as a rebellion against harsh, and many times uncalled-for, punishment for only minor infractions.

Also, in families with children constantly in trouble with the law, police officers usually find there is seldom any meaningful dialogue between parents and children, and just as seldom are there any joint family activities. The parents and children act less like a family and more like a group of people who all just happen to live under the same roof. In these families, the parents seldom know, or even seem to care, where their children are, whom they are with, or what they are doing. The parents in families with problem children are also usually so involved with their own lives that their children are often looked upon as inconveniences that the parents only very rarely allow to interfere with their jobs or leisure activities. And in some cases, the parent or parents are simply struggling so hard to make ends meet that they just don't have time between jobs for their children. Lastly, because of the lack of family activities, the boredom in these homes is often extreme. And it is many times this boredom that causes children to get into trouble, usually out of a desire to do anything to spark some excitement.

"A lot of the kids we see don't have any family activities," said Detective Jan Cotton, a police officer who has worked for many years with problem children. "Because of this they are bored and often fall into the trap of doing something bad just to break the monotony."

In families with well-behaved children, however, the parents have, from the beginning, set down rules and guidelines for their children, and know that discipline is needed, but that it doesn't have to be harsh and brutal. They understand that it isn't the severity of punishment that makes it work, but the certainty of it. Misconduct in these families is never overlooked or ignored, and the parents always take corrective action immediately upon seeing it. In addition, the parents of law-abiding children always know where their children are, whom they are with, and what they are doing. Parents in these families also understand the value of love and positive reinforcement. They praise their children for good behavior and are not reluctant to show affection.

This showing of affection, however, doesn't mean giving children anything they ask for. Parents of these children know when to say no, and also realize the value of making their children earn things rather than simply having everything given to them. I recall, for example, an incident in which, as a patrol officer, I assisted a juvenile detective serving an arrest warrant on a juvenile for possession of stolen property. After the detective had taken their son away, along with a truckload of stolen items, the parents seemed genuinely stunned and showed me the car, clothing, stereo, and other things they had bought for their son, then assured me that they gave him money whenever he asked for it. "Why would he want stolen property?" they asked. They simply couldn't understand it. A few questions, though, about their son's friends, his activities, and where he went in the evenings showed me that the parents and son had not had any meaningful dialogue or interaction in years.

Additionally, in families with well-behaved children, self-discipline is taught by giving all members duties to carry out, and by teaching children to value individual responsibility. Also, the parents always make time for their children to talk with them about themselves and their problems, to talk about setting and reaching goals, or just simply to talk. They also make time to do things with their children, to involve themselves and their children in school and community activities, to reinforce the feeling of family and unity. But most important, in families with law-abiding children the parents are good role models who set the example for their children.

For those who think that being a good parent seems like a lot of hard work and trouble, they are right. But, as a police officer who has seen hundreds of families with problem children, I can assure them that raising law-abiding children is not nearly the trouble that raising problem children can be, because for the parents of problem children the trouble never stops. Quite often, problem children grow up to become problem adults who expect their parents to continue supporting them, to continue bailing them out of trouble and out of jail, and to continue taking care of them as if they were still children.

As an example of this, a study in Chicago showed that 34 percent of boys sent to the local juvenile court later went to jail or prison as adults, while in New York City 78 percent of those with lengthy juvenile records, it was found, were arrested as adults, and more than a third became serious career criminals. As another example, I had a case once in which I caught a 29-year-old burglar inside a closed Shell service station helping himself to the supplies and equipment. After arresting him and taking him down to the lockup, I hung around a bit talking to one of the jail officers. The burglary suspect was brought down to the telephone to make his call, and I could overhear him talking to his mother, crying that if she would help him just this one more time, he would never get into trouble again. Later, when his case came up for trial, I met his mother, who told me she had been bailing her son out of trouble ever since he was 12. She told me she had spent untold thousands of dollars on attorneys, court fines, and bailbondsmen. Finally, her son, besides being convicted of the burglary, was convicted of being a habitual criminal and given a lengthy additional, and consecutive, prison term (an additional 30 years in Indiana) since he had been arrested over a hundred times and convicted of several felonies.

What to Do When Children Get into Trouble with the Law

Of course, even in families with well-behaved children, even in families where the parents have done everything parents should do, occasionally circumstances or events will cause a previously law-abiding child to get into trouble with the law. Police officers, however, have witnessed enough of these cases to develop certain common strategies for bringing children back to proper behavior.

Parents in families with law-abiding children, for example, never simply brush off a serious infraction and pretend it isn't important. They instead treat any such offense as a matter of concern, as something the child should not have done, but as something he or she can learn from. These parents sit down with their children and have a serious talk. The children are made aware that the parents don't approve of whatever the offense was, and that they are expected to never do that sort of thing again.

But one of the most crucial things that parents of these children do is try to find the cause for the problem, and then, if possible, correct it. Just as important, they also decide on some type of punishment for the offense, a punishment that fits the seriousness of the misbehavior. But once the punishment is done and the children recognize their mistake, the matter is dropped. The children are not treated differently because of one mistake, and are not constantly told how they have disappointed everyone.

And yet, while these strategies and actions are certainly in the best interests of both parents and children, far too often police officers see parents who think they are doing the right thing

Extent of Juvenile Crime

Many people believe that juveniles are responsible for a large percentage of the crime in their neighborhood. But is this true? Just how much crime are juveniles really responsible for?

Actually, the truth is that juveniles are responsible for quite a lot of crime. While making up only about 11 percent of the population, juveniles aged 10 through 17 are responsible for almost 28 percent of the serious crime in the United States. This, however, is only an overall average, and to find the extent of juvenile involvement in specific types of crimes the national arrest figures can be used as a guide. These figures indicate juveniles aged 10 through 17 are responsible for:

9 percent of murders

14 percent of aggravated assaults

16 percent of rapes

25 percent of robberies

31 percent of larcenies

32 percent of burglaries

47 percent of arsons

34 percent of vehicle thefts

instead do what is probably one of the worst things they can do. Far too many parents immediately shield their children, and themselves, through denial, insisting that their children wouldn't do whatever it is they have been accused of doing, and maintaining that the police or complainants are just picking on them for no reason. I have seen parents do this over and over until the children finally do something so serious their behavior can no longer be denied, and then the parents can't seem to understand how things have deteriorated so much. Some parents though, police officers find, never stop shielding their children. They get them out of the juvenile hall time after time, and then, once they become adults, bail them out of jail time after time, always maintaining that their children are just being picked on, and never seeing the damage they themselves have done by preventing their children from paying the consequences for their actions.

"Don't overprotect your children," advises police officer Shirley Purvitis, who has spent many years working with children. "But also don't rush in with punishment until you know all the facts."

The experiences most police officers have with children in trouble with the law demonstrate that any previously well-behaved child can almost always be brought back to proper behavior, but also that it is nearly impossible to change the behavior of a child who has gotten into trouble with the law because of a lifetime of parental neglect. I'm not saying that there has never been a case in which some young person was turned around after a lifetime of parental neglect, only that these cases have been few.

Children Who Care for Themselves

A special concern of parents, especially as more and more families become two-income families, is children who must care for themselves. It is estimated that every day, 12 million children between the ages of 5 and 13 are left to take care of themselves for at least several hours. And this should be a concern to parents because it has been found that these children are three times more likely than other children to engage in delinquent behavior.

Boredom and a sense of isolation, research shows, are the greatest instigators of delinquency for these children. The best advice available is to make sure children's time is taken up by both household tasks and activities they find interesting. Also, having a neighbor or friend either looking in on or telephoning children taking care of themselves is an excellent idea. And for their own safety, parents should review the following safety rules concerning any youngsters left on their own for any length of time:

- Instruct them never to open the door to strangers.
- Also, instruct them never to enter the home if the door is a jar or a window is broken.
- Make sure they know escape routes out of the house in case of fire or other emergency, and where to go in such an emergency.
- Make certain they know how to use the telephone, and whom to call in case of an emergency.
- If your children think someone is following them home, there should be some safe place they know to go instead of into the house, where they could be trapped.
- If someone calls on the telephone, they should know never to tell anyone they are alone.
- Your children should check in with you or someone else immediately upon getting home.

Gangs

Just the word *gang* terrifies many adults. They envision youths involved in murders, robberies, rapes, and drugs. And unfortunately, much of this fear is based on fact.

While becoming a serious national concern in only the last few decades, gangs have actually been a part of America for over 100 years. But in the past 20 years they have become more organized and more violent. Every day there is another news story about some heinous crime committed by a gang, and in some inner-city areas simply trespassing on a gang's turf can result in an assault or even a murder. A number of gangs in the last decade have even taken over control of drug trafficking on their turf. And more disturbing, a new trend with gangs is to recruit children only 8, 9, or 10 years old to work as lookouts or to sell drugs for them, knowing that if these children are caught, nothing really serious will be done to them. Confirming the danger of belonging to a gang, the 589 convicts interviewed for *The Figgie Report* felt that belonging to a gang was a leading cause for crime, ranking only behind drugs (including alcohol) and unemployment.

Membership in a gang should also concern parents because it will often initiate children into the world of crime. In *The Figgie Report* more than half of the convicts said they were under the age of 14 when they began their criminal careers and 9 percent said they were less than 10. The report also found that criminals who began their careers at an early age often became perpetrators of a high volume of crimes. In addition, it has been found in a number of other studies that the earlier criminals start their careers, the more difficult it is to rehabilitate them.

Frank Radke, commanding officer of the Gang Crimes Section of the Chicago Police Department, had the following gloomy news at a conference on gang crime: "Today we are arresting more gang members than ever before; we are getting more convictions than ever before; and we are getting longer sentences than ever before; but ironically, we have more gangs than ever before."

The increase in gang membership can be attributed to several causes. With gangs becoming involved in drug trafficking there is a large amount of money to be made, and this attracts many new members. Also, gangs give kids with no future some status in the neighborhood, and in addition give inner-city kids protection from other gangs. In a February 2002 report, The U.S. Department of Justice estimated that more than 24,500 gangs are active in the United States.

How does a parent go about keeping a child from joining a gang?

In affluent, or even middle-class, neighborhoods, it is fairly easy because the opportunities available there to kids can offer them many more activities now and than gangs can. But in poorer neighborhoods, where the kids have nothing now and even less to look forward to, the lure of big money (at least compared with what they could make legitimately) and status is hard to compete against. I'm not really sure that in these neighborhoods there is a viable alternative as attractive, and so the answer lies in correcting the social conditions that perpetuate the problems in these neighborhoods. I must admit that if I were a youth in one of these neighborhoods, and had little education, inadequate verbal skills, and no hope for a really bright future, I might be tempted to join a gang. But still, parents should do their best to inculcate a sense of values and personal responsibility in their children. It may be hard for a child to make his or her way in a war zone, but with the help of supportive parents who are good role models it is at least possible. Others have done it.

The solution to the gang problem, like the ultimate solution to America's drug problem, is beyond the control of the police. We can only patrol bad neighborhoods, keep the peace as much as possible, and arrest criminals. We can't change the condition of neighborhoods or make the feelings of hopelessness disappear. This will take changes in society that require curing causes rather than fighting symptoms.

Best Advice

The best information the police have about keeping children from getting into trouble with the law is that while raising well-behaved and law-abiding children may be a lot of hard work and trouble, it is not nearly the trouble that raising problem children can be.

11

MISSING PERSONS

WAITING PERIODS AND PRIORITIES

Until the early 1980s the only people who knew the truth about missing person investigations, the truth that there was a serious problem in the way American police departments handled missing person investigations, were those who had reported a missing person. The truth was that at that time, many American police departments did very little when citizens reported a runaway or missing person to them. They did very little because they knew from experience that 80 to 90 percent of these missing persons, particularly juvenile runaways, returned home on their own within a day or two. Yet, for years experts have estimated that over a million runaways live on the street. In 2001, that estimate reached 1.3 million.

Most police departments also used the fact that most runaways and missing persons returned on their own to justify instituting a 24-hour waiting period before they would even take a missing person report: 24 worrisome, heart-wrenching hours for the parents or spouse of a loved one who had suddenly, and quite often unexpectedly, become a missing person. The parents or spouses were forced to worry for 24 hours that their loved one might be injured or ill, or that a runaway or missing child could fall victim to drugs, crime, sexual exploitation, child pornography, child prostitution, or death. These latter fears, incidentally, are not baseless. Research by the Family Research Laboratory at the University of New Hampshire found that 11 to 23 percent of all runaways fall

211

prey to prostitution, and that 25 percent of these will take part in pornographic productions.

The 24-hour waiting period instituted by most police departments, however, saved tremendous amounts of time and work for these departments, allowing them to disregard the 80 to 90 percent of missing persons who actually did return home on their own, but was quite often incomprehensible to the parents or spouses of the other 10 to 20 percent. It was incomprehensible to the parents of a child who had never been a runaway or discipline problem, or to the spouse of someone who had never given any indication of being unhappy and who had suddenly become a missing person.

The parents of missing children, often stunned when they found themselves facing this waiting period, many times found, however, that after the 24 hours they faced another, even larger, roadblock because of something else that had become an accepted fact by many American police departments, something often used as justification for doing very little about the problem of runaways. This was the belief that the million or so runaway children who didn't return on their own and were living on the street were just too many to do anything about. Beginning in the 1960s and continuing for many years, so many teenagers, it seemed, were running away to New York, to California, or to Florida that no police department could handle the volume of runaway cases.

As to the problem of finding missing adults, many police departments reasoned that, after all, they were adults and most had left on their own and really didn't want to be found anyway, so there was no real justification for expending large amounts of time and energy searching for them either. Because of these facts, for a number of years when a missing person was reported to many police departments, the report was taken, filed away, and that was it. The missing person case in these departments remained open, but no officer was assigned to it and no one was responsible for its solution. In many cities in America, only with missing preschool-age children, or in obvious cases of foul play,

Missing Children Support Groups

If the police are unsuccessful in locating a missing child, parents should consider contacting one of the dozens of missing children support groups, many of which have been formed by individuals whose own children disappeared. These groups can be beneficial not only because of the emotional support they offer, but also because they can advise parents of resources beyond the police that are available to assist them, resources the average citizen may be unaware of. Those wishing to learn the name of a group in their area should call their local victims advocate group, their local police department, or contact:

National Center for Missing & Exploited Children
Charles B. Wang International Children's Building
699 Prince Street
Alexandria, VA 22314-3175
1-800-843-5678
FAX 703-274-2200
www.missingkids.com

In addition to contacting one of these support groups, parents of missing children should leave a message for their child on the National Runaway Switchboard and check to see if their child has left a message for them. The telephone number of the National Runaway Switchboard is:

1-800-621-4000

was an investigation and search conducted, and in extreme cases fliers were printed up and sent to other police departments.

Parents and spouses with no previous experience in dealing with missing persons were quite often shocked by many police departments' priorities when they discovered that if they reported their automobile stolen or their house burglarized, the police department would immediately send a uniformed officer to the scene to take a report, assign a detective to the case, and then expend a considerable amount of time and effort attempting to locate the missing property. Yet, if a child, spouse, or other person was missing, a report would be taken, but only after 24 hours, and that was the extent of the police department's involvement in the case. Because of this situation, parents or spouses who didn't want to have to simply wait and hope that the missing loved one returned home on his or her own were forced to hire private investigators or to go through one of the private organizations that deal with missing persons. These private investigators and organizations, however, didn't, and still don't, have the resources or investigative ability of the police. They don't have access to the vast, interconnected police computer system or to the high-tech forensic laboratories, and often they don't have the experience that comes from years of police work. Therefore, they many times have no success in finding the missing person.

Runaway Statistics

The National Center for Juvenile Justice performed an analysis of more than 40,000 records in the National Juvenile Court Data Archive. They found that:

- Juvenile courts handle three runaway cases for every 1,000 children aged 10 to 17 in their jurisdiction.
- Girls are more likely than boys to be runaways.
- The majority of juvenile runaways are age 14 to 16.
- More children run away in medium-sized population areas than in large or small population areas.
- Recent statistics show that one in seven children aged 10 to 18 will run away.

But why do most children run away to begin with? Juvenile authorities find the most common reasons are:

- To escape some conflict at home.
- Fear of punishment over some misbehavior.
- Anger over actual punishment for some misbehavior.
- Changes in the family structure (parents divorcing, a parent remarrying, a new child, etc.).
- Feeling unloved or unwanted by family and friends.
- To escape sexual or physical abuse.

A Success Story

Until the early 1980s the benign neglect approach was probably the most common method used by American police departments for handling the missing person problem. But because of the publicity generated by the success of one police department in finding missing persons and runaways, many of these long-held attitudes finally began to change.

In the September 1983 issue of *The Elks Magazine,* an article about the Missing Person Unit of the Indianapolis Police Department. This article told how the unit had taken more than 1,500 reports of missing children in 1982, and how as of December 31, 1982, every single one of these children had been located and accounted for. Even more remarkable, the unit had also found all but 15 of the over 500 adults reported as missing in 1982, individuals who are much more difficult to locate because of their ability to travel and move about without arousing the suspicion that young people do. The story was soon picked up by other publications, and in the April 1984 issue of *Reader's Digest* another article appeared about the success of the Indianapolis Police Department's Missing Persons Unit, an article that reached millions of readers worldwide.

Because of the publicity generated by these articles many of the attitudes about finding missing persons finally began to change. The widespread publicity about the Indianapolis Police Department's success made it extremely difficult for police departments elsewhere to continue holding to their claim that nothing could be done about the problem of missing persons.

How the Police Find a Missing Person

But what exactly does the Indianapolis Police Department do to find a missing person? How were they able for many years to maintain a 98 to 99 percent success rate in finding missing persons?

"A large part of the reason for the success of our Missing Persons Unit is that it is not just a records-keeping unit," said former Indianapolis chief of police Paul Annee, who early in his career was assigned to the Missing Persons Unit. "Ours is an investigative unit that treats each missing person case as a case to be solved."

In addition to a central unit, the Indianapolis Police Department has full-time veteran detectives assigned to missing person investigations in each district (precinct), investigators who don't simply take reports and then file them away, but who spend their workday actually out looking for missing persons, running down leads, talking to neighbors, and checking teenage hangouts. They treat each case as seriously as any that can be reported to the police department, and follow the same procedures as with any other police investigation. They talk to family and friends. They canvass the neighborhood for anyone who might have seen something or know something about the disappearance. They attempt to gather facts from any physical evidence, such as notes, items left behind, etc. They regularly check the bus depot and other transportation centers. Basically, the detectives give each case the same energy they would give a robbery or burglary.

The ability of the Indianapolis Police Department to find large numbers of both missing persons and runaway children did not come about through some new advance in technology or through a breakthrough in police technique, but simply through old-fashioned police work, which involves a lot of knocking on doors, talking to people, and checking out leads. According to retired sergeant Joe St. John, former head of the Missing Persons Unit, the secret of Indianapolis's success can be stated very simply: "We find so many missing people because we take the reports immediately and then go right out looking for every single one of them. We never give up. We follow every lead, talk to every person who might have information, and just simply keep looking until we find them."

The Indianapolis Police Department also cooperates with other police agencies and with local, state, and national organizations that deal with missing persons, both providing them with information and requesting it in turn. As an outgrowth of a program started by the Indianapolis Police Department in the early 1980s, a program designed to form a central repository for information about missing children in central Indiana, the Indiana Missing Children Clearinghouse was born. Like clearinghouses now in many other states, this agency collects information on runaway and missing children from police departments throughout the state and then puts the information (which includes a picture, description, date of birth, area last seen in, etc.) into a monthly publication that is sent to police departments both inside and outside of the state, to public and private missing persons clearinghouses, and to any organization that requests copies.

But undoubtedly one of the most crucial things that the Indianapolis Police Department does differently from many other police departments is that it doesn't require a waiting period before taking reports. Reports are taken whenever a person calls, even if only minutes after noticing the loved one is missing, and are taken 24 hours a day. By taking missing persons reports without a waiting period, the Indianapolis Police Department can, within minutes of receiving the report, put the information out over the police radio. Time, it has been demonstrated on many occasions, can be critical to the success of finding missing persons. I recall, for example, a case in which I was called to take a missing person report on a 14-year-old girl. Within 30 minutes of putting her description out on the police radio two officers found her at the Greyhound Bus Station talking to one of the local pimps, who was attempting to recruit her.

"Our philosophy is to try to find runaways and missing persons before something can happen to them," said Sergeant St. John. "We try to find them while the trail is still warm. If people want to call us five minutes after they realize someone is missing, we'll take the report and start looking."

Sergeant St. John goes on to say that experience has shown that the sooner missing persons or runaways are reported, the easier it is for the police to find them, and in many cases quick reporting can save considerable work. Most runaways, for example, tend to stay, at least for a while, with someone they know, and whom their parents or friends also know. But if the missing person report is delayed a day or two, it gives runaways time to find new friends whom no one else knows about, and only makes locating them just that much more difficult.

Yet, while beginning a search immediately for runaway and missing children is important, Sergeant St. John and other missing person experts warn that it is just as important to begin searching immediately for missing elderly people. Quite often, elderly people who live with their children or in nursing homes wander away when no one is watching, and can become confused. It is imperative that there be no delay in reporting missing elderly people since they can come to harm just as easily as juveniles can.

But just as important as reporting a missing person right away is having the information available that the police will need when taking the report, such as:

- A complete description, including clothing the person was last known to be wearing
- A recent photograph
- Social Security number and date of birth
- Known friends and associates
- Locations the person is known to visit
- Automobile and license number, if applicable
- Any other information that may be helpful

Independent Actions

Even though the considerable publicity generated by the success of the Indianapolis Police Department has persuaded many other police departments to adopt their methods, many have still not done so. Many still have waiting periods and many still give missing person investigations low priority. For citizens in these communities, experts in the field of missing person investigation have some tips for independent actions that will increase the chances of a missing loved one being found:

1. The most important thing to remember is that the first 24 to 48 hours are crucial in a missing person investigation, particularly a missing or runaway child. It is during this time that the chances are best for finding the missing person. Therefore, don't delay taking actions of your own.

2. Upon discovering that a loved one is missing, maintain your composure and try to think clearly about where the person might have gone. Missing persons are not really missing, they're just not where they are supposed to be. Know who the loved one's friends are. Talk to them about where the person might be. If the missing person is a child, check with teachers about who the child's friends are at school and where they think the child might be. Check with neighbors. Have they seen the person or know where he or she might be?

3. Check your child's room and school locker. Are there letters or maps that might help decide where he or she has gone? What possessions are missing? Do these give a clue? Check recent telephone bills for long distance calls possibly made by the child. Check your child's computer, particularly e-mail and any chat rooms he or she might have visited.

4. To assist in determining where the person might have gone, be aware of, in addition to the loved one's friends, all the places the loved one is known to visit.

5. Because parents are often flustered when a child suddenly turns up missing, it is advisable to keep an identification file on

each child. The file should contain such things as a recent color photograph (in an ordinary pose and not in a Halloween costume, during a ballet exhibition, etc.), nicknames, birthmarks, weight, height, hair color, eye color, any medical conditions or disabilities, and a copy of the child's fingerprints and dental records. The National Center for Missing and Exploited Children reports that in half of its cases all they receive is a very general description, which, of course, only adds to the difficulty of finding missing children. However, with an in-depth description, and particularly with a recent, good-quality photograph, they report that the chances of finding a missing child increase greatly.

6. Try to notice and remember what your loved ones, particularly young children and the elderly, wear each day. Many people may not recall a face but will remember clothing. Also, for small children, sew their name and address into their clothing.

7. Know your child's school bus number and route in case he or she got off at the wrong stop. We had a case here in Indianapolis where a child didn't get off at the wrong stop, but fell asleep in the back of the bus and was overlooked by the driver when he parked the bus for the night. Knowing the bus number is vital in a case like this.

8. Even if the local police department has a waiting period before taking a missing person report, insist that they immediately enter a missing child's information on the FBI's NCIC computer network, a system that every police department in the United States has access to. There is no waiting period required for this, and if the local police don't want to do it, contact the nearest FBI field office. The Missing Children Act of 1982 mandates that they enter the information for you.

9. If no immediate success is realized, parents or spouses of missing person should consider having posters printed and distributed, and should also consider contacting one of the many private missing person organizations. Although these organizations may not have the resources or expertise of the police, no opportunity for finding a missing loved one should be overlooked. The National Center for Missing and Exploited Children

(1-800-843-5678) is a national clearinghouse for information on missing and exploited children.

10. The Office of Juvenile Justice and Delinquency Prevention has put together a 93-page book entitled *When Your Child Is Missing: A Family Survival Guide*, publication NCJ 170022. This book can be an invaluable resource for parents of missing children. It is available free and can be obtained at:

http://www.ncjrs.org/jjmec.htm#170022

Or by writing or calling:

Juvenile Justice Clearinghouse
PO Box 6000
Rockville, MD 20849-6000
1-800-638-8736

In addition to the tips above, there is another thing one can do to make finding missing persons easier. A number of police departments and missing person organizations sponsor finger-printing of young children. As noted above, fingerprints should be placed in your child's identification file. Then, if your child should turn up somewhere far away, positive identification by the police agency finding him or her is possible. This has proven many times to be a valuable precaution, and would also be an advisable precaution for elderly persons in nursing homes or under home care. In addition, dental records have been shown many times to be important in identifying a missing person. Obtain a copy from the family dentist and place it in your child's identification file.

Parental Kidnapping

A number of studies have suggested that many of the children listed each year as missing or runaways are actually not, but instead are the victims of parental kidnapping (the unlawful taking of a child by a noncustodial parent). A recent study suggested that 49 percent of abducted children were not abducted by strangers but by a family member, 43 percent of these family members being female and 80 percent being one of the parents. In a December 2001 report, the U.S. Department of Justice states that approximately 350,000 children are abducted each year by family members. However, less than 10 percent of these cases are reported to the police. Unfortunately for the child, though, the police find that in many cases the noncustodial parent doesn't really want the child as much as he or she wants to hurt the other parent, and as a consequence children abducted by their noncustodial parent can become the victims of neglect and abuse, making parental kidnapping an even more serious offense.

The case of a child missing through parental kidnapping, however, should be handled in the same way as a child missing for any other reason. The custodial parent should immediately contact the police and, after making a report, insist that the child's information be put onto the FBI's NCIC computer network. For their report the police will need the same information as for a runaway or missing person report, such as a description, when and where last seen, a recent photograph, etc. But in addition, the police will need as much information as possible about the noncustodial parent, such as address, place of employment, car and license number, addresses of family and friends, etc.

In parental kidnappings, however, besides notifying the police it is also advisable to retain an attorney (either privately hired or through the local legal services office). An attorney can be very helpful in obtaining child custody orders and in petitioning courts for a child's return in the event the child is located in another state or jurisdiction. In addition, an attorney acquainted with child custody disputes can assist in overseeing the law enforcement efforts. For example, if criminal charges are filed (parental kidnapping is a crime in all 50 states) and the noncustodial parent flees the state, an attorney can see that a federal warrant for "unlawful flight to avoid prosecution" is obtained, and the FBI can then join in the search for the child and his or her abductor.

There are several extremely important things that custodial parents can do to prevent a parental kidnapping, or at least increase the chances of a quick recovery in the event of a parental kidnapping:

- Children should be taught how to dial their home telephone number from anywhere.
- Schools, day-care centers, baby-sitters, and so on should be made aware of custody orders and any dangers of parental kidnapping. Insist that they never release a child to anyone without notifying you.
- An up-to-date list should be kept on the noncustodial parent, including address, telephone number, description, Social Security number, place of employment, car type, license number, and any information available on family and friends.
- Any threats of abduction should be reported to the police. Often, a noncustodial parent may not know that such an action is a crime, and a call or visit from the police can many times be helpful.
- Once a child kidnapped by a noncustodial parent has been reported to the police, ask the officer in charge of the investigation to use the Federal Parent Locator Service (FPLS) to search for the abductor. The FPLS is operated by the U.S. Department of Health and Human Services and is authorized by the Parental Kidnapping Prevention Act of 1990 for use in tracing a parental-kidnapping suspect.

For those concerned about a possible parental abduction of a child, the National Center for Missing and Exploited Children (see sidebar for address and telephone number) has prepared an excellent 128-page book entitled *Family Abduction*. I heartily recommend it.

Those who, after reporting a parental abduction, find themselves running into bureaucratic opposition or a lack of interest by the police can still do considerable investigative work on their own. Most of the procedures below can be done legally through an attorney:

- Obtain the telephone records of the abducting parent. A pattern of calls can show a destination.
- Check into the abducting parent's bank records. A transfer of funds will show a possible new home.
- Check credit card records, which can show the route of an abducting parent.
- Has the abducting parent registered a change of address at the post office?
- Have the abducted child's school records been transferred?
- If you believe your child is in a community, check with the local school system for new admittances. The child's date of birth can offset any new names that are given by an abducting parent.
- A civil suit against family members who helped in the abduction can often force their cooperation.
- If the arrest of an abducting parent is imminent, the custodial parent should be in the community so the child will suffer as little trauma as possible. Have your attorney establish your right to the child with the local authorities.
- Some parents who are anxious about the welfare of an abducted child, and who want to bypass the lengthy legal requirements necessary to have a parentally abducted child returned, will occasionally hire people to do a "snatch back." Be warned, however, that this can be very traumatic to the child and can also possibly jeopardize the legal standing of the custodial parent. Also, beware that the field of child finders is filled with rip-off artists who will take your money and deliver nothing.

Stranger Abduction

While it can be difficult enough dealing with the situation in which a child has run away from home or has been abducted by

International Parental Abduction

Although far rarer than ordinary parental abductions, in which the noncustodial parent takes a child to another community or state, international child abduction is much more serious because the perpetrator is usually outside the jurisdiction of American agencies. But even worse, the parent trying to have the child returned must depend on the cooperation and goodwill of a foreign government, which may or may not be a signer of the Hague Convention (a treaty meant to ensure the return of illegally abducted children). And while many countries have signed the treaty, there are many exceptions to its enforcement. Because of this, if your spouse should want to take your child to a foreign country, particularly if it is the spouse's country of origin, you should consider the following:

- How will a return to his or her roots affect the spouse?
- What are the laws of the country? Some countries require children to have their father's permission and women their husband's permission to travel.
- Is the country a signer of the Hague Convention? For a list of the countries that have signed the Hague Convention, go to http://travel.state.gov/hague_list.html.
- If your marriage is in trouble, do you have a decree giving you sole custody of the child? If you don't, many countries consider both parents to have legal custody.
- If you fear a child may be taken out of the country, contact the U.S. Department of State's Office of Children's Issues at 202-736-7000 to take advantage of the "Child Passport Issuance Alert Program," which will notify you in the event someone attempts to obtain a passport for your child. *(continued)*

International Parental Abduction (continued)

The U.S. Department of State, Bureau of Consular Affairs, (202) 647-4000, has a lengthy booklet explaining the procedures needed to stop an international child abduction, and how to have an abducted child returned from a foreign country. Ask for their publication 10862, "International Parental Child Abduction."

---

a family member, it is a much more terrifying experience to know that your child has been abducted by a stranger. While research shows that the vast majority of child abductions are committed by acquaintances or family members, usually a spouse or ex-spouse, abductions by strangers do occur and often have tragic consequences. One only has to recall the case of Adam Walsh, a child abducted and then beheaded. There was also a case recently in which a woman walked into Cook County (Illinois) Memorial Hospital and walked out with someone else's newborn infant. Although the baby was rescued by the police unharmed several days later, you can only imagine the terror the new mother must have suffered during the days of uncertainty.

The U.S. Department of Justice, in a June 2000 report, stated that their research shows that strangers commit 24 percent of all kidnappings of juveniles. While this report also said that only 2 percent of all juvenile kidnappings result in major injury or death, this is still a sizable amount when one considers the total number of kidnappings every year. And while some authorities may contend that this last figure is small in comparison with the yearly overall crime figures, I don't think that any number of children murdered, injured, or kidnapped for lengthy periods of time (often for sexual abuse purposes) is a small number. I'm sure every parent of a kidnapped child agrees. One can only imagine the pain suffered by parents like those of Polly Klass, and how they must grieve for their daughter, who was abducted by a stranger from their home in Petaluma, California, and murdered.

To prevent the possibility of a stranger abduction, there are a number of precautions parents can take:

- Instruct small children never to go anywhere with strangers unless it has been okayed by a parent or teacher, even if the strangers say that a parent has sent them or that a parent is ill or hurt. Have a code word so that your child will know you have really sent the stranger.
- Instruct small children never to help strangers, even if they appear to be in trouble. Instead, instruct the children to contact an adult they know to help the stranger. Serial rapist and murderer Ted Bundy used this ploy to abduct women, and it can only be assumed that someone would use it on children.
- If a stranger offers them candy, gifts, or the chance to walk with the stranger's adorable puppy, children should be instructed to ask a parent before accepting.
- Children should be encouraged to ride bicycles only with friends, never alone.
- Pay full attention if your child wants to tell you about a stranger who has acted oddly.

Best Advice

To ensure the safe return of missing persons, the best advice the police can offer is never to assume that missing persons will return on their own if enough time passes. The sooner a search begins for a missing person, the better the chances are of finding him or her.

12

THE POLICE
AND MOTOR VEHICLES

TRAFFIC TICKETS

Every year in our country, police officers issue millions of traffic tickets, and probably no common experience produces more negative feelings between the police and the public than the issuance of a traffic ticket. There are undoubtedly worse police encounters for a citizen, such as being arrested, but none more common than a traffic ticket. Citizens don't like receiving them and most police officers don't like giving them.

Many people may doubt the truth of the second part of the statement above since they have almost certainly seen hundreds of drivers they would have loved to give tickets to if they could. But police officers, driving in marked police cars, don't see nearly as many flagrant violations as private citizens do, and when a person can issue a ticket whenever he or she wishes, the desire to do so wears off fairly quickly. The truth is that during the years I served as a street uniformed sergeant and lieutenant, I had to constantly counsel my officers about the need to write a few tickets every month. While in Indianapolis (though I can't speak for other cities) there is no quota for traffic citations, tickets have to be written in certain areas to keep speeding, the disregard of traffic signals, and other violations under control. In addition, a certain, though very small, portion of most jurisdictions' income (including that of Indianapolis) stems from traffic violation fines.

Several years ago, when I worked as a street captain, I received a report each month that contained information on the productivity of the officers under my command, which averaged about 120 officers, and included how many traffic tickets each officer had written the previous month. On the average, 40 percent of these officers didn't write a single ticket, and another 20 percent wrote only one or two. This was always distressing to me since writing traffic tickets is part of these officers' duties, and I would have to constantly counsel my lieutenants and sergeants about the necessity of more closely monitoring their officers' activities.

And so, with the exception of uniformed traffic officers (motorcycle or radar officers), whose sole job it is to issue traffic tickets, most uniformed officers consider traffic tickets simply more tedious paperwork. Yet it is often the actions of stopped motorists themselves (as I will soon explain) that force an officer to take the time to issue a traffic ticket, even if originally he or she had only a warning in mind.

Be forewarned, however, that there are certain violations officers will almost always write a ticket for, even though they may not have written a single ticket during the entire preceding month. It's difficult to tell you what these violations are because they depend on the officers' experiences. I, for example, always wrote tickets when I saw a driver who refused to give the right-of-way to an emergency vehicle. I did this because I had experienced this violation a number of times when I was on an emergency run, but of course couldn't stop and write a ticket right then. An officer I knew who had once been a bus driver always wrote tickets for anyone parking in a bus zone, while another officer who had seen several children killed always wrote a ticket whenever he saw anyone pass a stopped school bus.

There are two times, however, when all police officers avoid writing traffic tickets, even for those individual sore spots talked about above. The probability, for example, of being stopped and issued a traffic ticket for a regular (not outrageous) traffic violation runs inversely proportional to the severity of the weather. The more severe or nasty the weather, the less likely it is that an officer will want to get out of his or her car to issue a traffic ticket. In addition, the 15 to 30 minutes before the three roll calls, which traditionally occur sometime between 5:00 and 8:00 A.M., 1:00 and 4:00 P.M., and 9:00 P.M. and midnight, when officers are heading back to the station to turn their duties over to the next shift, are a time of low probability for traffic tickets. These officers want to go home, not stay late and write a ticket.

"The brass is always on us to write some more tickets," said a uniformed district officer, "and if I see a violation and I'm not swamped I'll usually write one. But when it's time for me to go home you'd have to do something pretty bad to get me to stop you."

But suppose on a bright, sunny day, not close to roll call time, you are already 20 minutes late picking up your child at the babysitter. Suddenly, the traffic light up ahead turns yellow and so you stomp on the accelerator. The light flashes to red a moment before you reach the intersection, but you see no crossing traffic and so you zip through and on your way, a needless stop avoided. Or so you think. A siren suddenly blares behind you, and in your rearview mirror you see the flashing lights of a police car. What should you do?

Being Stopped by the Police

The first thing drivers should do, of course, is pull their vehicles over to the side of the road or, if on the interstate, into the breakdown lane. They should not, however, just pull their vehicles over to the side of the road, but also pull them as far as possible out of the traffic lane. Many drivers have been injured or even killed when they or their cars were struck by other vehicles after stopping too close to the roadway. If the drivers happen to be in the center or left lane, they should immediately put on their turn signal so the officers will know they are not ignoring or trying to escape them, and then let the police car's flashing lights and siren help them over. Most other drivers will be only too glad to move out of the way of the unfortunate driver. Police officers do understand if a motorist occasionally has to drive some distance before being able to pull safely off the roadway. Under no circumstances, though, particularly on an interstate, should the driver simply stop in the traffic lane. One of the most gruesome accidents I ever saw occurred when a woman's car quit running while on the interstate and she simply coasted to a stop in the traffic lane rather than pulling over into the breakdown lane. An 18-wheeler came barreling up behind her and didn't notice that her car was not moving until too late and slammed into the rear of it.

After pulling safely off the roadway, motorists will notice that the police car stops approximately a car length behind them and several feet farther out into the roadway than their car. Doing this forces vehicles approaching from the rear to drive around the police car, and thus gives the police officer a safe corridor for approaching the driver's side of the stopped car.

Depending on the neighborhood, time of day, and characteristics of the motorists, police officers may employ several other safety procedures. Officers may, if it is dark, shine the police car's spotlight into the rearview mirror of the stopped car. This denies the driver a clear view of the officer's movements. As officers approach a stopped car, motorists may notice them touching the trunk lid. Police officers do this to be certain the trunk is shut and locked. A number of police officers have been ambushed and killed by criminals hiding in the trunk. If it is dark, officers will also likely shine their flashlights into the rear seat as they approach the driver's window, again to check for hazards.

Properly trained police officers, when making a traffic stop, will always stand just to the rear of the driver's door while talking to motorists. They do this for several reasons. Ffirst denies the driver an opportunity to strike the officer with the car door, but, more importantly, it forces the driver, who is sitting facing forward, to turn his or her head in order to speak to the officer, which puts the driver in a position of tactical disadvantage if he or she should have any aggressive intent.

Often, motorists who are unused to being stopped by the police will feel uncomfortable talking over their shoulders, and will want to get out of their cars and talk face-to-face. These drivers also usually want to follow the officer back to the police car and stand just outside the driver's door as the officer writes the ticket. Although it is certainly an understandable reaction from people who are used to dealing with others face-to-face, police officers nevertheless try to discourage stopped drivers from doing this because it not only negates their own tactical advantage, but also compromises the stopped driver's safety. Passing motorists, often distracted by the flashing lights and trying to see what is happening, can easily not notice the driver standing in the roadway.

For reasons that have always baffled me and most other police officers, some motorists keep their driver's license either in the glove box or under the front seat of the car. Some motorists, however, also keep firearms and other weapons in these locations, so, when being stopped by the police, it is always advisable to wait until the officer has approached the vehicle and asked for your driver's license before reaching under the seat or into the glove box—but even then only after telling the officer exactly what you are doing.

To the average citizen who has absolutely no aggressive intent against police officers all of these precautions may seem to border on paranoia. But these officers are not paranoid. They are simply following occupational safety precautions similar to the precautions practiced by anyone in a profession with a certain level of danger. A study done by the FBI showed that from 1991 to 2000 almost 16 percent of the police officers killed in the line of duty were killed during traffic stops, while the same study showed that almost 10 percent of the assaults on police officers also occurred during traffic stops. Properly trained police officers recognize the dangers inherent in their occupation, even from seemingly innocent encounters.

A nearly heart-stopping example of how an innocent traffic stop can suddenly turn deadly occurred to me one evening when, while working as a uniformed district sergeant, I noticed a car with no taillights. When I turned on the police vehicle's flashing lights and siren to stop the car, though, it suddenly raced away. After a long chase (during which I was accidentally blacked out on my radio by a dispatcher giving out another chase in another part of the city), the car crashed as it tried to make too sharp of a turn into an alley, and pinned itself between a telephone pole and a house. The car, as it turned out, contained three professional hit men who had been brought down from Chicago by people wanting to take over the local drug trade. These men had shot more than a dozen people in the previous week and we were all looking for them. I was awarded Officer of the Year for this catch, though, as in many good catches a good deal of luck was involved. I could just as easily have been killed if the three hit men hadn't been pinned in the car and stunned from the crash. The car was loaded with guns. I really hadn't been prepared for what happened since I had originally thought it would be just a simple traffic stop.

Traffic Violator Cues

While police officers cannot legally stop motorists for no reason, certain driver actions, though not illegal in themselves, alert police officers that they should observe these drivers carefully for traffic violations. Many officers, for example, watch closely any motorists who display rudeness and disregard for other drivers, since these motorists have been found to be much more likely to violate traffic laws. Officers also watch for drivers who appear inattentive or distracted, because too often they disregard traffic ordinances.

In addition to watching motorists, though, police officers closely observe certain types of vehicles, particularly those engineered for high-speed driving. Few drivers of these vehicles, it has been found, can resist exceeding the speed limit, even though excessive speed is a major contributing factor to many accidents. For example, a study done by the Insurance Institute for Traffic Safety found a 34 percent increase in highway deaths during the year after many states increased the maximum speed limit from 55 to 65 mph. Many people simply don't realize (until too late) that higher speeds mean less reaction time.

And so, though driving a sporty and expensive car may enhance many people's social status, it also enhances the likelihood of making police officers more observant of their driving behavior. I have met a number of people who are convinced that the police, regardless of brand of car, especially watch for people in red cars. I don't think a car's color has much to do with attracting a police officer's attention, though police will, of course, closely watch a red (and any other color) sports car. Officers do, however, closely observe vehicles that have been modified to give them more speed, or the appearance of more speed, such as cars jacked up in the rear, cars with racing tires or slicks, and cars with cutouts on the hood.

"When I see a car that's all jacked up in the rear," said former traffic sergeant Stephen Gaunt, "I know it's somebody that if watched for a few minutes will probably do something illegal."

Speeding and Radar Detectors

Many of the drivers of high-performance cars, who find it difficult to resist the temptation to speed when the opportunity presents itself, often hope that by using a radar detector they can avoid being caught by the police. Every year thousands of these devices are sold by companies that promise buyers their product will warn them of any radar use by the police. These claims, however, are not always completely valid. Some police radar works with microwave radiation, and in heavily populated areas radar detectors are seldom totally effective since they are subject to a considerable number of false alarms due to microwave radiation leakage from alarm systems, industrial uses, and other sources. After too many of these false alarms, the users soon become complacent when the radar detector goes off, that is, until they hear the siren behind them. Yet, even for those drivers who don't become complacent, radar detectors still work more to the advantage of the police than to the owners. The Texas Transportation Institute of Texas A&M University did a study recently in which they found that when the police used radar that is detectable by radar detectors, the overall speed of trucks on the highway slowed significantly during the testing period, though when using undetectable radar the speed of trucks was not affected. It can be assumed the same holds for cars. Some localities are even now experimenting with having devices posted along highways that emit detectable radar, but don't really measure speed.

Whether or not radar detectors will give an advance warning, however, doesn't depend as much on the brand or type of radar detector as it does on the officer operating the radar device. Some officers, when using radar, leave the device operating constantly and simply measure the speed of vehicles as they pass through the beam. This type of radar operation, if done in flat, open areas, will usually allow radar detectors to warn the owner in time to slow down. Some officers, however, operate radar from the bottom of hills or around a curve in order to block out the beam, while others operate from behind objects that absorb the radar beam, and under these conditions radar detectors will often not warn a motorist until too late. Another method of using radar, activating the radar beam only when the officer has visually sighted a vehicle he or she wants to measure, will also activate radar detectors, but once again too late for the motorist to do anything, though it might warn drivers close behind.

One of the newer speed measurement devices used by police officers is the laser gun. I have seen radar detectors advertised that claim they can detect these laser guns. While this may be true, drivers should be forewarned that the beams from these laser guns are very thin and "target specific." What this means is that when the laser gun beam strikes the driver's car and the detector goes off, it's too late. The officer is measuring that driver's speed, and it's not a spillover from measuring another car.

"If you know how to work radar properly," said Traffic Sergeant Robert Patterson, "the beam will catch the drivers at the same time their radar detectors catch us, which is too late for them." Some officers report having drivers get so angry when they find themselves caught on radar that they have stomped on or smashed their radar detectors.

The locations monitored by radar officers can be selected for a number of reasons. Often, the police select the locations in response to citizen complaints of speeding, while other times they select areas where there have been several serious accidents attributed to speeding. When allowed to select on their own, though, many radar officers look for streets that have long stretches with no stops. The natural inclination of many drivers, particularly those driving sports cars, is to speed in these areas. Many of these drivers, however, are not as good behind the wheel as they believe they are and will often crash into other cars, pedestrians, or run off the road and hit fixed objects. Other radar officers pick areas close to interstate exits, where drivers who have become used to high speed on the interstate will usually exceed the speed limit. One radar officer, who said he had witnessed far too many needless injuries and deaths, told me he likes to select neighborhoods where the homes are built close to the road, since children are more likely to play in the street in these areas.

In addition to using police officers with radar to measure a vehicle's speed, a number of communities now use a device new in the United States (though used for some time in other countries), photo radar. This device, containing a radar unit, camera, and computer, takes pictures of the driver, the vehicle, and the license plate of vehicles exceeding the speed limit. The police department then mails a speeding citation to the vehicle's owner. (Many cities are also installing similar devices at traffic intersections where running red lights is common.) Some jurisdictions use aircraft to measure speed. The airborne officers measure the time it takes for a vehicle's front bumper to travel from one line on the highway to another one farther on. This information, fed into a special calculator that indicates the speed of the vehicle, is then radioed to police vehicles on the ground. Any motorist, therefore, who crosses a line painted across a highway for no apparent reason would do well to slow down immediately.

Leeways and Allowances

How fast can a driver go over the speed limit before being stopped by the police? What constitutes a legal stop at a stop sign? Is it okay for a driver to speed if many other drivers are also speeding and he or she wants to keep up with the flow of traffic? These are all questions drivers wonder about, and while most motorists know that the police give certain leeway, few know exactly how much this is.

No police department I'm aware of writes speeding tickets for only 1 or 2 mph over the speed limit, but the actual leeway given for traffic violations is not set nationally, and usually not even set statewide. Most police departments set their own policy, which the police never advertise since they know motorists would take advantage of this information and always go, for example, 8 or 9 mph above the speed limit in a community that has a 10 mph leeway. My own policy when I'm traveling is to set my cruise control at 4 mph over the posted limit, and I have never been stopped.

But citizens who are somehow aware of a local police department's policy in this regard should be warned that there are still certain areas and conditions under which even these guidelines do not apply. For example, in a community with a 10 mph speeding leeway, police officers may still write tickets for 7 or 8 mph over the speed limit in school zones or when weather conditions have made the streets hazardous. In addition, for those communities that allow "California stops," or slow rolls through stop sign or when making right turns on a red light, officers may still enforce complete stops in bad weather or when children are present. Also, if the police have received numerous complaints about traffic violations in a certain neighborhood, they will be much more strict in that area in order not to be called back. As for the advisability of speeding when many other cars are speeding, drivers should be warned that occasionally the police will select and stop one car in order that the other drivers will see the violator being ticketed, which, it is hoped, will then slow everyone else down.

Motorists' Actions

Upon being stopped by the police for a traffic violation, motorists inevitably, the police have found, take one of four actions trying to avoid getting a ticket, even though seldom will any of the four accomplish what the drivers had hoped for.

1. Excuses

For some motorists, the moment they see flashing lights in the rearview mirror their mind jumps into overdrive trying to come up with an excuse that will convince the officer they had no choice but to commit the violation. Unfortunately, the 20 or 30 seconds most motorists have is never enough time to come up with a really good, plausible excuse, and instead most drivers usually fall back onto something that undoubtedly later makes them blush to think they actually believed they could convince the officer of it.

Of course, if stopped motorists really do have a valid excuse for committing a traffic violation, they should certainly tell the officer about it. It still may not get them out of the ticket, but then again it may. If the excuse, however, is one of the below, motorists might as well not try because police officers hear these over and over:

- Someone was following them.
- Someone was tailgating them.
- The brakes failed (but work now).
- There is an emergency at home, at work, at the hospital, etc.

- They were disciplining a child in the rear seat.
- They were almost out of gas and hurrying to a gas station.
- They had to go to the bathroom and were hurrying to a gas station.
- A cramp made their leg straighten out and press the gas pedal.
- They could see both ways and there were no cars coming.
- They saw the police car and were trying to get out of its way in case the officer was on an emergency run.
- They were trying to swat a bee that had gotten into the car and they didn't see the traffic light, stop sign, etc.
- They were going too fast to stop.

Interestingly, I found when I worked as a uniformed patrol officer that most motorists, at least when they first used it, actually believed the excuse they were using was original with them, and most seemed insulted when I rolled my eyes and began writing the ticket. Every officer has heard all of the above excuses, and hundreds of others, hundreds of times. The problem with excuses is that the majority of them fall apart under the slightest investigation, or they are just plain silly.

2. Confusion

With this tactic, motorists pretend to be stunned when the officer approaches their car and usually say something such as, "Are you sure, Officer? A light?" They then lean out the car window and look behind them, seeming amazed when the officer points to the traffic signal. A little thought should make it obvious, though, why this ploy seldom works. Even on the off chance that an officer would believe the motorist actually didn't see the traffic light, stop sign, or whatever (about a 999 to 1 chance since police officers hear this on every seventh or eighth traffic stop), few officers would allow such an obviously unobservant and careless driver to leave without a traffic ticket, given in the hope that it will underscore the importance of being constantly alert and observant while driving.

3. Denial

This is the most common tactic drivers use. With this ploy, motorists simply look the officer in the face and swear they didn't commit whatever offense the officer is accusing them of, and usually suggesting, either implicitly or explicitly, that the officer (1) has obvious vision problems, (2) is suffering from hallucinations, or (3) has a quota to fill and is using them to do it.

The responses from the dozens of uniformed police officers I interviewed for this book overwhelmingly confirm that denial is the most irritating method drivers use when trying to get themselves out of a traffic ticket—and the most self-defeating. A majority of the officers stated that after motorists insult them by believing they are so simple-minded they can be convinced they didn't see a traffic violation they know occurred, they always issue a traffic ticket—even if originally they had only planned on giving a warning.

4. Indignation

The motorist has pulled to the side of the road and is now watching in the rearview mirror as the officer approaches, ticket book in hand. What to do?

Of course! The motorist knows the mayor! Well, not actually knows him, but the motorist did shake hands with him at an election rally several years ago. When the officer steps up to the car window the motorist immediately demands to know why he or she was stopped, and then makes it clear to the officer how upset the mayor is going to be when he hears of this.

The problem with this tactic, besides not working, is that after it doesn't work, a driver is faced with only three options:

- Grin sheepishly (and take the ticket).
- Say in a huff that the officer will be hearing from the mayor (and take the ticket).
- Increase the indignation (and still get a ticket). CAUTION: This option has the potential to backfire in a disorderly conduct arrest.

Indignant drivers don't impress or intimidate police officers simply because the police see this response on every fifteenth or twentieth traffic stop, and even more so because the officers have just witnessed the violation and know they are in the right. But most important, police officers know that if the person was really as important and connected as he or she claimed, there would be no reason to be indignant. The driver would just simply smile and thank the officer, then take the ticket and go get it fixed.

While most drivers will usually take one of the four actions above when stopped by the police, there is a seldom-used action that most admitted was uniformed police officers as the only thing motorists can do that will almost always convince officers to either let them go with no ticket or write them one for a lesser offense than was actually committed (for example, 41 mph in a 30 mph zone rather than the actual 52 mph, which will usually lower the fine). While this action should be obvious and the first thing drivers would naturally do, it isn't. It has only happened to me a couple of times in my career, and after talking to other officers I find this behavior is about as rare with them.

The action that will convince police officers you deserve a break is to simply look the officer in the face and admit the offense but, just as important, to also treat the officer with the same respect and politeness you would expect. The two or three times in 33 years it has happened to me, I had gone up to the car, my mind steeled and ready to respond to whichever of the four tactics the driver would choose to use, and was so flabbergasted by this blatant act of honesty that I let the driver go with just a "Please drive carefully."

For some reason many motorists believe that rudeness will work better. One of the major reasons why police officers don't like writing traffic tickets is because they are so often met with a hostile reaction (even by drivers using excuses or confusion once they find it isn't going to work). Often this hostility is accompanied by some sarcastic comment such as: "Why aren't you out catching criminals

Seat Belts

Although everyone of driving age has almost certainly seen at least one of the many public service announcements promoting the use of seat belts, police officers still find that every year thousands of the people injured in traffic accidents really didn't have to be, if they had only been wearing a seat belt or a child had been secured in a child safety seat. Every uniformed officer I interviewed for this book felt that only a fool would operate a motor vehicle without having everyone in it wearing a seat belt or in a child safety seat. (Several of the officers also expressed the same feeling about wearing a helmet when operating a motorcycle.) Keep in mind also that even though some states don't require passengers in the rear seat to be secured by a seat belt, in the event of a collision they become missiles that can severely injure or even kill passengers in the front seat. The officers I spoke with had hundreds of horror stories about adults and children needlessly propelled through windows, seriously injured, disfigured, or killed because they weren't wearing a seat belt or in a child safety seat.

As further evidence of the value of seat belts, according to researchers at Traffic Safety Now, the National Highway Traffic Safety Administration, and the National Safety Council: *(continued)*

rather than bothering honest citizens?" These motorists obviously don't know that every year careless drivers kill and injure many times more people than are killed or injured by criminals. In 2000, almost 42,000 people died in traffic accidents, which is close to as many as were killed in combat during the entire Vietnam War. And this doesn't include the hundreds of thousands who are maimed or injured each year in traffic accidents.

Seat Belts (continued)

- Seat belts reduce the likelihood of fatal or serious injury by 40 to 55 percent.
- Unrestrained passengers are two times more likely to be injured than seat-belted ones.
- Being thrown from a car increases one's chances by 25 times of being killed.
- Seat belt use is credited with saving at least 10,000 lives yearly, and 55 percent of the vehicle occupants killed in traffic accidents in 2000 were not buckled up.

As an officer who in the course of his career has been in over a dozen motor vehicle accidents and has totaled two police cars without being injured, I cannot say enough about the wisdom of wearing seat belts.

As a district officer I used to always stand on the curb at the rear of the stopped car to write the ticket. I didn't do this to see the license plate number (I always wrote that down as soon as I stopped the car). I did it to get away from rude, hostile drivers. On the other hand, whenever I encountered a motorist who greeted me with honesty, politeness, and respect, it was so refreshing that, like most of the other officers I interviewed, I gave the person a break seldom given to others.

But in addition to treating officers with politeness and respect, people have often asked me whether having a pro-police bumper sticker will increase the chances of getting a break from an officer who stops them for a traffic violation. Although many officers may say this has no effect on them, that isn't true. When an officer sees such a sticker, he or she will, either consciously or unconsciously, feel better about the driver, and if met by a friendly, honest person can hardly help but want to give that person a break.

Traffic Accidents

Even the most careful drivers, including those who have never been stopped by the police for a traffic ticket, can still have a momentary lapse in driving skills, or encounter another driver with such a lapse, and become involved in a traffic accident. According to the National Highway Traffic Safety Administration (NHTSA), the probability of being involved in an automobile accident during one's lifetime is more than 86 percent. These events are stressful, emotionally charged incidents that usually happen so seldom that drivers are often unaware of what to do when one does occur. (They are also expensive. The cost of all traffic accidents, for example, during 2000 was estimated by NHTSA to be well over $150 billion.) There are several immediate actions, though, that drivers should take in the event of a traffic accident.

If the motorists' cars are still drivable, and the accident only a minor "fender-bender" with no injuries, it is advisable to pull the vehicles off the roadway. While not only courteous to other drivers, this is also much safer for the motorists involved in the accident. Many minor accidents have become serious or fatal accidents when an approaching car has slammed into the stopped vehicles.

But probably the most significant thing to do at any accident scene is to stop as soon as safely possible and give needed first aid or, in the case of serious injuries, call for medical assistance. In addition, almost all jurisdictions require that motorists in accidents, whether there are injuries or not, stop and exchange driver and vehicle information. Attempting to leave the scene of an accident without exchanging driver and vehicle information for anything less than a life-threatening emergency can make the driver liable to both criminal and civil penalties. This doesn't negate the advice I gave in an earlier chapter about going to a safer location before exchanging information. The criminal and civil penalties above apply only to drivers trying to get away without giving their information to the other driver.

Most drivers, I've found, are not sure whether or not they should call the police when involved in an automobile accident.

Types of Accidents

Every year the police respond to millions of automobile accidents caused by a variety of factors. The Insurance Institute for Traffic Safety studied over 4,500 accidents in four major urban areas, and found that over 80 percent of these accidents could be attributed to six causes. They are, in order of their magnitude of occurrence:

1. Running a traffic signal
2. Struck from the rear when stopped or stopping
3. Running off the road (because of road conditions, speeding, or driver impairment)
4. Improper lane change
5. Struck while turning left
6. Collision while backing up

While the above was for all accidents, the National Highway Traffic Safety Administration analyzed only fatal accidents in 1999 and found four main causes:

1. Failure to keep in proper lane, or running off the road
2. Driving too fast
3. Failure to yield right-of-way
4. Driver inattention (using cell phone, eating, etc.)

The police, without question, should be called if someone is injured or if one of the vehicles is undrivable. But (though many police officers will probably gnash their teeth at this), my years as a police officer have shown me that, except in the case of very minor damage, it is usually in a motorist's best interests to have the police called to the scene of most accidents. The officer may not do more than just have the motorists exchange driver and vehicle information, but it is still important to have an officer there, and for you to get his or her name and badge number. Without an officer present at the accident scene, the details, and eventual fault, of an accident become simply one driver's word against another's. Even though many drivers may admit fault at the accident scene, later, when they discover that their insurance rates are going to skyrocket or that they might be dropped by their insurance company, details about what happened at the accident can, and often do, change. Having an officer there to see and hear what happened will usually discourage drivers from changing their stories.

Best Advice

The best advice the police can give concerning the operation of motor vehicles is always to obey traffic laws as closely as possible. It's a good idea to have a copy of the state driver's manual (or any reference used for the state driving test) in the glove box, and when you're waiting to pick up the children at softball practice or a spouse at work, occasionally thumb through it. This can keep you abreast of traffic regulations in your state. For those contemplating automobile travel between states I would recommend purchase of the book *Digest of Motor Laws*, which is published every year by the American Automobile Association. This inexpensive, yet very complete, paperback contains a listing of all the important traffic laws in each state and the provinces of Canada. Information concerning its purchase can be obtained at any local AAA club or by writing:

American Automobile Association
1000 AAA Drive
Heathrow, FL 32746-5603

However, if despite all your precautions you are still stopped by the police for a traffic violation, the best advice of all is to simply greet the officer with the same honesty, respect, and politeness you expect in return.

13

BEING ARRESTED

THE ARREST

You have been waiting in line for nearly an hour and are finally almost to the counter. Suddenly, a man crowds in front of you. After a moment of glaring at the back of his head, you say under your breath that the line forms at the rear. He hears you and says something surly over his shoulder, and so you say something surly back. Spinning around, he shouts a vulgar name and then shoves you. Just as you shout a vulgar name back and give him a shove, not to start a fight but only to show that you aren't afraid of him, a police officer appears and arrests you both.

You have just had a taxi bring you home from a party where you knew you would drink too much. As you hang up your coat, your ex-husband, who has the kids this weekend, calls from the hospital and says your six-year-old son has fallen, apparently breaking his arm in two places, and is crying hysterically for you. You call but find it will take at least an hour to get another cab. After several moments of indecision, you get into your car and drive very carefully, using extreme caution not to draw attention to yourself. But suddenly, you find yourself pulling up to a police sobriety checkpoint. Ten minutes later, you are under arrest and on your way to jail.

Impossible? Not at all. The cases above are two that I recall in which people who have never been arrested before are suddenly flung into the criminal justice system. The man was 35 years old and one speeding ticket was the extent of his acquaintance with the police, while the woman was 29 and had never had so much as a parking ticket.

The FBI, in its *Crime in the United States,* estimates that the police made almost 14 million arrests in 2000. Of this total, approximately 11 million were for misdemeanors (minor law violations such as those in the examples above). Although the names of the charges vary from state to state, misdemeanor arrests account for approximately 75 percent of all arrests made, and while these charges are minor when compared with felonies (serious crimes) such as robbery, burglary, or theft, a person arrested for a misdemeanor must still go through much of the same judicial process as a person arrested for a more serious crime. The advice in this chapter is restricted, however, only to misdemeanor arrests since they are the most common and likely type that average citizens experience. Moreover, in misdemeanor cases, police officers have wide latitude as to whether they make an arrest or not. Seldom do they have as much discretion with felonies. Felony arrests are much more serious matters, and a person arrested for a felony should immediately contact an attorney, preferably from jail and before talking to the police, and allow the attorney to handle any legal matters connected with the arrest. On the other hand, an attorney is not always needed by people arrested for a misdemeanor, that is, until after they are out of jail and preparing to go to court (see sidebar).

Best Response

During over 30 years as a police officer, I have arrested hundreds of people for misdemeanors. A number were, as in the examples above, simply law-abiding citizens caught up in situations that had gotten beyond their control. And yet, even though police officers arrest millions of people every year for misdemeanors, the truth is that most of them don't like making misdemeanor arrests because it means just a lot of paperwork. Misdemeanor arrests are simply not a high priority to most police officers because they don't contribute to an officer's record the way making felony arrests does. And while

An Attorney: Necessary or Not?

B efore someone who has been arrested goes to court, a number of crucial decisions must be made: how to plead, whether to have a jury trial, which attorney to hire, or even if an attorney is really necessary. Most of these decisions are beyond the scope of this book, except for one: whether or not an attorney is needed.

During over 30 years as a police officer, I haven't seen more than a dozen cases in which citizens who have gone to court without an attorney and pleaded guilty or were found guilty on a minor first offense received more than a suspended sentence or nominal fine. But during the same time I haven't seen a *single* case of a minor first offender (and very few second or even third offenders) who received more than a suspended sentence and nominal fine if that person did have an attorney. Judges are simply more receptive toward pleas for leniency from citizens who have hired attorneys, probably because they realize that such people have already spent a considerable amount of money on legal fees. In addition, judges, it must be remembered, are also attorneys and naturally like to encourage their use. I think this second reason is even more important than the first since people with public defenders (attorneys who serve indigent clients free of charge) also receive this favorable treatment.

One of the dozen cases I mentioned above particularly sticks in my memory. While working off-duty as a security agent, I arrested a woman for shoplifting a cheap necklace. She was 30, a mother of three, and had never been arrested. She appeared in court without an attorney and pleaded guilty. I suspect the judge was having a bad day because he sentenced her to 30 days in jail, a sentence that I, and even the prosecutor, felt was much too harsh, but we couldn't sway the judge.

My experience with the criminal justice system has shown me that while having an attorney may not always turn out to be necessary, not having one is a dangerous gamble.

officers, in the case of felonies, don't have as much discretion, and will usually (but not always) make an arrest, most jurisdictions have given police officers considerable discretion in the matter of making or not making misdemeanor arrests.

This discretion is theirs, officers find, because many laws are written in such a way as to give them wide latitude in their enforcement. Many laws, for example, say such things as "An officer may arrest for . . ." or "An officer can arrest for . . . ," but do not actually mandate an arrest. Some laws, on the other hand, make certain conduct illegal, yet don't define what the conduct is except in the broadest terms, leaving the interpretation up to the officer's discretion. This is because legislators know they cannot foresee all of the possible variations in the way a law is violated, and want the police to deal with each case in a fair and equitable way that allows for an arrest when necessary, but also allows for no arrest if the officers deem it proper.

While no records are kept of how many people the police don't arrest for misdemeanors, even though these people have committed clear violations of the law, any officer will tell you it is undoubtedly a substantial number. Consequently, you should realize there is a small, but real, possibility of talking a police officer out of making a misdemeanor arrest if you can convince the officer that:

- The violation you committed was an unintentional mistake, will be corrected, and you will never commit it again.
- You will not cause any more problems that would require the officer to return.
- You are simply a rational, reasonable person caught up in circumstances beyond your control.

In contrast to the conditions above, police officers seldom release anyone who they believe will go right back to doing whatever it was the police were called to stop, will become a danger to themselves and others if released, or will embarrass the police by flaunting their bad judgment in releasing the individual.

In addition, there is one other situation. "I've been talked a few times into letting someone go that probably should've been arrested," said a veteran street officer. "But if I have to put my hands on someone, they might as well stop talking because there's no way I'm going to let them go after that."

The chances, therefore, that an officer can be talked out of a misdemeanor arrest increase with the reasonableness of the solution offered to the officer. The solution must include an offer to correct the violation and go directly home (if away from home) and, most important, must include an assurance that the violation will not be repeated. All of this, incidentally, must be related to the officer in a reasonable, rational tone. Nothing is more self-defeating than being loud, rude, abusive, or threatening. Interestingly, the police find that every year a much larger number of people will talk their way into jail than talk their way out. Often, an officer is on the borderline and can't decide whether a person should be arrested or not, and the person will be so rude and obnoxious that it pushes the officer into making the arrest.

In addition, there are several other self-defeating actions that will ensure that a police officer cannot be talked out of a misdemeanor arrest, even if he or she was originally undecided about a citizen's fate. For example, you should never flee or physically resist the police, even if the officers are completely wrong, unless you are threatened with serious injury or death. There are powerful legal and administrative remedies that can be taken if police officers abuse their power and authority. Police officers can be sued, arrested, or both, as the Rodney King case demonstrated.

Fleeing or resisting the police, incidentally, is not only self-defeating but also dangerous. Police officers have the training, experience, equipment, and backing of the law to use whatever reasonable force is necessary to overcome resistance when making a misdemeanor arrest in good faith (which simply means the arrest doesn't have to be legal and valid, only that the officers believe it is). In addition, the act of fleeing or resisting is also usually a separate charge in itself that can be added to the original arresting charge. It is very possible to be found innocent of the original arresting charge but still to be found guilty of fleeing or resisting the arrest.

Arguing with a police officer, while usually not a separate criminal charge like fleeing or resisting, is just as futile and self-defeating. In over 30 years I have never seen a single case in which a citizen has successfully argued a police officer out of an arrest. But yet, while arguing may be futile, a person should still try talking to the officers calmly and rationally. In most misdemeanor situations, with people quite often screaming all around them (since the majority seem to be public-order violations), police officers are glad to find someone willing to speak calmly and rationally, and will usually listen to what that person has to say. Although admittedly the times have been few, I have occasionally been talked into releasing a person who spoke calmly and rationally, especially when that person offered to do something that would solve the problem I had been called to settle.

The Three "C's"

In many situations, such as the two at the beginning of this chapter, police officers have no choice but to make an arrest, especially if there is a complaintant demanding it and the officers have witnessed the misdemeanor. And, of course, in most jurisdictions, even though police officers do not have to make misdemeanor arrests, they still have the discretion to do so if they wish. If this happens, it is imperative that you spend as little time as possible in custody, because while the Bill of Rights should have included the right of a citizen under arrest to be held in a sanitary detention facility with an assurance of personal safety, this is simply not the case in the majority of jails and detention facilities in America. Most are overcrowded (the Bureau of Justice Statistics reports that in 2000, the overall jail capacity in the United States was over 100 percent), unsanitary, and populated by individuals only a step

Give Me a Break!

L ike most police officers, I'm very careful about whom I don't arrest when grounds are there for an arrest. A very frightening experience taught me this. It was close to my roll call time one evening, and I was slowly cruising back to turn in my car and go home. Suddenly, as I turned onto a main thoroughfare, I saw a car in front of me weaving from curb to curb. Damn! I thought, turning on my emergency equipment to stop the car. Why now? I'm ready to go home!

The driver was drunk, of course, but when I asked him to step out of the car, he began begging me to give him a break. He only lived, he said, a hundred feet up the road. I checked his driver's license and found he was telling the truth. I stood there in the roadway for a few moments in indecision, but finally decided that since it was so close to my time to go home, and since a drunk driving arrest would take at least an hour, I'd let him go ahead and pull up into his driveway and then go to bed.

He thanked me, put his car in gear, and then floored the accelerator, swerving over into the opposing lane of traffic and running an oncoming car into a ditch. Luckily, no one was hurt, and there was no damage to either car, but from that moment on, my standards for releasing people became much, much stricter.

above being a prima facie case for Darwin. In addition, a survey by the Bureau of Justice Statistics found that almost 60 percent of all inmates in state prisons (who often stay in local jails while on trial and whom a number of states are now housing in local jails because of overcrowding in the prisons) have been in situations that required a test for AIDS, and 2.1 percent of all male inmates nationally were HIV-positive. This is five times the rate in the U.S. general population. However, the HIV rate among female prisoners was even higher, at 3.4 percent. These, incidentally, are national averages. The inmate HIV rate in various states can run as high as nearly 10 percent. In addition, the overcrowding of most jails and prisons also makes controlling such diseases as tuberculosis, which killed 36 inmates several years ago in New York, much more difficult. But diseases aside, 16.2 percent of all state prisoners are believed to be mentally ill, and it has been found that mentally ill prisoners are more likely to have been confined for a violent crime than other inmates. Lastly, because of the intensely crowded conditions of most local jails, authorities cannot always keep new arrestees separated from hardened criminals.

While the chance of contracting AIDS is certainly small, jail rapes do occur, though no one knows how many there are because this is not something jail keepers like to talk about. In addition, due to their immunity-weakened condition, it is possible these AIDS-infected prisoners have other communicable diseases. But, of course, far more likely than disease is simply intimidation by other prisoners or a nonsexual assault. Therefore, an arrested person should, in order to ensure personal safety and welfare, spend as little time as possible in one of these facilities.

What is the secret for doing this?

The answer is a simple, commonsense approach that should be obvious, but apparently isn't since few people do it. To get through America's criminal justice system as quickly and smoothly as possible, a person must know and practice the three "C's":

- A cool head
- A calm voice
- A cooperative attitude

An interesting side of human nature, police officers find, is that seldom will professional criminals give them much trouble once arrested, yet officers can expect trouble at least 8 times out of 10 when making public-order arrests (disorderly conduct, public intoxication, etc.). Professional criminals know that the three "C's" are solid advice, and use them to their advantage, while most of the people arrested for public-order violations, if given the same advice, are more likely to jump up and scream that they would rather hold a dead rat in their mouth than cooperate with the police, even though the latter would be to their benefit.

Practicing the three "C's," however, doesn't mean admitting guilt or giving the officers incriminating evidence. Police officers generally advise citizens of their constitutional rights against self-incrimination immediately after placing them under arrest. These include:

- The right to remain silent
- The warning that anything said can be used as evidence against them
- The right to consult with an attorney before being asked any questions, and the right to have an attorney present during the questioning
- If they cannot afford an attorney, one will be appointed for them free of charge before any questioning takes place

"It has been my experience that when it becomes obvious that the police cannot be dissuaded from an arrest, it is usually in a citizen's best interests to exercise the right to remain silent," said a former police officer who is now a criminal defense attorney.

Interestingly, though, few people arrested for misdemeanors, particularly first-timers, ever exercise their right to remain silent. Instead, most talk and talk and talk, usually to their own detriment.

Getting Released

Exercising the right to remain silent, however, should never be carried to the point of refusing to give personal information to the police or jail personnel. Being uncooperative about information such as name, address, date of birth, and so on will only prolong an arrested person's stay in the detention facility. Remaining silent also doesn't apply to talking about serious medical conditions or medicine needs. Upon being arrested, you should immediately tell the police of any such problems. An arrested person becomes an officer's responsibility, and the officer will see that medical needs are attended to.

From the scene of an arrest a citizen is usually transported to the county jail or other detention facility, where the arrest will be logged, and the arrested person searched, fingerprinted, and photographed. These are all procedures the police have a right and obligation to perform, and will perform, regardless of whether the citizen cooperates or not. Because a quick release is imperative, it is in a citizen's best interest to practice the three "C's" and not resist these procedures.

And yet, even though incarcerated, an arrested person cannot legally be held incommunicado, and so in most jurisdictions a citizen under arrest is guaranteed one completed telephone call. Arrested citizens should therefore be certain the person they contact is someone who, if needed, can get them released. In addition, the Constitution and a number of high court rulings have stated that all arrested persons, except for those arrested on certain specific charges, are entitled to be considered for bail, and that this consideration should be based on the likelihood of that person's returning to court. The amount of bail is usually fixed within a few hours of arrival at the detention facility (depending on how busy they are), and it is during this time that a cool head, calm voice, and cooperative attitude can be most beneficial since it can speed up the process considerably. But more important, most large jurisdictions have programs that allow them to release minor offenders with community roots on personal recognizance (a simple written promise to appear in court, rather than bail). A belligerent, uncooperative person, though, will often not be considered for this type of release.

A release on personal recognizance is not automatic, however, just because it is your first arrest. Jurisdictions that use personal recognizance releases have guidelines for when a person is eligible that are usually based on both the severity of the crime and the risk factor you present for not returning to court. A more severe misdemeanor charge is one that involves drugs or injury to another person. For risk factors, it is in your favor if you live with a spouse or child, have a telephone listed in your name (showing community roots), have been employed for more than one year, and your arrest is for a public-order violation (drunkenness, disorderly conduct, and so on) or a property charge (minor theft).

If you do not meet the requirements for a personal recognizance release, but don't have enough negative risk factors to require that you post a surety bond through a bailbondsman (this type of bond is usually required for people with a high likelihood of not returning for court proceedings since bailbondsmen will go and find them and bring them back), you may be eligible for what is called a cash bond. With this type of bond, 10 percent of the bail amount must be put up in cash (personal checks are usually not accepted because of the problem of bad checks), and it is refundable when you show up for court.

Getting Someone Released

The truth is (though few people seem to know it), the most practical action for someone witnessing a family member's or friend's arrest is to return home and wait until that person calls. This is also true if a person is contacted by someone other than the arrested person and told of the incident. An arrested person will be allowed a telephone call and there is really not much point in immediately proceeding to the police station since there are a number of time-consuming procedures an arrested person must go through before he or she can be considered for release. In a number of cases I have seen people race to the jail, almost beating the police there, then sit for hours before the arrested person is considered for release, only to find that they have to go home anyway for money or some documents. The length of time it takes for the procedures arrested people must go through depends on both the time of the arrest (on weekend nights, for example, jails are crowded and the work backed up and slow) and whether or not alcohol was involved in the arrest (some jurisdictions require that enough time pass for the arrested person to sober up before being considered for release). In addition, because of the strong likelihood that a person, if arrested for the first time on a misdemeanor charge, will be released on personal recognizance, the most help he or she will usually need is simply a ride home.

If, however, because of the nature of the charge or a person's lack of community roots, a surety bond is required, you must usually contact a bailbondsman, and pay a percentage of the bond, which is not recoverable. Dealing with bailbondsmen can be a frightening experience since many operate out of low-rent locations close to the jail and often appear to be rough individuals. It is difficult to give advice on how to locate a reputable bailbondsman because the people who regularly use them, and could therefore give a recommendation, are not the type of individuals with whom average citizens would socialize. Also, police departments usually discourage their officers from recommending bailbondsmen since this could be viewed as a possible conflict of interest. Still, it wouldn't hurt to ask a police officer for a recommendation. If this doesn't work, however, bail can usually be arranged for a fee (in addition to the bail bond cost) through a criminal attorney.

Going to Court

After their release from jail, many citizens mistakenly believe that forfeiting their cash bond will take the place of appearing in court, or that not appearing in court after being released on personal recognizance will be treated as a matter quickly forgotten. This is often not the case. In many jurisdictions not only will the cash bond be forfeited, but a rearrest warrant will be issued. At this point several things can happen. The officers, depending on how energetic they are and on how much trouble the citizen gave them, may go to the citizen's home or place of business once the warrant is issued and take him or her back into custody, or the officers may simply allow the warrant to go on the computer file. Thousands of arrests are made every year off the computer file during traffic violation stops or during routine records checks for licenses, permits, etc. This can be both embarrassing and expensive. Court dates should always be taken very seriously.

Complaints Against the Police

Police officers have millions of contacts every year with citizens, most of them stressful: someone has been assaulted, robbed, or burglarized; someone has received a ticket; someone has been arrested. Because these contacts deal with negative matters, citizens often leave disgruntled, and occasionally want to complain about some police action or inaction. Many times the complaints are over procedural matters, something the citizens felt the officers should or should not have done, and often citizens will file complaints over police actions that were legal and proper but which they simply didn't like. Misconceptions about what the police can and cannot do make up a large percentage of the complaints filed against them, and it is for this reason the majority of these complaints are found to be without basis.

Police work, however, because of the nature of the job, does occasionally attract individuals who cannot handle the power of the office, and who, therefore, abuse both their authority and the citizens with whom they come in contact. Citizens not only should, but have an obligation, to report any police officer who violates their constitutional rights or who physically or verbally abuses them. Different communities have different mechanisms for doing this, but all have a place where one may complain about abusive officers. Only when citizens promptly bring this type of behavior to the attention of police officials can they identify individuals whose employment should be terminated. Some people may doubt this, but the truth is that, probably more than anyone else, police officers dislike this type of individual representing law enforcement, and want very much for citizens to report them. As I mentioned earlier in this book, police departments have tried during the last few decades to improve their public image, and all police officials know that one police officer abusing his or her authority can undo the work of a hundred good police officers. Therefore, police departments are much more likely now to discipline or discharge bad police officers. Part of my job when I was the police department's executive officer was to terminate probationary officers who proved to be unfit for the job. Although it was never fun, I always knew that by doing it I was making the job easier for the rest of us, and so I never flinched from it.

Best Advice

Where misdemeanor violations are concerned, the best advice the police can offer is that a cool head, calm voice, and cooperative attitude are the surest way for citizens to avoid, or, if avoidance isn't possible, at least quicken, a trip through America's criminal justice system.

14

CITIZEN INVOLVEMENT IN CRIME PREVENTION

CITIZEN EXPECTATIONS

Law enforcement can often be a very frustrating occupation because there is seldom any closure to a police officer's job. A firefighter, for example, goes to a fire and puts it out, closing the task, seldom being called back to fight the same fire. Police officers, on the other hand, arrest a criminal, and he or she is soon back out on bail committing more crimes. Police officers go to a home to settle a domestic disturbance, knowing they will be back the very next weekend for the very same problem. A police officer's job never seems to be completed. On occasion, though, police officers do get satisfaction from the job.

One of the most satisfying things I experienced as a street uniformed officer was the very obvious relief that came over people when the police arrived at the scene of an incident where immediate action was necessary, where someone was perhaps trapped in a wrecked car, seriously injured and in need of medical attention, or where a person had a seizure or some other medical problem. It is often heard that people are never glad to see the police, but this isn't always so. The truth is they are occasionally very glad to see the police, because until the police arrive at the scene of an emergency, the people present, who often have no idea what should be done, realize that they are responsible for helping the victim, particularly if he or she is a family member or friend. These people often suffer guilt and anxiety since they aren't sure of the correct thing to do. But once the police arrive, they feel greatly relieved because the responsibility for action then passes from them to the police, who are, of course, trained and equipped to handle such emergencies. Citizens are also usually just as happy to see the police if they happen to be passing through a high-crime area or suspect that a crime is about to occur with them as the likely victim.

The police can be counted on in many situations. Still, there is only so much they can do, especially to thwart crime. The truth is that most police departments are understaffed, overworked, and simply spread too thin to be effective in preventing many crimes. Most police departments must depend on assistance from the public in order to have any real impact on reducing and preventing crime.

The understaffed condition of many police departments was not always so. During the 1960s and early 1970s, federal and state grant money flowed into police departments in huge, unprecedented amounts. Many departments used this money to hire extra officers. This money, however, has since dried up, and the 1980s were a time of shrinking budgets and tight control of money, causing the layoff of police officers in many police departments. The 1990s weren't any better, nor are the 2000s.

There was a large hoopla in the press several years ago when the crime bill was passed by Congress and signed by the president. There was talk of plunging crime rates and drastic reductions in the criminal population. However, I doubt if the effects of this law will ever be as dramatic as advertised. While supporters of the bill claimed it would eventually put 100,000 new police officers on the street, this is very unlikely. The reason for this is that the crime bill pays for only part of the expense of new officers, and cash-strapped cities must come up with the remainder of the money. The point is that if the cities had this extra money, they would already be hiring more officers.

But, of course, there was also money in the bill for other law enforcement functions. And while I like the part in the crime bill about supplying money to build more prisons, anyone who has ever dealt with federal grant money knows that actually getting the money is a long, tortuous process. I doubt very much if the crime bill will have a dramatic effect on the crime rate, the number of police officers, or the financial crunch of the cities.

Citizen Volunteers

Yet, while seeing large cuts in local law enforcement budgets and subsequent layoffs during the 1980s and 1990s, America at the same time saw a growing crime rate that brought about increased demands for uniformed police service. Allocating more and more of their remaining officers to street patrol in order to meet the increasing public demand caused many police departments to cut back, or to cut out entirely, certain important auxiliary functions, such as crime analysis, victim assistance, and crime prevention. But even in the face of these large budget cutbacks, several thousand local police departments have found that they don't have to cut back on auxiliary services. Instead they have developed a method for maintaining these integral functions while still meeting the increased demand for more police officers on street patrol. They are able to do this through citizen volunteers.

"Because of the budget constraints under which we must operate, it is safe to say we could not do without civilian volunteers," said A. Tony Fisher, former chief of police of Takoma Park, Maryland, whose department uses civilian volunteers in many areas.

Documenting this trend toward the use of volunteers in law enforcement, a survey conducted by the American Association of Retired Persons (AARP) found that over 600,000 citizens in the United States engage in some type of volunteer work for local law enforcement agencies. Over half of these volunteers, it was found, were 55 years of age or older. Nearly unanimous among the police chiefs contacted during this survey was the belief that this trend will continue to grow and spread in the coming years, with many chiefs saying that volunteers in their departments were having a definite impact on the crime rate.

Volunteer work, though, even volunteer work in police departments, is not new to America. In the eighteenth and nineteenth centuries most law enforcement agencies depended heavily on citizen posses to help them track down and apprehend criminals. However, with the advent of large, organized police departments at the beginning of the twentieth century the need for citizen participation lessened until in the middle of the twentieth century it practically disappeared. The budget and manpower problems of the last 15 to 20 years, though, have brought citizen volunteers back.

Types of Volunteer Work in Law Enforcement

The types of volunteer work done in the estimated 2,000 to 3,000 local police departments in the United States now using citizen volunteers vary with the locality and needs of the agency. There is a unit, for example, of the Colorado Springs Police Department that has received many prestigious awards, including a coveted Presidential Commendation and selection as an Exemplary Law Enforcement Assistance Administration Project. While this high level of performance is praiseworthy in itself, even more impressive is that the members of this unit are not police officers, but citizen volunteers, citizens who hold other full-time jobs or who are retired, yet who put in 10 to 15 hours a week of volunteer work for the Colorado Springs Senior Victim Assistance Team. The members of this unit are responsible for crisis intervention, support, and reassurance to elderly crime victims; for the referrals of these victims to social service agencies; for help in replacing items broken during a crime, such as eyeglasses, hearing aids, canes, windows, and locks; and for assistance in the replacement of stolen identification, credit cards, food stamps, Social Security checks, etc.

Colorado Springs also has many other volunteers who work in such areas as tracking runaways, victim contact, and providing clerical assistance in a number of units. "These volunteers free our police officers to do those duties only they can do," said

Colorado Springs chief of police Lorne C. Kramer. "And in this time of tight budgets, we figure this amounts to a substantial financial savings."

The Maricopa County (Phoenix), Arizona, Sheriff's Department, with a force of over 3,000 citizen volunteers in 57 separate units, has one of the largest and most diversified citizen volunteer programs in America. But before citizens receive an assignment to one of this department's many volunteer units, which include an air posse, a mounted posse, desert and mountain trackers, and many other specialized units, each new volunteer receives 48 hours of basic instruction in first aid, CPR, patrol procedures, and radio communications. Then, for volunteers who wish them, there are many specialized training courses, such as crowd control, desert survival, and crime prevention.

Many large-city police departments now also have crime analysis units that are staffed with civilian volunteers. These volunteers update crime location pin maps, sort and categorize crime reports, and perform many other clerical functions. Because of the assistance of citizen volunteers, police officers doing crime analysis in these departments are able to devote more of their time to actually analyzing crime and, with this increased time, are able to decipher crime patterns and suspect information. Thus, detectives and uniformed officers can see whether crimes committed in one precinct are similar to crimes committed in other parts of the city, which can suggest a common perpetrator. Also, occasionally the police in one precinct will know who committed a crime, but don't have enough evidence yet to arrest him or her. Through analysis of similar crimes, though, it can be determined whether he or she may be committing crimes in other precincts, where there may be plenty of evidence but no suspect. With the information supplied from the crime analysis unit the police have someone to match the evidence against. While all of this crime analysis could be done by uniformed officers and detectives, it is tremendously time-consuming, and having a crime analysis unit to do it leaves more time for the officers to perform other vital work.

Citizen volunteers, however, not only assist in making crime analysis units more effective, but because of shrinking police department budgets and manpower can often make the difference between a unit existing or being disbanded. Many top law enforcement administrators agree with the police chief who, when asked about citizen volunteers, said, "If it wasn't for the volunteers, our department simply wouldn't have a crime analysis unit."

Other police departments use citizen volunteers in almost as many positions as there are units within a police department. For example, citizen volunteers in Takoma Park, Maryland, along with staffing the crime analysis unit, provide victim assistance, maintain the police department's statistics, and assist in numerous administrative tasks. Virginia Beach, Virginia, uses volunteers in such positions as personnel and training aides, crime analysis, alarm unit, pawnshop unit, and transportation aides. In Indianapolis, Indiana, the retired head of a May Company department store's personnel office previously volunteered his time to assist the police department's personnel branch.

Finally, almost all major, and many medium and small, police departments use volunteers as police reserves (estimated nationally to total 250,000), who often have the same power and much of the same training as regular police officers. The reserves assist police departments with routine patrol, prisoner transportation, and many other areas of law enforcement. For younger people interested in police work, many police departments also sponsor cadet and police explorer scout (Boy Scout) programs, along with police summer camp.

Crime Watch and Crime Stoppers

While there are many citizens actively working in volunteer law enforcement tasks, there are many other citizens who are just as tired of increasing crime and who would like to do something to help, but simply do not have the time, have a physical disability that prohibits them from volunteering, or for some other reason cannot take part in one of the many law

Police Corps

For a number of years there has been talk in law enforcement circles about the creation of a police corps. This group would be made up of college graduates who could have their college loans forgiven by working for a certain period of time in law enforcement.

From my experience as head of a police department's personnel branch, I feel this is an excellent idea since it would give police departments a new pool of highly educated people to draw from as recruits. Police work is an extremely complex field these days, and society has always granted police officers immense power. It only makes sense to want to have only the best qualified and most educated people performing this job.

Respected criminologist Lawrence Sherman, however, in an article that appeared in the *Wall Street Journal,* opposed the idea of a police corps on a number of grounds, including the belief that it would be a tremendous waste of money since police departments would only receive service from these individuals for the few years it takes them to work off their loans. We operate now, however, under the same problem, in that we are never sure how long a recruit will want to stay. Unlike the military, we don't have any way to keep people who don't want to stay. I think, however, that many of these people would enlist for life. Being a member of a police department is like belonging to a large family, with everyone looking out for everyone else, and leaving it brings about the same pain as a divorce or death in the family. The police corps, I believe, is an idea from which law enforcement can only benefit.

enforcement volunteer programs. For these people there is still vital volunteer work that does not require leaving the home, doing clerical work, or even having a specialized skill, but only requires being observant. It is participation in a Neighborhood Crime Watch program.

Operating in most major communities, the Crime Watch program acts as extra eyes and ears for the local police. Its members watch for suspicious people and activities in their neighborhood, and then report them to the police. A survey several years ago estimated that there were over 15,000 Neighborhood Watches or block clubs in the United States, and the police have found that those neighborhoods that have an active Crime Watch program or block club have been able to have a significant impact on the crime in their area. A 1997 study confirms this. A research team from the University of Chicago found that, regardless of racial makeup, neighborhoods where the residents looked out for each other had fewer incidents of violent crime. I have never heard of a neighborhood that was sorry they had joined Crime Watch or formed a block club. If there is no organization in your community, start your own block club. It can be great for social as well as crime fighting functions.

Some block clubs, however, have gone beyond their traditional role of simply acting as extra eyes and ears for the police department. Some now also act as volunteer victim assistance aides, and call on crime victims after a crime to see if there is anything they need help with. Some also escort victims to court, and assist them in understanding the complexities of the criminal justice system. Some also reassure crime victims, stay with them for a while after the crime, and assist the victims in obtaining any help or compensation available.

Along with the Crime Watch program, however, there is another very successful crime prevention program that citizens who have little or no time for volunteer work can also take part in: Crime Stoppers. Now an international organization with chapters in many metropolitan areas around the world, this program offers both cash rewards and a guarantee of anonymity to callers with information about crime. Far too often, the police find, citizens who have vital information

A Crime-Fighting Program That Works

In the early 1970s, Police Officer Greg MacAleese watched with dismay as crime in Albuquerque, New Mexico, seemed to be getting worse and worse. He knew that somewhere there were dozens of people with the information necessary to bring many of the city's criminals to justice, but that these people were either afraid or unmotivated to come forward. Hoping to solve this problem, in 1976 MacAleese formed the first chapter of Crime Stoppers, a crime fighting program that offers both a guarantee of anonymity and cash rewards for anyone with information on unsolved crimes.

From this single program, Crime Stoppers has now grown to over 1,100 programs worldwide, and boasts over $5 billion in narcotics and stolen property recovered and over 815,000 cases solved. Almost everywhere Crime Stoppers has been tried, it has become an invaluable addition to the community's crime-fighting efforts.

For readers wanting more information on Crime Stoppers, contact:

Crime Stoppers International, Inc.
PO Box 614
Arlington, TX 76004-0614
1-800-245-0009
www.c-s-i.org

about crime don't come forward with this information because of the fear of retaliation (which actually happens much less than people believe), or because they have no real motivation to come forward (cash rewards may change that). But more often, citizens with information don't come forward because they don't want to be dragged into the criminal justice system and forced to give statements to the police, attend line ups, testify in court, etc. With Crime Stoppers none of this is necessary. Callers are not asked to identify themselves, but are instead given a code number for identification, and in those situations in which the information they give leads to an indictment (rather than a conviction, as most rewards require), a cash reward is paid at some agreed-upon public place (usually by a civilian member of the Crime Stoppers board), where the citizen identifies him-or herself only by the code number.

Guardian Angels

Unlike crime watch and block clubs, the Guardian Angels espouse a much more aggressive stance against crime in the neighborhoods, including walking patrols and the holding of criminal suspects for the police. This is an organization that has run into a lot of opposition from local police departments because of the fear of neighborhoods regressing to vigilantism. I doubt this is a real possibility in most communities and believe that if they stay within legal boundaries, the Guardian Angels should be a welcome addition to the citizen volunteers of any community, but particularly in high-crime communities where the police protection is spread thin.

Best Advice

The best information the police can offer about crime prevention is that the key to all successful programs is not so much the work of the police as the participation of the public.

A FINAL THOUGHT

As long as there is a large drug problem in this country, there will be a large crime problem. The two parallel each other in both magnitude and seriousness. But citizens don't have to become victims of this drug-related crime, or victims of crimes unrelated to drugs. Every crime has a risk attached to it, and people can, with the information provided in this book, raise the level of risk for criminals and thereby dramatically reduce the chances of becoming crime victims. They can feel secure in the fact that crime is much less likely to happen to those who are knowledgeable about cops, crooks, and crime.

EPILOGUE:
WHEN IS IT SAFE?

As CRIME BECOMES more and more an unwanted, but seemingly unavoidable, part of our society, a question many concerned citizens ask police departments is "When is it safe?"

According to the FBI's *Crime in the United States*, one reported major crime occurred in America every 2.7 seconds in 2000. But since this figure is based on only reported crimes, it is probably merely 30 to 40 percent of the actual number of major crimes, with a more likely rate being one major crime every second or less. The chances of becoming the victim of a crime, therefore, are much better than the chances of winning on a scratch-off lottery card. Fortunately, this figure of one major crime every second or less is only an overall average, and rather than the smooth, even intervals this statistic would seem to indicate, crime actually shows a tendency to be either high or low during certain periods and in certain localities, depending on a number of variables.

While it is always advisable to follow standard security precautions, such as installing dead-bolt locks on all outside doors, never carrying or flashing large amounts of cash, and locking car doors while driving, citizens should also be aware of the various factors that can increase the likelihood of crime, and take extra precautions when these are present. By using this information, citizens can significantly reduce the chances of becoming the victim of a crime.

In a yearly poll by the National Opinion Research Center, an average of over 40 percent of those people questioned each year say they are afraid to go out alone at night, even within a mile of their own home. While some might scoff at the idea of being afraid of the dark, the belief that crime is more prevalent at night is well grounded in fact. Manpower studies done by many large city police departments have shown that more than half of all calls for the police occur within the eight-hour period from 7:00 P.M. to 3:00 A.M., even though this is only one-third of the day. To address this problem, most large-city police departments have established special task forces to augment their manpower during these peak demand hours, and have reevaluated previous staffing levels.

"Police departments are obligated to have officers available whenever citizens call," said former deputy chief of operations James E. Campbell. "Looking at our records of calls for service, I find we simply can't justify equally dividing the officers into three shifts."

While the number of calls to a police department can be used to measure the level of overall crime in a community, a measure often used by researchers to determine the level of violence in a community is assaults on police officers. A community with many assaults on the police is a violent community where no one is safe from attack. This crime, like most others, shows a marked increase after dark. According to the FBI's *Law Enforcement Officers Killed and Assaulted*, a 10-year review from 1991 to 2000 showed that more than half of all the assaults on and murders of police officers in the United States occurred between the hours of 8:00 P.M. and 4:00 A.M., though this also comprises only one-third of the day. The same review shows that Friday, as might be expected, the day of most violence, while Sunday appears to be the day of least violence.

The time of year, in larger units of measure, has also been found to have an effect on the crime rate. Analyzing 12 years of data from the National Crime Survey, researchers for the U.S. Department of Justice have found a seasonal variation in the likelihood of some crimes. Rape, for example, was found to be much more likely during the summer than during other times of the year, as were aggravated assault, larceny, and vehicle theft. Robbery, on the other hand, showed a marked increase at the end of the year, due very likely to the large amount of cash around because of holiday shopping.

Professor John L. Cotton of Purdue University also studied this rise in certain crimes during the summer months. In a paper presented to an annual meeting of the American Psychological Association, he related the results of his research of crime in a large midwestern city. Comparing the city's daily crime records with reports of maximum temperature from the National Weather Service, he discovered a correlation between violent crime and maximum temperature. The hotter the weather, he found, the more violent the crimes.

While warm weather has been shown to have a significant effect on the number of violent crimes, cold weather, and especially extremely cold weather with large amounts of snow, has been shown to have the opposite effect on property crimes. The same large midwestern city in which Professor Cotton conducted his study experienced during an extraordinarily harsh winter several years ago the only day in memory on which not a single burglary was reported.

"Really bad weather can be a blessing to us," said a veteran burglary detective. "Usually, the worse the weather is, the less crime we have to deal with."

The claim that weather has an effect on crime probably won't raise many eyebrows, yet the belief that the moon can have an effect on human behavior is something scoffed at by many people. Police officers, however, don't laugh. They have witnessed far too many times the large increase in police runs during the full moon. The author of the book *The Lunar Effect*, Arnold Lieber, a psychiatrist in Miami, Florida, also doesn't laugh. Instead, he tells of his study of homicides in Florida and Ohio. Through his research, Dr. Lieber was able to show a relationship between increases in the homicide rate and the presence of either a full or new moon. A number of scientists, however, have contested Dr. Lieber's findings, saying there is no scientific evidence for a lunar effect. But whether or not the moon really does have an effect on human behavior is not as significant as the fact that many police officers believe it does and so prepare themselves accordingly. Their attitudes and heightened vigilance are believed by some to be part of a self-fulfilling prophecy.

Certain locations within a community can also affect the likelihood of crime. While no one has to tell people that in economically depressed areas of a city they are much more likely to be robbed or assaulted, the largest proportion of violent crimes, it has been found, occur on a street other than the one on which the victim or friends live. The second most likely location for a violent crime, unfortunately—and this is a good reason to review carefully the advice in Chapters 2, 3, and 6—is the victim's own home. Next highest are parking lots and garages, followed by school buildings, bars, and public transportation. For property crimes, not including the victim's or a friend's home, the locations that most affect the likelihood of crime are (in order of occurrence) a parking lot or garage, a commercial building, and a bar. Thus, crime can occur nearly everywhere.

The desire to escape increasing crime has for the last several decades led people to flee large metropolitan areas into the suburbs and rural areas, this flight usually based on the belief that the likelihood of crime in these new environments will be less. Recently, though, a number of news stories have appeared that would seem to indicate such flight has been futile, that crime has now followed people to the suburbs and rural areas. While it is admittedly true that crime has increased in recent years in both the suburbs and rural areas, the likelihood of crime in these areas is still much lower than in large metropolitan areas. In 2000, for example, the overall crime rate in America's 52 largest cities (over 250,000 population) was almost twice as high as in suburban counties, and almost three times as high when compared with rural counties.

Since crime is almost always present to some degree regardless of where a person lives, a question often asked of police departments is whether there is any group of people more responsible for crime than any other, a group that could be considered a pivotal variable in the likelihood of crime. There are several such groups. One group I've pointed out in nearly every chapter is drug abusers. They are responsible for a tremendous amount of crime. Yet identifying a drug abuser isn't always that easy.

There is another group of individuals, though, who are also responsible for a large amount of crime but who are much more easily identified. In the United States in 2000, almost 45 percent of all those arrested for violent crimes and almost 60 percent of all those arrested for property crimes were under the age of 25, even though this age group accounts for only about a third of the country's population. According to *Report to the Nation on Crime and Justice*, for most individuals property crime arrests peak at age 16, while violent crime arrests peak at age 18.

There is also a third group who tends to be responsible for crime in highly disproportionate numbers, and whose identity shouldn't surprise most people. These are recently released inmates from penal institutions, and career criminals out on bail. A study of people on pretrial release by the Bureau of Justice Statistics in 75 of America's most populous counties found that 18 percent of these people were rearrested for a felony while on pretrial release; but even more shocking, 75 percent of these criminals, though arrested while on pretrial release, were then released again (undoubtedly to commit more crimes). A study by the U.S. Department of Justice found that 62.5 percent of all released state prison inmates were rearrested for a serious crime within three years of their release. I don't think I have to tell you that the three groups above contain many of the same individuals, with a large number of serious criminals belonging to all three groups.

The leniency of our nation's court systems has also often been blamed for the prevalence of crime in our society, and, from a police officer's point of view, there is undoubtedly some truth to this claim. However, there are other variables that are less known, but which can still have a sizable effect on the crime rate, an example being the policy of a local police department on arrest. This effect of arrest policies was studied in an experiment that used a group of Minneapolis police officers. During this experiment, depending on the date, the officers would do one of the following when dispatched to a domestic disturbance in which someone had been assaulted:

- Attempt to mediate the dispute and counsel the parties.
- Send the assailant away for several hours (the standard practice of most police departments for less serious assaults).
- Arrest the assailant.

The Police Foundation, which conducted the experiment, analyzed 314 separate incidents. They found that the assailants who were arrested were only half as likely to repeat the violence in the following six months as were the assailants who were either counseled or sent away for a few hours.

Even though the above study dealt only with assaults that occurred during family disputes, and even though other researchers have given alternate explanations for the decrease in reported violence, the significant implications of this experiment are apparent. In response to these findings, a number of police departments across the country have instituted policies that now require arrests in certain situations.

In addition to all of the studies and findings above, the FBI lists several other factors they believe are responsible for the amount of crime in a community, though these are usually features of a community people have little or no control over. They include:

- Stability of the population (number of transients)
- Family cohesiveness
- Community attitudes about crime
- Crime reporting procedures

A last variable is one that brings us full circle. It is perhaps the variable that has the largest effect on the crime rate of any community: the prevalence of illegal drug use in that community. The high economic cost to drug abusers of maintaining their drug habit seldom allows them to pay for it out of legitimate earnings, and so a serious drug habit almost always leads to crime. This makes it inevitable that the more illegal drug use there is in a community, the more crime there will be. This reason alone, even without considering the damage drug abuse does to the youth of our communities, should be enough to make all citizens want to enthusiastically support efforts in both the schools and the community to fight drug abuse.

While all of the facts and figures presented in this book may seem to paint a gloomy picture of crime in our country and of one's chances of being a victim, this isn't necessarily true. If you understand what makes crime happen, you are much better prepared to avoid or stop it. If you understand how to make a crime look very difficult and risky to a criminal, your chances of being a victim are greatly reduced. But, you must rely on real, factual information about cops, crooks, and crime, and not on information from novels and movies. I hope that I've been able to provide you with that.

INDEX